THE
CRYSTAL BIBLE

THE
CRYSTAL BIBLE

A DEFINITIVE GUIDE TO CRYSTALS

Judy Hall

WALKING STICK PRESS

Cincinnati, Ohio

First published in Great Britain in 2003 by Godsfield Press Ltd,
Laurel House, Station Approach, Alresford, Hampshire SO24 9JH, UK

Distributed to the trade markets in North America by
Walking Stick Press, an imprint of F&W Publications, Inc.
4700 East Galbraith Road, Cincinnati, OH 45236
Tel: 1-800-289-0963

10 9 8 7 6 5 4 3 2 1

Designed and produced for Godsfield Press by The Bridgewater Book Company

Additional photography by Mike Hemsley at Walter Gardiner Photography

Printed and bound in China

ISBN: 1-58297-240-0

NOTE: An asterisk* placed after a word indicates that the word or
term may be looked up in the Glossary section (see pages 378–383)
for a full explanation.

CAUTION: The information given in this book is not intended to act
as a substitute for medical treatment, nor can it be used for diagnosis.
Crystals are powerful and are open to misunderstanding or abuse.
If you are in any doubt about their use, a qualified practitioner should
be consulted, especially in the crystal healing field.

CONTENTS

CRYSTAL REFERENCE

CRYSTAL DELIGHTS

Everyone is attracted to gemstones. Diamonds, Rubies, Emeralds, and Sapphires are prized the world over. These are indeed precious stones; they uplift the heart. Their brightness is what most people think of when they hear the word "crystal." Equally prized are the semiprecious stones such as Carnelian, Garnet, Rock Crystal, and Lapis Lazuli. They have been used for ornamentation and as a symbol of power for thousands of years. But such crystals were valued for more than their beauty—they each had a sacred meaning. In ancient cultures their healing properties were as important as their ability to adorn.

Crystals still have the same properties today but not all are as flamboyant as gemstones. There are quieter, less outwardly attractive crystals that are nonetheless extremely powerful. Gemstones themselves can easily be overlooked when in their natural, uncut state but their attributes remain the same, and an uncut Sapphire, for instance, which costs a fraction of the price of a faceted stone, is as effective as the most scintillating cut gem.

Most people are familiar with the crystals that have been around for years such as Amethyst, Malachite, and Obsidian but nowadays new crystals such as Larimar, Petalite, and Phenacite are finding their way into

stores. These are "stones for the New Age." They have made themselves known to facilitate the evolution of the earth and all those upon it. These crystals have an extremely high vibration that raises consciousness and opens the higher chakras* to communicate with other dimensions. Knowing how to use these crystals is vital if you are to make use of the gifts they offer.

This book has been divided into sections that will help you to find your way around the crystal kingdom. Containing everything you could ever need to know, these sections tell you about the delights of crystals, their healing use and decorative features, how they were formed, and how to take care of them. There is a Crystal Reference at the front so that you can look up a particular crystal by the name by which you know it, and then find its properties in an extensive Directory section, which also enables you to identify crystals. The comprehensive Index at the back is cross-referenced to symptoms and attributes; you can use this to find a crystal for a specific task, or for your particular purpose. The Glossary on pages 378–383 defines terms that you may not be familiar with.

Crystals come in numerous shapes and many of these have now been given names that signify their function, such as channeling or abundance crystals. If you want to identify a particular facet shape or to know what a certain type of crystal looks like, browse through Crystal Shapes. This section is followed by Quick Reference pages that give you useful information such as the Body and Zodiac Crystal Correspondences, Gem Remedies, Healing Layouts, and a Love Ritual.

CRYSTAL BACKGROUND

The more you understand about crystals, the more effective they are.
In this section you will find background information on how crystals are
formed, advice on how to choose and care for your crystals; how to use
them for healing and decoration, and the way to dedicate them.

Dedicating and programming your crystals helps them to work more
efficiently. It is part of the ritual of working with crystals. As crystals are
powerful beings in their own right, they need to be approached with
respect. If you do this, they will be only too pleased to cooperate with
you. Many people like to have a "crystal day" when they cleanse their
crystals and then meditate with them to attune more strongly to their
energy. Doing this regularly enables your crystals to talk to you and to
show you how you can use them to enhance your life and well-being.

Taking the time to cleanse your crystals is extremely important.
Crystals are efficient absorbers and transmitters of energy. One of their
functions is to cleanse and transmute negative energies. If you leave
your crystals to do this without regular cleansing, most become
saturated and unable to do their work, though a few are self-cleaning.

CRYSTAL FORMATION

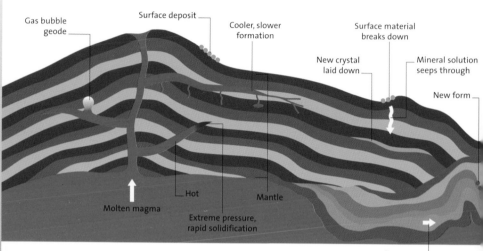

Gas bubble geode

Surface deposit

Cooler, slower formation

Surface material breaks down

New crystal laid down

Mineral solution seeps through

New form

Molten magma

Hot

Mantle

Extreme pressure, rapid solidification

Pressure

A crystal is a solid body with a geometrically regular shape. Crystals were created as the earth formed and they have continued to metamorphose as the planet itself has changed. Crystals are the earth's DNA, a chemical imprint for evolution. They are miniature storehouses, containing the records of the development of the earth over millions of years, and bearing the indelible memory of the powerful forces that shaped it. Some have been subjected to enormous pressure, others grew in chambers deep underground, some were laid down in layers, others dripped into being—all of which affects their properties and the way they function. Whatever form they take, their crystalline structure can absorb, conserve, focus, and emit energy, especially on the electromagnetic waveband.

THE CRYSTAL LATTICE

Because of chemical impurities, radiation, earth and solar emissions, and the exact means of their formation, each type of crystal has its own specific "note." Formed out of an array of minerals, a crystal is defined by its internal structure—an orderly, repeating atomic lattice that is unique to its species. A large or small specimen of the same type of crystal will have exactly the same internal structure, which can be recognized under a microscope.

This unique geometric crystal lattice is how crystals are identified and means that some crystals, such as Aragonite, have several very different external forms and colors, which at first glance could not possibly be the same crystal. However, because the internal structure is identical, they are classified as the same crystal. It is this structure, rather than the mineral or minerals out of which it is formed, that is crucial to crystal classification. In some cases the mineral content differs slightly, creating the various colors in which a particular crystal can be found.

While a number of crystals may be formed out of the same mineral or combination of minerals, each type will crystallize out differently. A crystal is symmetrical along an axis. Its regular external planes are an outward expression of its internal order. Each matching pair of faces has exactly the same angles. The internal structure of any crystalline formation is constant and unchanging.

Crystals are built from one of seven possible geometric forms: triangles, squares, rectangles, hexagons, rhomboids, parallelograms, or trapeziums. These forms lock together into a number of potential crystal shapes, which have generic names based on their internal geometry. As the name suggests, a hexagonal crystal is formed from hexagons built into a three-dimensional shape. A collection of squares forms a cubic crystal, triangles a trigonal, and rectangles a tetragonal

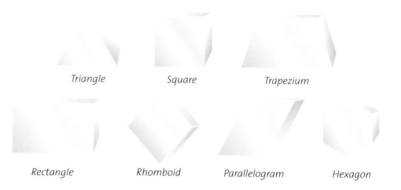

Triangle   Square   Trapezium

Rectangle   Rhomboid   Parallelogram   Hexagon

crystal, while rhomboids form an orthorhombic crystal, trapeziums a triclinic, and parallelograms a monoclinic crystal. The outer form of the crystal will not necessarily reflect its inner structure.

At the heart of a crystal is the atom and its component parts. An atom is dynamic, consisting of particles rotating around a center in constant motion. So, although a crystal may look outwardly serene, it is actually a seething molecular mass vibrating at a certain frequency. This is what gives a crystal its energy.

THE EARTH'S CRUST

The earth began as a whirling cloud of gas, out of which was created a dense dust bowl. This contracted into a white-hot, molten ball. Gradually, over eons, a thin layer of this molten material, magma, cooled into a crust—the earth's mantle. The crust is relatively about as thick as the skin on an apple. Inside that crust, the hot, mineral rich, molten magma continues to boil and bubble and new crystals form.

Some crystals, such as Quartz, arise from the fiery gases and molten minerals in the earth's center. Superheated, they rise toward the surface, propelled by stresses caused by movement of huge plates on the earth's surface. As gases penetrate the crust and meet solid rock, they cool and solidify—a process that may take eons or may be fast and furious.

If the process has been relatively slow, or if the crystal grows in a gas bubble, then large crystals can grow. If the process is fast, then the crystals are small. If the process stops and starts, effects such as phantom or self-healed crystals are possible. If the process is exceptionally fast, a glass-like substance, such as Obsidian, is formed rather than crystals. Crystals such as Aventurine or Peridot are created at high temperatures from liquid magma. Others, such as Topaz and Tourmaline, are formed when gases penetrate adjoining rocks.

Yet other forms arise when magma cools sufficiently for water vapor to condense into a liquid. The resulting mineral-rich solution lays down crystals such as Aragonite and Kunzite. When it penetrates fissures in surrounding rock, the solution is able to cool very slowly and lay down large crystals and geodes such as Chalcedony and Amethyst.

Aragonite ("sputnik" form)

Crystals like Garnet are formed deep in the earth when minerals melt and recrystallize under intense pressure and enormous heat. These crystals are known as metamorphic because they have undergone a chemical change that has reorganized the original lattice.

Calcite and other sedimentary crystals form from an erosion process. Rocks at the surface break down and mineralized water dripping through rock or traveling as a river lays down weathered material as new crystals, or the minerals become cemented together. Such crystals are often laid down in layers on a "bedrock" and tend to be softer in texture.

Crystals are often found still attached to the bedrock on which they formed or cemented together as a conglomerate. This bedrock is known as the matrix.

CRYSTAL DECORATION

Crystals are highly decorative, especially when shaped and polished, although some stones are stunning in their natural form. You can now buy decorative objects wrought from an enormous variety of precious stones, all of which greatly enhance their surroundings, especially if you choose them for their esoteric properties too.

Amber jewelry

Gemstones such as Emeralds and Sapphires are vibrant stones. They make excellent jewelry, for men as well as women, but all crystals can enhance your environment and look superb as well. A carefully placed crystal can magically transform its surroundings.

Wearing gems used to be a royal or priestly prerogative. The high priest of Judaism wore a breastplate set with precious stones. It was much more than a badge of office; it conveyed power to the wearer. As far back as the Stone Age, men and women wore crystal jewelry and talismans. They had a protective as well as a decorative function, guarding their wearer against harm.

Crystals today carry the same power and jewelry can be selected not just on the basis of its outward attraction. Wearing crystals, or simply having one in close proximity, can boost your energy (Orange Carnelian), clean your space (Amber), and attract wealth (Citrine). Carefully positioned, crystals can change your life. You can choose stones to enhance your intuition (Apophyllite), increase mental abilities (Green Tourmaline), and boost confidence (Hematite). You can select abundance (Tiger's Eye) and healing (Smithsonite), or attract love (Rhodonite).

CRYSTAL PROTECTION

Certain crystals, such as Smoky Quartz and Black Tourmaline, have the ability to absorb negativity and electromagnetic smog*. They put out pure, clean energy. Wearing a Black Tourmaline around your neck protects you against electromagnetic emanations, including cell phones and computers, and turns back psychic attack*. Amber and Jet jewelry will also protect your energies.

A large Smoky Quartz cluster or shaped point can look stunning as a decorative object, belying its practical cleansing purpose. Place one between you and a source of electromagnetic smog or geopathic stress* or position it on your desk. An Amethyst geode has the same effect. If you find that computers have a debilitating effect on you, place a Fluorite cluster or a piece of lustrous Lepidolite beside it, and you will be amazed at the difference in how you feel—and your computer will work more in harmony with you.

*moky
*Quartz
lestial

CRYSTAL ATTRACTION

A large Citrine geode is highly decorative. A beautiful object in its own right, it will not only attract wealth but will also help you to keep it. Place it in the Wealth Corner of your home (farthest left rear corner from the front door).

Citrine geode

19

Selenite is one of the newer stones. Its pure white, finely ribbed form looks angelic and, not surprisingly, it attracts angelic energy into your life. It can link you to your soul's purpose. You can pop it under your pillow, but it is at its most beautiful as a pillar with the sun behind it or set on a light box.

Many transparent crystals have their effect heightened by being placed on a light box or catching the sun. Care should be taken as clear Quartz, for instance, focuses the sun's rays and may start a fire, and colored crystals can fade in sunlight.

Selenite

SEMIPRECIOUS STONES

Semiprecious stones have as much power as gemstones. Some are found in several colors, which can affect their attributes. Topaz, which sheds golden light on your life's purpose, is often used for rings. In its blue form, it can be worn at the throat because it stimulates the ability to put your thoughts into words.

Herkimer Diamonds have a clarity and sparkle every bit as attractive as Diamonds themselves, and they come in bigger and more affordable sizes. Many Herkimers display wonderful rainbows in their depths. Used for earrings, they heighten your intuition and increase your creativity. But their power is such that it is better to wear them in your ears for a few hours only. Wearing them for too long can set your head buzzing and may cause insomnia. Peridots are known as "poor

Herkimer Diamond

man's Emeralds," but this visionary stone has the power to ameliorate jealousy and anger, reduce stress, and release negative patterns. As with many stones, in its unpolished form it could easily be overlooked. But faceted and polished, it is a jewel fit for a queen.

BRINGING LOVE INTO YOUR LIFE

If you are seeking love, crystals will help. Place a large piece of Rose Quartz in the Relationship Corner of your house (farthest right rear corner from the front door), or put a piece beside your bed. Its effect is so powerful it might be wise to add an Amethyst to regulate the attraction. You can also wear Rhodochrosite jewelry—its softly banded pink is pretty as well as potent. Love will soon come your way.

Amethyst geode with Snow Quartz crystal

21

CRYSTAL HEALING

Malachite

Crystals have been used for millennia to heal and bring balance. They work through resonance and vibration. To gain maximum benefit from crystal healing, you need to be properly trained or to be treated by someone who is well qualified and experienced. But you can find benefit in crystals for common ailments and they are effective first-aid remedies, especially when made into gem essences (see page 371).

Some crystals contain minerals that are known for their therapeutic properties. Copper, for instance, reduces swelling and inflammation. Malachite has a high concentration of copper, which aids aching joints and muscles. Wearing a Malachite bracelet allows the body to absorb minute amounts of copper in exactly the same way as a copper bracelet does. In ancient Egypt, Malachite was powdered and applied to wounds to prevent infection. Today it is a powerful detoxifier but, as it is toxic, it should only be applied externally. This property of toxic crystals to detoxify is rather like the homeopathic principle of "like cures like." Crystals safely deliver infinitesimal, vibrational doses of something that, taken in large quantities, would be poisonous.

Crystals are used in modern medical practices. They are piezoelectric, which means that electricity, and sometimes light, is produced by compression. This property is harnessed in ultrasound machines, which use a piezoelectric crystal to produce a sound wave. Sound is now being applied at the leading edge of surgery. A tightly focused beam of ultrasound can cauterize wounds deep within the body and blast tumors apart without the need for invasive procedures. Shamans and crystal healers of old were familiar with this ability of crystals to focus sound and light vibrations into a concentrated ray, which was then applied for healing. Rotating a crystal wand on the skin causes compression, which releases a focused beam to the organ beneath.

Carnelian

Ancient healers also knew that, whereas some crystals are either energizing or calming, there are crystals that will both sedate an overactive organ and stimulate a sluggish one. Magnetite, with its positive and negative charge, does exactly this. It sedates an overactive organ and stimulates an underactive one. There are crystals that will heal quickly, but may provoke a healing challenge, while others work much more slowly. If you want to deal with pain—a signal that something is wrong in your body—you can do this with crystals. Pain could result from an excess of energy, a blockage, or a debility. A cool and calming crystal such as Lapis Lazuli or Rose Quartz will sedate energy, whereas Carnelian will stimulate it, and Cathedral Quartz is excellent for pain relief no matter what the cause.

Lapis Lazuli

Crystals are excellent for dealing with headaches. Lapis Lazuli will quickly draw off a migraine headache. But you need to know from where the headache stems. If it is caused by stress, Amethyst, Amber, or Turquoise placed on the brow will relieve it. If it is food-related, however, a stone that calms the stomach, such as Moonstone or Citrine, will be appropriate.

23

HOLISTIC HEALING

Crystals heal holistically. That is to say, they work on the physical, emotional, mental, and spiritual levels of being. They realign subtle energies and dissolve dis-ease*, getting to the root cause. Crystals work through vibration, rebalancing the biomagnetic sheath* that surrounds and interpenetrates the physical body and activating linkage points to the chakras* that regulate the body's vibrational stasis (see page 364). By bringing the chakras back into balance, many states of physical and psychological dis-ease can be ameliorated.

Most illnesses result from a combination of factors. There will be dis-ease at subtle levels. This dis-ease may be emotional or mental, or a sign of spiritual unease or disconnection. There may be misaligned connections between the physical body and the biomagnetic sheath. Other energetic disturbances may be caused by environmental factors such as electromagnetic smog* or geopathic stress*. Simply placing a Black Tourmaline or Smoky Quartz crystal between you and the source of geopathic or electromagnetic stress can magically transform your life. But you may need to go deeper into the cause of dis-ease. Crystals gently deal with the cause rather than merely ameliorating the symptoms.

Larimar

You can lay crystals on or around your body for ten to thirty minutes (for sample layouts see pages 365 and 374), or use them like a reflexology tool to stimulate points on your feet—Larimar is particularly useful for this as it locates the source of dis-ease. Crystal eggs (see page 331) can also be used on the feet. Crystal wands are helpful if you need to stimulate a point on the body. Rotated gently, they lift pain and dis-ease. Throughout the Directory you will find crystals to treat illnesses and imbalances on all levels.

Crystals have been connected with particular parts of the body and its organs for thousands of years (see page 368). Many of the connections come from traditional astrology, both Western and Eastern. Traditional Chinese Medicine and Indian Ayurveda, both over 5,000 years old, still use in modern medical prescriptions crystals that appear in formulas in ancient texts. Hematite, for instance, is said to calm the spirit and so combats insomnia. But it is also used for blood disorders as it is believed to cool the blood, arresting bleeding. Hematite is used by modern crystal healers to relieve those same conditions.

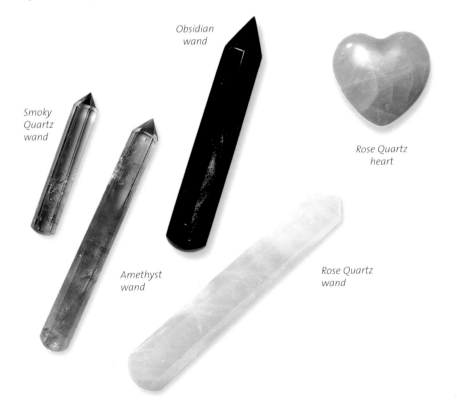

Obsidian wand

Smoky Quartz wand

Rose Quartz heart

Amethyst wand

Rose Quartz wand

CHOOSING A CRYSTAL FOR HEALING

To choose a crystal, or crystals, for healing, you can work from symptoms to deeper cause (preferably with advice from a qualified crystal healer). Each entry in the Crystal Directory lists the conditions it heals at the physical, emotional, psychological, mental, and spiritual level. The Index has a comprehensive cross-reference to help you link symptoms with relevant crystals.

So, for instance, if your symptom is a digestive problem, you could choose a Citrine point to aid healing. Laying it on your abdomen, or wearing it on your little finger, which connects to the small intestine meridian*, could calm your digestion. The crystal works directly on the physical body. However, at a deeper level, digestive problems could well relate to a lack of abundance. Money worries often translate themselves into dis-ease*. Citrine is the stone of prosperity. It attracts wealth and abundance into your life (especially when placed in the left corner of you home that is farthest from your front door). Wearing a Citrine reenergizes you and stimulates motivation and creativity—which brings abundance.

At a deeper level still, fears around money often stem from a feeling of being unsupported by the universe. This fear is not merely emotional dis-ease, it is spiritual disconnection. Citrine's ability to activate the crown chakra*, which is where the spiritual connection is made, could enable you to strengthen your trust in the universe.

Angelite

Citrine

Having identified spiritual disconnection as a probable root cause of your dis-ease, you might then want to look to other crystals that will support that level of your being. Stones such as Petalite and Phenacite link you to a spiritual reality with a very high vibration. Phenacite aids in grounding the spiritual into everyday life but, if this is your first experience of working with crystals to stimulate spiritual contact, it may be too powerful for you. A better choice might be Angelite or Celestite, which gently attune you to the celestial realm*. Angelic presence induces a powerful sense of being supported by the universe.

Brown Celestite

As some crystals support each other and others cancel each other out, care should be taken when using crystals for healing. If in doubt, consult a qualified crystal healer.

SOURCING YOUR CRYSTAL

The best source for your crystal is a local store where you can browse at your leisure. Such stores are usually listed in Yellow Pages under Crystals, Gemstones, or Minerals. The Internet can also point you in the right direction—although there are hundreds of thousands of entries and it can take time and persistence to narrow a search down. There are also Mind-Body-Spirit, Healing, and Crystal and Mineral fairs where you will find crystals for sale. These are listed in Lepidiary Journal, Mind-Body-Spirit journals, or advertised locally.

CRYSTAL SELECTION

Within these pages, you will find crystals that are familiar and others that you have never seen before. With so many crystals to choose from, it can be difficult to know which is the right one for you. If one is gifted to you, it makes it easy. But if you wish to buy one for yourself, browsing through this book first will be invaluable.

If you want to choose a crystal for a specific purpose, the Directory and the Index will help you to find exactly the right one. Look up possibilities in the Index and then check out the crystals themselves in the Directory. If you have no idea what you want your crystal for, but are attracted to the idea of wearing one, then your date of birth is a good starting point and you will find your birthstones on pages 362–363. You can select one that resonates to your zodiac sign, earthing celestial energies.

You can also pick out a crystal at random. Trust your intuition. Browse through the Directory until one attracts your attention and go out and buy that type. There will no doubt be several in the store to choose from. The crystal that speaks to you will be right (never buy from a source that does not let you handle the stones first and, if buying through the Internet, ensure that crystals can be returned if inappropriate—see page 27). Handle several, allow yourself to be drawn to one, or put your hands into a tub of crystals until one sticks to your fingers. If that crystal makes you tingle, it is the one for you. Remember that big or outwardly beautiful is not necessarily most powerful. Small, rough crystals can be extremely effective.

Before you use your crystal, remember to cleanse it first (see page 31).

PROGRAMMING YOUR CRYSTAL

Crystals need to be dedicated to the purpose for which you use them.
Dedicate a new crystal as soon as you have cleansed it (see pages 30–1).
This focuses the energy.

Hold the crystal in your hands. Picture light surrounding it. (If you
find this difficult, hold your hands in front of a light source.) Say out
loud: "I dedicate this crystal to the highest good of all. May it be used
in light and love."

To program your crystal, hold it. Let yourself be open to higher
guidance. Consider the purpose for which you wish to use it. Be specific.
If you want it to attract love, describe exactly what kind of love you are
looking for. If you are seeking healing, say precisely for which condition
and what you want to happen. When you have formulated your
program, attune to the crystal. Ensure that this is exactly the right
crystal for the purpose. When you are totally in tune, say out loud:
"I program this crystal for [your purpose]."

Then put the crystal in a place where you will see it frequently
or keep it in your pocket. It can be helpful to hold it two or
three times a day, or more. You may need to
repeat the programming several times.

*Crystals are highly
responsive. Hold in the palm
of your hand for dedication,
programming, or to select
the right crystal for you*

CRYSTAL CARE

Many crystals are fragile or friable. Crystals that are layered or clustered can separate. Crystals such as Selenite are water soluble. Polished surfaces or natural points are easily scratched or damaged. Tumbled stones are more durable. Endless hours turning in fine grit gives them a tough surface. You can keep tumbled stones together in a bag but other crystals should be kept apart.

When not in use, wrap your crystals in a silk or velvet scarf. This prevents scratching and protects the crystal against absorbing foreign emanations. Crystals need to be cleansed when you buy them and after wearing or using for healing. Always cleanse jewelry that comes to you from someone else, as it can hold their negative vibrations and pass them on to you.

A few crystals never need cleansing. Citrine, Kyanite, and Azeztulite are self-cleaning. Clear Quartz and Carnelian cleanse other crystals, and are especially useful for delicate and friable stones, but may need cleaning themselves afterward.

Tumbled stones can be kept in a small bag

CRYSTAL CLEANSING

Crystals that are not friable or jointed can be held under running water or immersed in the sea or in salt water. As you do so, hold the intention that all negativity will be washed away and the crystal reenergized. Placing the crystal in the light of the sun or moon for a few hours can also recharge its batteries provided it is not a stone that fades in sunlight and care is taken not to focus the rays where they could start a fire—remember that the light from the sun moves around in an arc as the day progresses.

Friable crystals or clusters can be left in sea or rock salt overnight. Gently brush every speck of salt off afterward as they could damage the crystal, especially in a damp atmosphere.

Certain crystals have the ability to cleanse other crystals. Keep a Carnelian in a bag of tumbled stones and you will never need to cleanse them using any other method. A small crystal can be placed on a Clear Quartz cluster and left overnight.

You can smudge* crystals or pass them through the light from a candle. You can also visualize them surrounded by light, which purifies and reenergizes them.

One of the easiest ways to purify a crystal is to use a purpose-made cleanser available over the Internet. You only need to put a drop or two on the crystal, or spray it with an atomizer of water to which a few drops of cleanser have been added—this does not damage friable crystals if sprayed lightly.

Cleanse crystals in water or salt

31

CRYSTAL MEDITATION

Meditating with a crystal is one of the easiest ways to attune to its energy. Cleanse your crystal before beginning so that its energies will be pure. Meditation is a way of shutting off mind chatter. It has many benefits—alleviating stress, lowering blood pressure, etc.—but it also allows you to get to know your crystals. In the stillness of meditation, the crystals talk to you.

Meditation is like opening a door to another world, especially if you choose a crystal that has fault lines* and occlusions* within it. You lose yourself within the crystal. In the peace that follows, solutions and insights rise up into awareness. It is beneficial to meditate with each of your crystals in turn, taking a few days to tune into each one and come to know it fully.

Some people like to have a "crystal day" when they tune into each of their crystals. Start with the red crystals to energize and awaken, moving through the rainbow spectrum into orange, yellow, green, blue, purple, violet, and clear. This brings you to the highest crystal vibration and you could well feel blissed out*. You may need to earth your energies again with one of the black crystals. Earthing, or grounding, your energies after meditation is important as you may otherwise feel floaty and not quite here. Boji Stones are excellent for this as they settle you into your body instantly but gently, and immediately bring you fully present.

Agate   *Amber*   *Sulphur*   *Peridot*   *Agate*   *Amethyst*   *Fluorite*

32

CRYSTAL MEDITATION EXERCISE

Making sure that you will not be disturbed, especially by a phone, settle yourself comfortably with your crystal. Hold it in both hands or place it on a low table in front of you.

Breathe gently, letting each out-breath be a little longer than the in-breath. As you breathe out, let go of any stress or tension you may be feeling. As you breathe in, let peace flow with your in-breath passing right through your body. Allow your breathing to settle into an easy rhythm.

With softly focused eyes, look at your crystal. Notice its color, its shape, its weight if you are holding it. Feel its vibrations passing into your hands. Allow yourself to wander within the crystal, exploring its inner planes. When you are ready, close your eyes. Quietly contemplate the energies of the crystal and let it teach you about itself.

When you have completed the meditation, open your eyes and put the crystal aside. Place your feet firmly on the floor. To ground yourself, hold a Smoky Quartz or Boji Stone.

CRYSTAL DIRECTORY

Crystals come in all shapes and sizes, and the same crystal may occur in several forms or colors, or be known by several names. The appearance of many crystals is enhanced by cutting or polishing, but they are as effective in the raw state. A crystal in the raw may be difficult to identify as many of its characteristics are less easy to spot.

Throughout this Directory you will find crystals illustrated in various forms and colors to make identification easy. You will be able to see what a rough crystal looks like when it has been cut and faceted or tumbled. You will see large clusters and small points, polished palm stones, and geodes.

Crystals can be used for healing or environmental enhancement as well as personal adornment. Their subtle vibrations affect the physical, emotional, mental, psychological, and spiritual levels of being. They bring out particular qualities, and open the gateway to spiritual understanding. This Directory contains all the knowledge—practical and esoteric—you need to access their miraculous properties and to position stones for the greatest benefit.

CRYSTAL ATTRIBUTES

Within this section you will find all the information you need on the general attributes of each crystal, together with its psychological, mental, emotional, and spiritual effect and its use in healing—all of which are cross-referenced in the Index. You will also learn how to place your crystal for maximum effect.

Each crystal is listed with all the colors it takes on and the names by which it is known. Where there is more than one color or a form of the crystal that has additional properties, these are listed after the main entry. Thus, the general properties of each crystal are shown under the generic heading, followed by the crystal's unique attributes.

You can also use the Directory to select a crystal for healing, protection or some other purpose. The Index will help you here. Look up the condition for which you need the crystal. You will probably find several page references. Look at each crystal in turn and note which one has the strongest attraction for you. This will be the most appropriate.

Chalcedony geode

IDENTIFYING A CRYSTAL

The sources for each crystal are shown in the box beneath the heading, together with a description of its color, appearance, and size. This means that if you happen to pick up or are given a crystal, you can identify it.

If you need to identify a crystal, look at it closely. Note its color and its form. Does it have clear crystals with faceted points? Is it rough or has it been tumbled smooth? Is it dense and grainy or translucent? Look through the illustrations until you spot the one most like your stone. The photographs in the Directory show many but not all of the colors in which each crystal is available. If your crystal is similar in appearance and is one of the colors listed but not shown in a photograph, then this is most probably a correct identification. (If you are in any doubt, most crystal stores will be pleased to help you further.)

CRYSTAL BEINGS

Many crystals contain beings or guardian spirits who actively want to work with you to use your crystal to its fullest potential. Meditating with your crystal (see page 32) puts you in touch. You may find that the being is in another dimension with which the crystal forms a bridge. Some crystals have their own angel or connect with higher beings.

Blue Chalcedony being

AGATE

*Natural
Agate (sliced)*

COLOR	Clear or milky white, gray, blue, green, pink, brown, often artificially colored
APPEARANCE	Waxy and soft, usually banded, sometimes translucent with small crystals, various sizes. Often sold as artificially colored slices that have no additional therapeutic properties
RARITY	Common
SOURCE	United States, India, Morocco, Czech Republic, Brazil, Africa

ATTRIBUTES Formed from microscopic crystals of quartz laid down in bands, this is a very stable crystal. Agates are grounding stones, bringing about an emotional, physical, and intellectual balance. They aid in centering and stabilizing physical energy.

Agate has the power to harmonize yin and yang, the positive and negative forces that hold the universe in place. A soothing and calming stone, Agate works slowly but brings great strength. Its multiple layers can bring hidden information to light.

Psychologically, Agate gently facilitates acceptance of one's self. This builds self-confidence. It aids self-analysis and perception of hidden circumstances, bringing to your attention any dis-ease* that is interfering with your well-being.

Agates enhance mental function as they improve concentration, perception, and analytical abilities, leading to practical solutions. Agate's love of truthfulness encourages speaking one's own truth. Agates with clear crystals can stimulate memories.

Emotionally, this crystal overcomes negativity and bitterness of the heart. It heals inner anger, fostering love and the courage to start again. It is useful for any kind of emotional trauma. It creates a sense of safety and security by dissolving internal tension.

Spiritually, Agate raises consciousness and links into collective consciousness and awareness of the oneness of life. It encourages quiet contemplation and assimilation of life experiences, leading to spiritual growth and inner stability.

HEALING Agate stabilizes the aura*, eliminating and transforming negative energies. Its cleansing effect is powerful at the physical and emotional levels. Placed on the heart, it will heal the emotional dis-ease that prevents acceptance of love. Placed on the abdomen or taken as an elixir, Agate stimulates the digestive process and relieves gastritis. It heals the eyes, stomach, and uterus; it cleanses the lymphatic system and the pancreas; it strengthens blood vessels and heals skin disorders.

POSITION Hold or place on appropriate body location.

SPECIFIC COLORS AND TYPES In addition to the generic properties, specific colors have additional properties:

Blue Agate (natural)

Blue-Green Agate is usually artificially made glass and has no therapeutic properties.

Green Agate

Green Agate enhances mental and emotional flexibility and improves decision-making. It is useful in resolving disputes.

Pink Agate promotes love between parent and child. Position over the heart for optimum effect.

Pink Agate

Botswana Agate Found only in Botswana, this Agate is excellent for anyone connected with fire or smoke. It is beneficial for smokers and those who want to quit smoking. Botswana Agate looks to solutions rather than dwelling on problems. It helps you to explore unknown territory and your own creativity. At a mental level, it helps you to see the bigger picture. At an emotional level, it gently releases repression. This agate often has nodules or ovoids and, being gray and usually found as a nodule, it looks like the brain, with which it resonates. It is particularly useful in helping the body to assimilate oxygen, benefiting the circulatory system and the skin. It also aids depression. At a nonphysical level, it stimulates the crown chakra*, bringing energy into the auric field.

AGATE: **BLUE LACE AGATE**

Polished and tumbled

Raw

COLOR	Pale blue with white or darker lines
APPEARANCE	Banded, often small and tumbled
RARITY	Readily available
SOURCE	As Agate

ADDITIONAL PROPERTIES Blue Lace Agate is a wonderful healing stone. Its soft energy is cooling and calming, bringing peace of mind. It is particularly effective for activating and healing the throat chakra*, allowing free expression of thoughts and feelings. It opens the way to experience of the higher energies. This is one of the great nurturing and supportive stones. It will neutralize anger, infection, inflammation, and fever.

Psychologically, Blue Lace Agate counteracts the repression and suppression of feelings that stem from fear of being judged and rejected. Judgment is often present in the parent–child relationship, both in childhood and adulthood. As a result, feelings are held back and the lack of self-expression blocks the throat chakra and may affect the chest—the feeling being of suffocation. Blue Lace Agate gently dissolves the old pattern of repression and encourages a new mode of expression. It is useful for helping men to release and accept their sensitivity and feeling natures.

Mentally, Blue Lace Agate assists with verbal expression of thoughts and feelings and counteracts mental stress. Emotionally, the peaceful energies exuded from this stone neutralize feelings of anger.

Spiritually, Blue Lace Agate clears the throat chakra so that the highest spiritual truths can be expressed. It is a stone that links thought to the spiritual vibration and brings in deep peace.

HEALING Blue Lace Agate is a powerful throat healer. Its property of counteracting blocked self-expression releases shoulder and neck problems, thyroid deficiencies, and throat and lymph infections. It lowers fevers and removes blockages of the nervous system, and treats arthritic and bone deformity, strengthening the skeletal system and healing fractures. It also aids capillaries and the pancreas. As an elixir, it treats brain fluid imbalances and hydrocephalus. Blue Lace Agate can also be used to enhance sound healing—it focuses and directs sound to the appropriate place.

POSITION As appropriate, particularly at the throat.

AGATE: **DENDRITIC AGATE**

ALSO KNOWN AS TREE AGATE

Shaped and polished

COLOR	Clear, brown, green
APPEARANCE	Transparent with fern-like markings, often small and tumbled
RARITY	Readily available
SOURCE	United States, Czech Republic, India, Iceland, Morocco, Brazil

ADDITIONAL PROPERTIES Dendritic Agate is known as the stone of plenitude. It brings abundance and fullness to all areas of life, including business and agriculture. It can be used to enhance the yield of crops or to maintain the health of house plants.

Dendritic Agate creates a peaceful environment, both inner and outer, and encourages the enjoyment of each moment. This crystal has a particularly strong connection with the plant kingdom and can enhance communication with that realm. It deepens your own connection to the earth.

However it is used, Dendritic Agate works slowly and takes time to be fully effective.

Psychologically, Dendritic Agate encourages you to remain centered in times of strife or confusion, bringing stability. It lends you perseverance and the ability to see difficulties as a challenge.

Spiritually, Dendritic Agate urges you to remain connected with your roots as you grow. Dendritic Agate opens and aligns the chakras*, enabling them to integrate higher consciousness.

HEALING At a subtle level, Dendritic Agate heals dis-ease caused by chakra imbalances. Within the body, Dendritic Agate resonates with anything that branches, such as blood vessels and nerves. It heals the nervous system and conditions such as neuralgia. This stone treats skeletal disorders and aligns the skeleton to one's physical reality. Dendritic Agate reverses capillary degeneration and stimulates the circulatory system. Placed on the site of injury or pain, it provides pain relief. It is a useful stone for healing plants and the earth itself. It stabilizes the vortices within the earth's energy field and can overcome geopathic stress* or "black ley lines*."

POSITION Hold or place on the appropriate point. Wear for long periods to gain maximum benefit. Tuck into plant pots.

AGATE: **FIRE AGATE**

*Natural
formation*

COLOR	Brownish red, orange, blue, green
APPEARANCE	Swirling, luminescent, small stone
RARITY	Obtainable from specialist stores
SOURCE	United States, Czech Republic, India, Iceland, Morocco, Brazil

ADDITIONAL PROPERTIES Fire Agate has a deep connection to the earth and its energy is calming, bringing security and safety. With strong grounding powers, it supports during difficult times.

Fire Agate has a strong protective function, especially against ill-wishing. Building a protective shield around the body, it returns harm back to its source so that the source understands the harm it is doing.

Physically, Fire Agate, as its name suggests, links to the fire element and aids sexual endeavors, fires up the base chakra* and stimulates vitality on all levels. Psychologically, Fire Agate dispels fear and instills deep security.

Holding a Fire Agate encourages introspection, effortlessly bringing up inner problems for resolution. It helps to eliminate cravings and destructive desires and can be useful in treating addictions.

Spiritually, this protective stone aids relaxation so that the body "mellows out," enhancing meditation. Said to represent absolute perfection, it instills spiritual fortitude and aids the evolution of consciousness.

HEALING This stone heals the stomach, the nervous and endocrine systems, and circulatory disorders. It aids eyes, strengthening night vision and clearing vision at the inner, intuitive levels and outer, physical levels. It resonates with the triple-burner meridian* and can be applied to bring it back into balance, reducing hot flashes and removing heat from the body. Fire Agate brings vitality into the body, preventing energy burn-out. Placed on a blown chakra*, it gently brings it back online. At a subtle level, Fire Agate clears etheric blockages and energizes the aura*.

POSITION Fire Agate can be worn for long periods, or placed on the head or body as appropriate.

AGATE: **MOSS AGATE**

Polished

Tumbled

COLOR	Green, blue, red, yellow, brown
APPEARANCE	Transparent or translucent with branching markings like foliage or moss, often small and tumbled
RARITY	Common
SOURCE	United States, Australia, India

ADDITIONAL PROPERTIES A stabilizing stone strongly connected with nature, Moss Agate is said to refresh the soul and enable you to see the beauty in all you behold. It is helpful in reducing sensitivity to weather and to environmental pollutants. This stone is extremely beneficial for anyone employed in agriculture or associated with botany.

A birthing crystal, Moss Agate assists midwives in their work, lessening pain and ensuring a good delivery. It is a stone of new beginnings and release from blockages or spiritual fetters.

47

A stone of wealth, Moss Agate attracts abundance.

Moss Agate can act with a dual purpose. It helps intellectual people access their intuitive feelings and, conversely, assists intuitive people in channeling their energy in practical ways.

Psychologically, Moss Agate improves self-esteem and strengthens positive personality traits. It releases fear and deep-seated stress. It helps to develop strength and the ability to get along with others, and encourages expanding one's personal space and growth. It strengthens the ability to try one more time, inspiring with new ideals after a period of stagnation.

Mentally, Moss Agate promotes self-expression and communication. It balances the emotions, reducing stress and lessening fear. It encourages trust and hope, being a highly optimistic stone. It is helpful for anyone suffering from depression through life circumstances or brain imbalances. No matter how difficult those circumstances may be, Moss Agate gives insight into the reason behind them.

HEALING Moss Agate speeds up recovery. It can be used to counteract long-term illness. It is anti-inflammatory, cleanses the circulatory and elimination systems, encouraging the flow of lymph, and boosts the immune system. Moss Agate eliminates depression caused by left–right brain imbalance. It helps prevent hypoglycemia and dehydration, treats infections, colds and flu, and lowers fevers. It is anti-inflammatory and reduces swelling in lymph nodes. As an elixir applied to the skin, Moss Agate treats fungal and skin infections.

POSITION Place or hold on the appropriate point in contact with the skin.

AMAZONITE

Polished and tumbled

Raw

COLOR	Blue, green
APPEARANCE	Opalescent with veins, various sizes, sometimes tumbled
RARITY	Common
SOURCE	United States, Russia, Canada, Brazil, India, Mozambique, Namibia, Austria

ATTRIBUTES Amazonite has a powerful filtering action. At a physical level, it blocks geopathic stress*, absorbs microwaves and cell phone emanations, and protects against electromagnetic pollution. It should be placed between you and the source of any pollution or taped to a cell phone. At a mental level, it filters the information passing through the brain and combines it with intuition.

This is an extremely soothing stone. It calms the brain and nervous system and aligns the physical body with the etheric*, maintaining optimum health. It balances the masculine and feminine energies and many aspects of the personality. It is a stone that helps you to see both sides of a problem or different points of view. At an emotional level, Amazonite soothes emotional trauma, alleviating worry and fear. It dispels negative energy and aggravation.

Spiritually, an elixir of Amazonite is extremely beneficial to all levels of consciousness. The stone itself assists in manifesting universal love.

HEALING Amazonite heals and opens both the heart and throat chakras* to enhance loving communication. It also opens the third eye* and intuition. The stone dissipates negative energy and blockages within the nervous system. It is beneficial in osteoporosis, tooth decay, calcium deficiency, and calcium deposits, balancing the metabolic deficiencies that create these conditions. The elixir rectifies calcium problems. Amazonite also relieves muscle spasms. A major property is the protection it affords from the health hazards of microwaves and other sources of electromagnetic smog*.

POSITION Hold or place over the affected point, or wear to protect against microwaves. Place near computers or tape to your cell phone.

AMBER

Shaped

Yellow, clear

COLOR	Golden brown or yellow—green is artificially colored
APPEARANCE	Opaque or transparent resin, insects or vegetation trapped inside, various sizes
RARITY	Easily obtained
SOURCE	Britain, Poland, Italy, Romania, Russia, Germany, Myanmar, Dominica

ATTRIBUTES Strictly speaking, Amber is not a crystal at all. It is tree resin that solidified and became fossilized. It has strong connections with the earth and is a grounding stone for higher energies. Amber is a powerful healer and cleanser that draws dis-ease* from the body and promotes tissue revitalization. It also cleans the environment and the chakras*. It absorbs negative energies and transmutes them into positive forces that stimulate the body to heal itself. A powerful protector, it links the everyday self to the higher spiritual reality.

Psychologically, Amber brings stability to life but also motivates by linking what is wished for to the drive to achieve it. Its warm, bright energies translate into a sunny, spontaneous disposition that nevertheless respects tradition. It can help counteract suicidal or depressive tendencies.

Mentally, Amber stimulates the intellect, clears depression, and promotes a positive mental state and creative self-expression. It brings balance and patience and encourages decision-making, being a useful memory aid. Its flexibility dissolves opposition. Emotionally, Amber encourages peacefulness and develops trust. Spiritually, Amber promotes altruism and brings wisdom.

HEALING Amber is a powerful chakra cleanser and healer. At a physical level, it imbues the body with vitality and has the power to draw disease out of the body. By absorbing pain and negative energy, Amber allows the body to rebalance and heal itself. Amber alleviates stress. It resonates with the throat, treating goiters and other throat problems. It treats the stomach, spleen, kidneys, bladder, liver, and gallbladder, alleviates joint problems, and strengthens the mucus membranes. As an elixir and for wound healing, it is an excellent natural antibiotic. It can stimulate the navel chakra and help in grounding energies into the body.

POSITION Wear for prolonged periods, especially on the wrist or throat, or place as appropriate. If treating babies or children, it is beneficial for the mother to wear the stone first.

AMETHYST

Purple Amethyst

COLOR	Purple to lavender
APPEARANCE	Transparent, pointed crystals. May be geode, cluster, or single point. All sizes
RARITY	One of the most common crystals
SOURCE	United States, Britain, Canada, Brazil, Mexico, Russia, Sri Lanka, Uruguay, East Africa, Siberia, India

ATTRIBUTES Amethyst is an extremely powerful and protective stone with a high spiritual vibration. It guards against psychic attack*, transmuting the energy into love. A natural tranquilizer, Amethyst blocks geopathic stress* and negative environment energies. Its serenity enhances higher states of consciousness and meditation. Amethyst has strong healing and cleansing powers, and enhances spiritual awareness. Traditionally, it was worn to prevent drunkenness and has a sobering effect on overindulgence and physical passions, supporting sobriety. It overcomes addictions and blockages of all kinds. Used at a higher level, Amethyst opens to another reality.

Amethyst is extremely beneficial to the mind, calming or stimulating as appropriate. When you meditate, it turns thoughts away from the mundane into tranquility and deeper understanding. Mentally, it helps you feel less scattered, more focused and in control of your faculties. It enhances the assimilation of new ideas and connects cause with effect.

This stone facilitates the decision-making process, bringing in common sense and spiritual insights, and putting decisions and insights into practice. Mentally, it calms and synthesizes, and aids the transmission of neural signals through the brain. It is helpful where insomnia is caused by an overactive mind and protects against recurrent nightmares. Amethyst enhances memory and improves motivation, making you more able to set realistic goals. It can help you to remember and understand dreams and facilitates the visualization process.

Amethyst balances out highs and lows, promoting emotional centering. It dispels anger, rage, fear, and anxiety. Alleviating sadness and grief, it supports coming to terms with loss.

Amethyst is one of the most spiritual stones, promoting love of the divine, giving insights into its true nature, and encouraging selflessness and spiritual wisdom. It opens intuition and enhances psychic gifts. This is an excellent stone for meditation and scrying* and can be placed on the third eye to stimulate it. Sleeping with Amethyst facilitates out-of-body experiences* and brings intuitive dreams. It transmutes "lower" energies to the higher frequencies of the spiritual and etheric* realms.

HEALING Amethyst boosts production of hormones, and tunes the endocrine system and metabolism. It strengthens the cleansing and eliminating organs and the immune system. An excellent cleanser for the blood, Amethyst relieves physical, emotional, and psychological pain or stress, and blocks geopathic stress. It eases headaches and releases tension. This stone reduces bruising, injuries, and swellings, and treats hearing disorders. It heals dis-eases of the lungs and respiratory tract, skin conditions, cellular disorders, and dis-eases of the digestive tract. It is beneficial for the intestines, regulating flora, removing parasites, and encouraging reabsorption of water. Amethyst treats insomnia and brings restful sleep.

At a subtle level, Amethyst balances and connects the physical, mental, and emotional bodies*, linking them to the spiritual. It cleanses the aura* and transmutes negative energy, and stimulates the throat and crown chakras*. It is helpful for people about to make the transition through death. Amethyst can stabilize psychiatric conditions but should not be used in cases of paranoia or schizophrenia.

POSITION Wear or place as appropriate, especially as jewelry. Clusters and geodes can be placed in the environment and single points are used in healing. Place the point in toward you to draw in energy, and away from you to draw off energy. Amethyst is especially beneficial worn over the throat or heart. For insomnia or nightmares, place under the pillow. Amethyst fades in sunlight.

Amethyst point

55

SPECIFIC COLORS

In addition to the generic properties, the following colors and
forms have additional properties:

Violet-Lavender Amethyst has a particularly high vibration.
Double-terminated lilac crystals take you into beta brain waves.
They also stimulate and then calm the throat and heart chakras.
Violet "flowers" bring light and love into the environment.

*Lavender
Amethyst
flower*

Chevron Amethyst is one of the best third-eye* stimulators. It
enhances inner, intuitive vision and outer, physical vision, and out-of-
body journeys. It has powerfully focused energy that dissipates and
repels negativity. This stone cleanses the aura and aids in auric
diagnosis. It has a strong healing field, bringing harmony to the organs
of the body and stimulating the immune system. It helps you to find
and implement a positive answer to any problem.

Pineapple Amethyst has small nodules covering the sides
above which emerge the termination points. Looking like the
turrets of a castle in a fairytale, it facilitates contact with
the mythic and fairytale realms and stimulates the
imagination. It is a powerful archetypal healer for
family and collective myths.

*Amethyst
wand*

*Pineapple
Amethyst
cluster*

AMETRINE

Polished   *Raw*

COLOR	Purple and yellow
APPEARANCE	Transparent crystal, combination of Amethyst and Citrine, often small and tumbled
RARITY	Readily available though obtained from only one mine
SOURCE	Bolivia

ATTRIBUTES Ametrine powerfully combines Amethyst and Citrine. It is fast and effective in its action, and is particularly useful in long-standing illness as it brings insight into causes of dis-ease*. Ametrine connects the physical realm with higher consciousness. This stone facilitates and protects during astral travel* and relieves psychic attack*. It clears stress and tension from the head, calming the mind and bringing greater focus to meditation. Ametrine opens

57

the third eye, promoting healing and divination. It unites masculine and feminine energies.

Psychologically, Ametrine enhances compatibility and acceptance of others. It shows where everyone is linked, overcoming prejudice. An extremely energetic stone, it stimulates creativity and supports taking control of one's own life. It is a stone that can overcome apparent contradictions.

Mentally, Ametrine brings clarity, harmonizing perception and action. It strengthens concentration and aids thinking things through, encouraging exploration of all possibilities, bringing creative solutions. It takes the intellect beyond everyday reality to link into higher awareness.

Emotionally, Ametrine releases blockages, including negative emotional programming* and expectations, facilitating transformation, bringing insight into underlying causes of emotional distress. Ametrine promotes optimism and a well-being that is not disturbed by stressful external influences.

HEALING Ametrine gets to the bottom of things. Its powerful cleansing properties disperse negativity from the aura*, and toxins from the body. An exceptional blood cleanser and energizer, it regenerates the physical body and strengthens the immune system, aids the autonomic nervous system and physical maturation, stabilizes DNA/RNA, and oxygenates the body. Ametrine heals chronic fatigue syndrome (CFS)*, burning sensations, depression, gastric disturbances and ulcers, fatigue and lethargy, tension headaches, and stress-related dis-ease. It releases blockages in the physical, emotional, and mental subtle bodies*.

POSITION Wear directly on the body for prolonged periods, placing on solar plexus. Holding Ametrine brings deep-seated issues to the surface so that they can be communicated and healed.

ANGELITE

*Sliced and
lightly polished*

COLOR	Blue and white, sometimes flecked with red
APPEARANCE	Opaque and often veined like wings, largish stone
RARITY	Easily obtained
SOURCE	Britain, Egypt, Germany, Mexico, Peru, Poland, Libya

ATTRIBUTES Angelite is one of the "stones of awareness" for the New Age. It represents peace and brotherhood. As its name suggests, Angelite facilitates conscious contact with the angelic realm*. It enhances telepathic communication and enables out-of-body journeys*

to take place while still maintaining contact with everyday reality.

Angelite is a powerful stone for healers because it deepens attunement and heightens perception. It also provides protection for the environment or the body, especially when taken as an elixir.

Angelite is formed from Celestite (see page 96) that has been compressed over millions of years, and it shares many properties with that stone.

Psychologically, Angelite helps you to speak your truth, whatever it may be. It also helps you to be more compassionate and accepting, especially of that which cannot be changed. It alleviates psychological pain and counteracts cruelty. Mentally, Angelite has been used to enhance astrological understanding and to bring deeper understanding of mathematics. It also facilitates telepathic contact between minds.

Spiritually, Angelite is filled with compassion. It transmutes pain and disorder into wholeness and healing, opening the way for spiritual inspiration. It creates a deep feeling of peace and tranquility. It helps connect to universal knowledge and raises awareness. Angelite facilitates the rebirthing process, stimulates healing, and opens psychic channeling*.

HEALING Applied to the feet, Angelite unblocks meridians* and energetic pathways. It resonates with the throat, alleviating inflammation and balancing the thyroid and the parathyroids. This soothing stone repairs tissue and blood vessels, balancing the fluids within the physical body, and can act as a diuretic. It is useful in weight control, and relates particularly to the lungs and arms. Angelite can cool the pain of sunburn. At a subtle level, Angelite balances the physical body with the etheric realms.

POSITION Hold or place on the body as appropriate.

ANHYDRITE

*Natural
formation*

COLOR	Clear, blue, gray
APPEARANCE	Long bladed or short crystals, usually on matrix
RARITY	Obtained from specialist stores
SOURCE	Italy

ATTRIBUTES Anhydrite gives support and strength on the physical plane. It promotes acceptance of the physical body as a transient vessel for the soul. It helps you face with equanimity what tomorrow may bring. It is useful for people who have difficulty in coming to terms with incarnation and who long for the "post-death" state. Teaching acceptance of all that life has brought, releasing a hankering for the past, it assists past-life healing, showing the gift in all that has been.

HEALING Anhydrite treats disorders of the throat, especially those caused by a difficulty in expressing oneself through a physical body. It removes retained or excess fluid and disperses swelling.

POSITION Place on the throat or over the thymus gland.

APATITE

Blue

COLOR	Yellow, green, gray, blue, white, purple, brown, red-brown, violet
APPEARANCE	Opaque, sometimes transparent, glassy, hexagonal crystal, various sizes, often tumbled
RARITY	Blue readily available, yellow rare
SOURCE	Mexico, Norway, Russia, United States

ATTRIBUTES Apatite has inspirational properties. The interface point between consciousness and matter, it is a stone of manifestation and promotes a humanitarian attitude, inclining toward service. Apatite is attuned to the future, yet connects to past lives. It develops psychic gifts and spiritual attunement, deepens meditation, raises the kundalini*, and aids communication and self-expression on all levels.

Psychologically, Apatite increases motivation and builds up energy reserves. It induces openness and social ease, encouraging extroversion, dissolving aloofness and alienation. It draws off negativity about oneself and others. It is helpful for hyperactive and autistic children.

Stimulating creativity and the intellect, Apatite clears confusion and helps to access information to be used personally and for the collective good. Apatite expands knowledge and truth and eases sorrow, apathy, and anger. It reduces irritability and overcomes emotional exhaustion. By releasing energy in the base chakra*, it clears frustration and endorses passion without guilt.

HEALING Apatite heals bones and encourages formation of new cells. It aids absorption of calcium and helps cartilage, bones, teeth, and motor skills and ameliorates arthritis, joint problems, and rickets. This stone suppresses hunger and raises the metabolic rate, encouraging healthy eating; heals the glands, meridians, and organs; and overcomes hypertension. It balances the physical, emotional, mental, and spiritual bodies, and the chakras, eliminating overactivity and stimulating underactivity. Used with other crystals, Apatite facilitates results.

POSITION Wear on skin over affected part, or place as appropriate.

SPECIFIC COLORS
In addition to the generic attributes, the following colors have additional properties:

Blue Apatite connects to a very high level of spiritual guidance. It facilitates public speaking, enhances group communication, opens the throat chakra, and heals the heart and emotional dis-ease.

Yellow Apatite is a great eliminator, especially of toxins. It activates the solar plexus and draws off stagnant energy. Yellow Apatite treats CFS*, lethargy, and depression, and overcomes lack of concentration, inefficient learning, and poor digestion. It removes cellulite and treats the liver, pancreas, gallbladder and spleen. At an emotional level, it neutralizes stored anger. Yellow Apatite elixir is an appetite suppressant.

Yellow Apatite

APOPHYLLITE

White cluster

COLOR	Clear, white, green, yellowish, peach
APPEARANCE	Cubic or pyramidal crystals, may be transparent or opaque, small single crystals to large clusters
RARITY	Readily available
SOURCE	Britain, Australia, India, Brazil, Czech Republic, Italy

ATTRIBUTES Apophyllite has a high water content which makes it a very efficient conductor of energy and a carrier of the Akashic Record* (the esoteric record of all that has occurred and will occur, including past-life information). Its presence in a room enhances the energies as it is a powerful vibrational transmitter. Apophyllite creates a conscious connection between the physical and the spiritual realms. During out-of-body journeys*, it keeps a strong connection with the physical body, allowing information to be transmitted from the spiritual realm into the physical. This spiritual stone enhances clear sight, stimulating intuition and enabling the future to be accessed. It is an excellent stone for scrying*.

Psychologically, Apophyllite promotes introspection into one's own behavior, and the correction of imbalances or flaws that are perceived. It abandons pretence and breaks down reserve. This is a stone of truth, bringing recognition of one's true self and allowing that to be shown to the world.

Mentally, Apophyllite has a calming effect. It is an effective stress reducer, releasing mental blockages and negative thought patterns. It has the effect of reducing desire. At a spiritual level, Apophyllite imbues universal love into analysis and the decision-making process so that the mind becomes attuned to the spirit.

Emotionally, Apophyllite releases suppressed emotions. It overcomes anxiety, worries, and fears. It calms apprehension and allows uncertainty to be tolerated.

Spiritually this stone calms and grounds the spirit. It has strong links to the spiritual realm, while at the same time allowing you to feel comfortable within your body. It facilitates journeys out of the body and spiritual vision. With its connection to the Akashic Record, it eases journeys into past lives.

HEALING Apophyllite is regarded as the stone *par excellence* to assist Reiki* healing. It facilitates taking the patient into a deeper state of relaxation and receptiveness, and, at the same time takes the healer out of the way so that the transmission of healing energy to the patient is purer.

Apophyllite works on the respiratory system and, when held to the chest, can stop asthma attacks. It neutralizes allergies and promotes the regeneration of the mucus membranes and the skin. Placing an Apophyllite crystal on each eye rejuvenates the eyes. Apophyllite is especially useful in healing matters of the spirit and in helping the spirit to come to terms with being in a physical body.

POSITION Place as appropriate. Single Apophyllite pyramids can be placed on the third eye* when channeling or meditating. When scrying*, look into the crystal from the corner of the eye.

SPECIFIC COLORS AND FORMS
In addition to the generic attributes, the following colors have additional properties:

Green Apophyllite

Green Apophyllite activates the heart chakra* and promotes a forthright heart, especially regarding decisions in matters of the heart. It absorbs and then transmits universal energy. This stone opens the heart chakra and allows absorption of universal energies. It helps those undertaking fire walking as it facilitates a meditative state and cools the feet after the walk. It releases hypnotic commands* and other control mechanisms from present or past lives.

Apophyllite Pyramid

Apophyllite Pyramids are powerful energizers. They enhance spiritual vision and open the third eye. Looking through the base of the pyramid toward the apex opens a "star gate."* Like all pyramids, they have powers of preservation and can be used to charge up objects or other crystals. Made into an elixir, Apophyllite pyramids bring light and energy into the heart.

AQUAMARINE

Clear, raw

COLOR	Green-blue
APPEARANCE	Clear to opaque crystal, often small and tumbled or faceted
RARITY	Readily available
SOURCE	United States, Mexico, Russia, Brazil, India, Ireland, Zimbabwe, Afghanistan, Pakistan

ATTRIBUTES Aquamarine is a stone of courage. Its calming energies reduce stress and quiet the mind. It harmonizes its surroundings and protects against pollutants. In ancient times it was believed to counteract the forces of darkness and procure favor from the spirits of light. It was carried by sailors as a talisman against drowning.

67

Psychologically, Aquamarine has an affinity with sensitive people. It has the power to invoke tolerance of others. It overcomes judgmentalism, gives support to anyone who is overwhelmed by responsibility, and encourages taking responsibility for oneself. It creates a personality that is upright, persistent, and dynamic. It can break old, self-defeating programs.

Aquamarine calms the mind, removing extraneous thought. It filters information reaching the brain and clarifies perception, sharpens the intellect, and clears up confusion. With its ability to bring unfinished business to a conclusion, Aquamarine is useful for closure on all levels. It clears blocked communication and promotes self-expression. This stone is helpful in understanding underlying emotional states and interpreting how you feel. It soothes fears and increases sensitivity.

Spiritually, Aquamarine sharpens intuition and opens clairvoyance. A wonderful stone for meditation, it invokes high states of consciousness and spiritual awareness and encourages service to humanity.

Aquamarine shields the aura* and aligns the chakras*, clearing the throat chakra and bringing communication from a higher plane. It also aligns the physical and spiritual bodies.

HEALING Aquamarine is useful for sore throats, swollen glands, and thyroid problems. It harmonizes the pituitary and the thyroid, regulating hormones and growth. This stone has a general tonic effect. It strengthens the body's cleansing organs and aids the eyes, jaw and teeth, and stomach. It is useful for counteracting short- or long-sightedness and calms overreactions of the immune system and autoimmune diseases such as hay fever.

POSITION Hold or place as appropriate. Can be placed on the eyes or used as an elixir.

ARAGONITE

Brown "sputnik"
form

White "fan"
form

White "coral"
form

COLOR	White, yellow, gold, green, blue, brown
APPEARANCE	Several forms, usually small. Chalky and fibrous or translucent or transparent with distinct protrusions like little sputniks
RARITY	Easily obtained
SOURCE	Namibia, Britain, Spain

ATTRIBUTES Aragonite is a reliable earth-healer and grounding stone. Attuned to the Earth Goddess, it encourages conservation and recycling. This stone transforms geopathic stress* and clears blocked ley lines* even at a distance. With its ability to center and ground physical energies, it is useful in times of stress. Aragonite stabilizes the base and earth chakras*, deepening connection with the earth. It gently takes you back into childhood or beyond to explore the past.

Psychologically, Aragonite teaches patience and acceptance. It combats oversensitivity. Good for people who push themselves too hard, it facilitates delegating. Its practical energy encourages discipline and reliability, and develops a pragmatic approach to life.

Mentally, this stone aids concentration on the matter at hand, and brings flexibility and tolerance to the mind. It gives insight into the causes of problems and situations. Emotionally, Aragonite combats anger and emotional stress. It provides strength and support.

Physically, Aragonite is a stone that makes you feel comfortable and well within your own body. It combats dis-ease*, especially the nervous twitching and spasms that come out of inner unrest. It is a stabilizing stone that grounds and centers within the body.

Spiritually, Aragonite stabilizes spiritual development that is out of control. Calming and centering, it restores balance and prepares for meditation by raising vibrations to a high spiritual level and bringing energy into the physical body.

HEALING Aragonite warms the extremities, bringing energy through the body. It treats Reynaud's Disease and chills. It heals bones, aids calcium absorption, and restores elasticity to discs. It also ameliorates pain. Aragonite stops night twitches and muscle spasms. It strengthens the immune system and regulates processes that are proceeding too fast. It is useful for grounding floaty people into their body. Aragonite can be placed on a map to heal stress lines in the earth.

POSITION Hold or place over affected part, or bathe with elixir. Place under pillow to combat restlessness at night. Makes a useful hand comforter. Can be worn as a pendant for grounding.

ATACAMITE

*Atacamite
on matrix*

COLOR	Deep turquoise
APPEARANCE	Tiny crystals on matrix—resembles Chrysocolla
RARITY	Quite rare but becoming more widely available
SOURCE	United States, Australia, Mexico, Chile

ATTRIBUTES Atacamite is a newly discovered crystal and its properties have not yet been fully explored. (If you meditate with an Atacamite crystal, it will tell you how it wants to work for you.) It is sometimes confused with gem Chrysocolla and may share some properties with this crystal.

What is known is that Atacamite forcefully opens the third eye*, creating powerful visual images and a strong spiritual connection.

71

Despite its forcefulness, it is a very safe crystal to use to stimulate spiritual vision and aid visualization. It is a stone of great clarity. Used in meditation, it takes the soul safely to the highest possible levels.

Atacamite restores lost spiritual trust and promotes a connection to higher guidance. It is a useful stone to hold when journeying out of the body, especially to the higher spiritual spheres.

Atacamite works willingly to open the higher heart chakra*, bringing more unconditional love into your life, and to stimulate the thymus gland and immune system functioning.

HEALING Atacamite purifies the kidneys, removing fear, and promotes elimination at all levels. It is a powerful cleanser for the etheric body and the brow chakra. It can be used to heal the genitals and is said to improve resistance to herpes and venereal disease. Placed on the throat, Atacamite heals the thyroid gland, opening the throat chakra and removing the blockages to self-expression that can lie behind hypothyroidism. With its calming green color, it is also beneficial for the nervous system, overcoming stress and frayed nerves at a subtle level.

POSITION Place on the third eye* to stimulate visualization or over organs as appropriate. Hold in hands for meditation or journeying.

AVENTURINE

Blue, raw

COLOR	Green, blue, red, brown, peach
APPEARANCE	Opaque, speckled with shiny particles, all sizes, often tumbled
RARITY	Readily available
SOURCE	Italy, Brazil, China, India, Russia, Tibet, Nepal

ATTRIBUTES Aventurine is a very positive stone of prosperity. It has a strong connection to the devic kingdom* and is used to grid* gardens or houses against geopathic stress*. Wearing Aventurine absorbs electromagnetic smog* and protects against environmental pollution. Taped to a cell phone, it acts as a protection against its emanations. This crystal defuses negative situations and turns them around.

Psychologically, Aventurine reinforces leadership qualities and decisiveness. It promotes compassion and empathy and encourages perseverance. It takes you back into the past to find sources of dis-ease*. This stone relieves stammers and severe neuroses, bringing understanding of what lies behind the conditions. Aventurine stabilizes one's state of mind, stimulates perception, and enhances creativity.

73

It sees alternatives and possibilities, especially those presented by other people. This stone brings together the intellectual and emotional bodies. Aventurine calms anger and irritation. It stimulates emotional recovery and enables living within one's own heart.

Physically, Aventurine promotes a feeling of well-being. It regulates growth from birth to seven years. It balances male–female energy and encourages regeneration of the heart. Spiritually, Aventurine protects the heart chakra*, guarding against psychic vampirism* of heart energy.

HEALING Aventurine benefits the thymus gland, connective tissue, and nervous system; it balances blood pressure and stimulates the metabolism, lowering cholesterol and preventing arteriosclerosis and heart attacks. It has an anti-inflammatory effect and helps ease skin eruptions and allergies, relieves migraine headaches, and soothes the eyes. Aventurine heals the adrenals, lungs, sinuses, heart, and muscular and urogenital systems. As an elixir, it relieves skin problems.

*Peach
Aventurine
(raw)*

POSITION Hold or place on appropriate point.

*Green
Aventurine
(tumbled)*

SPECIFIC COLORS

In addition to the generic attributes, the following colors have additional properties:

Blue Aventurine is a powerful mental healer.

Green Aventurine is a comforter and heart healer, and general harmonizer, protecting the heart. It brings things back into control and is useful in malignant conditions. It settles nausea and dissolves negative emotions and thoughts. An all-round healer, bringing in well-being and emotional calm.

*Red
Aventurine
(raw)*

AZEZTULITE

Raw, opaque

COLOR	Colorless or white
APPEARANCE	Clear or opaque quartz with striations, usually small
RARITY	Rare and expensive
SOURCE	North Carolina (one seam, mined out)

ATTRIBUTES A rare and light-bearing crystal, Azeztulite is a stone for the New Age. Its extremely pure vibration, one of the most refined in the mineral kingdom, is attuned to the highest frequencies. It brings higher frequencies down to the earth to aid spiritual evolution.

This crystal expands your consciousness. If you are ready, it can lift your awareness and vibrations to a higher level. As Azeztulite raises your vibrations, it helps you to give out a positive vibration to benefit others. Azeztulite never requires cleansing and is always energized.

This crystal should be handled with care if you are not used to working in the spiritual realms or at high frequencies. The vibrational shift it induces is powerful and can have unpleasant side effects until it has been fully assimilated. Using other spiritual crystals such as Ametrine and Aquamarine prepares the way. Old patterns should be dissolved and emotional cleansing completed before undertaking this shift. The opaque form of Azeztulite has a less fine vibration and can be a useful staging post on the way to working with the more transparent form of the crystal.

Spiritually, Azeztulite facilitates meditation, instantly inducing a state of "no mind" and providing a protective spiral around the physical body. It stimulates the kundalini* to rise up the spine. A stone of vision and inspiration, Azeztulite opens the third eye and the crown and higher crown chakras* reaching up to spiritual levels. It tunes into spiritual guidance from the future, assisting in making important decisions.

Azeztulite activates the ascension points at the base of the spine, middle of the abdomen, and center of the brain to shift to a higher vibration while still in the physical body. Used on the third eye*, it helps you to see the future.

HEALING At a physical level, this crystal treats cancer, cellular disorders, and inflammation. It aids the chronically sick by revitalizing purpose and restoring the will. Most of Azeztulite's healing work is at the spiritual vibration, working on the chakra connections to higher reality and facilitating a vibrational shift.

POSITION Third eye, crown, or as appropriate.

AZURITE

Raw

COLOR	Deep blue
APPEARANCE	Very small, shiny crystals (not visible when tumbled), often small tumbled stone
RARITY	Easily obtained, often in combination with Malachite
SOURCE	United States, Australia, Chile, Peru, France, Namibia, Russia, Egypt

ATTRIBUTES Azurite guides psychic and intuitive development. It urges the soul toward enlightenment. It cleanses and stimulates the third eye* and attunes to spiritual guidance. This crystal enables journeys out of the body to take place easily and safely. It raises consciousness to a higher level and gives greater control over spiritual unfoldment. It facilitates entering a meditative and channeling* state. Azurite is a powerful healing stone, facilitating psychosomatic understanding of the effect of the mind and emotions on the body.

Mentally, Azurite brings about clear understanding and new perspectives, and expands the mind. It releases long-standing blocks in communication and stimulates memory. Azurite challenges your view of reality and lets go of programmed belief systems to move into the unknown without fear, reaching deeper insights and a new reality. Old beliefs gently rise into the conscious mind to be tested against truth.

Emotionally, Azurite clears stress, worry, grief, and sadness, allowing more light into the emotions. It transmutes fear and phobias, and brings in understanding of why they occurred in the first place. It calms someone who talks too much out of nervousness, or encourages someone who holds back from self-expression.

HEALING Azurite treats throat problems, arthritis and joint problems, aligns the spine, and works at a cellular level to restore any blockage or damage to the brain. It heals kidney, gallbladder, and liver problems, and treats the spleen, thyroid, bones, teeth, and skin and aids detoxification. It encourages the development of the embryo in the womb. Azurite has a special resonance with the mind and mental processes, mental healing, and stress relief. It can energize and realign the subtle bodies* with the physical, clearing the chakras*. Azurite elixir ameliorates a healing crisis* where symptoms temporarily get worse before improving.

POSITION Wear touching the skin on the right hand or place as appropriate directly on the body, especially on the third eye. May induce palpitations. If so, remove immediately.

COMBINATION STONE

Azurite with Malachite combines the qualities of the two crystals and is a powerful conductor of energy. It unlocks spiritual vision, strengthens the ability to visualize, and opens the third eye. At an emotional level it brings deep healing, cleansing ancient blocks, miasms*, or thought patterns. It overcomes muscle cramps.

Azurite with Malachtite (tumbled)

BERYL

Blue *Golden*

COLOR	Pink, golden, yellow, green, white, blue
APPEARANCE	Prismatic crystals, may be transparent and pyramidal, all sizes
RARITY	Readily available in most forms but may be expensive
SOURCE	United States, Russia, Australia, Brazil, Czech Republic, France, Norway

ATTRIBUTES Beryl teaches you how to do only that which you need to do. It is the stone *par excellence* for dealing with a stressful life and shedding unnecessary baggage. It aids in tuning into guidance as to what you should be doing. Representing purity of being, Beryl helps to actualize potential and is an excellent stone for scrying*, and is often used for crystal balls. It opens and activates the crown and solar plexus chakras*.

Psychologically, Beryl enhances courage, relieves stress, and calms the mind. Mentally, with its ability to filter out distractions and to reduce overstimulation, it encourages a positive view. It discourages overanalysis and anxiety. Emotionally, Beryl reawakens love in those who are married but jaded.

HEALING Beryl aids the organs of elimination, strengthens pulmonary and circulatory systems, and increases resistance to toxins and pollutants. It treats the liver, heart, stomach, and spine, and heals concussions. Beryl is a sedative stone. As an elixir it can be used to treat throat infections.

POSITION Place as appropriate or use for scrying*.

SPECIFIC COLORS
In addition to the generic attributes, the following colors have additional properties:

Golden Beryl is a seer's stone and is used for ritual magic. It aids scrying and magical workings. This crystal promotes purity of being. It teaches initiative and independence and stimulates the will to succeed and the ability to manifest potential into reality. It opens the crown and solar plexus chakras*.

Golden Beryl (polished)

Morganite (Pink Beryl) attracts love and maintains it. It encourages loving thoughts and actions, creating space to enjoy life and living. As a pink stone it activates and cleanses the heart chakra, calms a stressed life, and benefits the nervous system. This stone helps you to

Morganite (Pink Beryl)

recognize the escape routes, closed-mindedness, and egotism that block spiritual advancement. It assists in becoming aware of the disregarded needs of the soul. Morganite also aids in recognizing unfulfilled emotional needs and unexpressed feelings. Morganite is a powerful stone for dissolving conscious or unconscious resistance to healing and transformation, clearing the victim mentality and opening the heart to receive unconditional love and healing. It holds the emotional body stable while psychosomatic changes take place. Used in healing, Morganite treats stress and stress-related illness. Oxygenating cells and reorganizing them, it treats TB, asthma, emphysema, heart problems, vertigo, impotence, and lung blockages.

Bixbite (Red Beryl) opens and energizes the base chakras.

(*See also* Emerald, page 126.)

BERYL: **CHRYSOBERYL**

Raw   Faceted

COLOR	Golden yellow, yellow with brown, green with red
APPEARANCE	Tabular transparent crystals. Alexandrite appears green in natural light and red in artificial light. Cat's Eye or Cymophane is banded or eye-like
RARITY	Chrysoberyl readily available, Cat's Eye may be expensive, Alexandrite rare
SOURCE	Australia, Brazil, Myanmar, Canada, Ghana, Norway, Zimbabwe, Russia

ATTRIBUTES A form of Beryl, Chrysoberyl is a stone of new beginnings. It brings compassion and forgiveness, generosity and confidence. Aligning the solar plexus and crown chakras*, it incorporates the mind into spiritual endeavor and opens the crown chakra, increasing both spiritual and personal power, and is excellent for creativity.

Psychologically, Chrysoberyl strengthens self-worth and releases outworn energy patterns. Mentally, Chrysoberyl helps you to see both sides of a problem or situation and to use strategic planning. Emotionally, it encourages forgiveness for those who have perpetrated injustices.

HEALING Used with other crystals, Chrysoberyl highlights the cause of dis-ease. It supports self-healing, balances adrenaline and cholesterol, and fortifies the chest and liver.

SPECIFIC FORMS
In addition to the generic attributes, the following forms of Chrysoberyl have additional properties:

Alexandrite is a crystal of contrasts. It opens intuition and metaphysical abilities, creates a strong will and personal magnetism. Regenerative, it rebuilds self-respect, and supports rebirth of the inner and outer self. Alexandrite centers, reinforces, and realigns the mental, emotional, and spiritual bodies. It brings joy, expands creativity, expedites change, and enhances manifestation. An emotional soother, Alexandrite teaches how to expend less effort. It stimulates imagery, including dreams and the imagination. In healing it aids the nervous system, spleen, pancreas, and male reproductive organs and regenerates neurological tissue. Alexandrite treats nonassimilation of protein, side effects of leukemia, and relieves tension from neck muscles. It has a powerful detoxifying action and stimulates the liver.

Alexandrite

Cat's Eye has magical properties. It is a grounding stone but stimulates the intuition. It dispels negative energy from the aura* and provides protection. It brings confidence, happiness, serenity, and good luck. Cat's Eye treats eye disorders and improves night vision. It relieves headaches and facial pain. Wear on the right-hand side of the body.

Cat's Eye

Cymophane is a form of Cat's Eye. It stimulates and stabilizes the intellect and supports flexibility of mind. It enhances unconditional love.

Cymophane

BLOODSTONE

ALSO KNOWN AS HELIOTROPE

Tumbled

Raw

COLOR	Red-green
APPEARANCE	Green quartz flecked with red or yellow jasper, often medium tumbled stone
RARITY	Readily available
SOURCE	Australia, Brazil, China, Czech Republic, Russia, India

ATTRIBUTES As its name suggests, Bloodstone is an excellent blood cleanser and a powerful healer. It is believed to have mystical and magical properties, controlling the weather and conferring the ability to banish evil and negativity and to direct spiritual energies. In ancient times Bloodstone was said to have been an "audible oracle,"* giving off sounds as a means of guidance. It heightens the intuition and increases creativity. An excellent grounding and protecting stone, Bloodstone keeps out undesirable influences. It stimulates dreaming and is a powerful revitalizer.

Psychologically, Bloodstone gives courage and teaches how to avoid dangerous situations by strategic withdrawal and flexibility. It encourages selflessness and idealism and aids the recognition that chaos precedes transformation. Bloodstone assists you in acting in the present moment.

Mentally, Bloodstone calms the mind, dispels confusion, and enhances the decision-making process. It can revitalize the mind if you are mentally exhausted. This stone assists in adjusting to unaccustomed circumstances.

Emotionally, Bloodstone helps in grounding the heart energy. It reduces irritability, aggressiveness, and impatience. Spiritually, Bloodstone assists in bringing spirituality into everyday life.

HEALING Bloodstone is an energy cleanser and immune stimulator for acute infections. It stimulates the flow of lymph and the metabolic processes, revitalizes and reenergizes when body and mind are exhausted, purifies blood, and detoxifies the liver, intestines, kidneys, spleen, and bladder. Bloodstone benefits blood-rich organs, regulates and supports blood-flow, and aids the circulation. It reduces the formation of pus and neutralizes overacidification. It is helpful in cases of leukemia as it supports the blood and removes toxins. The ancient Egyptians used it to shrink tumors. Bloodstone can be used to heal the ancestral line. It cleanses the lower chakras* and realigns their energies.

POSITION As appropriate. Wear continually for good health. Place in a bowl of water beside the bed to ensure peaceful sleep. As an immune stimulator, tape over the thymus.

BOJI STONE

Raw

(Male)   *(Female)*

COLOR	Brownish, some blue
APPEARANCE	Metallic looking, smooth (female) or with square protrusions (male), small to medium size
RARITY	True Boji Stones can be difficult to obtain
SOURCE	United States, Britain

ATTRIBUTES Boji Stones are one of the most effective grounding stones. They gently but firmly return you to earth and into your body, grounding you in the present, especially after work in other spiritual realities. They are extremely useful for people who find it difficult to have more than a toehold in incarnation. They have a strongly protective function and are very useful for overcoming blockages.

The smooth stones have feminine energy, the protruded ones masculine energy. Boji Stones are balancers and energizers and a pair balances the male–female energy within the body and aligns the chakras and the subtle bodies*.

With their strong earth connection, Boji Stones are beneficial to plants and crops, but the stone may well disintegrate if left in the ground or exposed to the weather.

Psychologically, Boji Stones throw light on blockages at all levels. They clear blocked emotions and heal hurtful memories. They also reveal negative thought patterns and self-defeating behaviors for transformation. Going to the cause of psychosomatic disease, they dissolve blockages in the physical or subtle bodies. Holding a Boji Stone will align you to your shadow self, bringing up its repressed qualities so that you can gently release them and find the gift in them.

Physically, Boji Stones stimulate the flow of energy through the meridian systems of the body. Mentally, Boji Stones bring your attention to mental imprints and hypnotic commands from the past. Boji Stones can be emotionally stabilizing, but they tend to insist that any necessary work is done first.

HEALING Boji Stones heal energy blockages, relieve pain, and encourage tissue regeneration. They are useful when physical energy is low or when the condition is intractable. On a subtle level they realign the chakras* and repair and reenergize "holes" in the auric* body.

POSITION Hold a pair of Bojis in your hands for ten minutes or so, or place over a blocked or painful point. You can also grid* around your chair while meditating.

Blue Boji Stones have a high but grounded spiritual vibration. They are extremely useful when taking journeys out of the body as they facilitate traveling and guard the body until the soul returns.

CALCITE

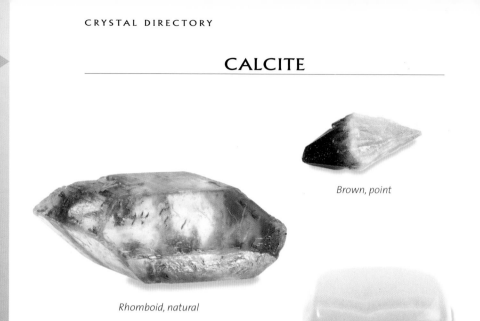

Brown, point

Rhomboid, natural

Mangano, tumbled

COLOR	Green, blue, yellow, orange, clear, brown, pink gray, red
APPEARANCE	Translucent and waxy, often banded (may be acid-treated to enhance color), all sizes sometimes tumbled
RARITY	Common
SOURCE	United States, Britain, Belgium, Czech Republic, Slovakia, Peru, Iceland, Romania, Brazil

ATTRIBUTES Calcite is a powerful amplifier and cleanser of energy. Simply having Calcite in the room cleans negative energies from the environment and heightens your energy. Within the body, it removes stagnant energy. The spectrum of colors cleans the physical and subtle bodies. Calcite is an active crystal, speeding up development and growth. This is a spiritual stone linked to the higher consciousness that facilitates the opening of higher awareness and psychic abilities, channeling, and out-of-body experiences. It accelerates spiritual development and allows the soul to remember experiences when it returns to the body.

Psychologically, Calcite connects the emotions with the intellect, creating emotional intelligence. Calcite has a positive effect, especially where someone has lost hope or motivation. It combats laziness, aiding in becoming more energetic on all levels.

Mentally, Calcite calms the mind, teaches discernment and analysis, stimulates insights, and boosts memory. It facilitates knowing which information is important, and then retaining it. Calcite confers the ability to change ideas into action. It is a useful stone for study.

Calcite alleviates emotional stress and replaces it with serenity. It is a stabilizing stone, enhancing trust in oneself and strengthening the ability to overcome setbacks. On a subtle level, a layout of the appropriate colors of Calcite cleanses, balances, and energizes all the chakras*.

HEALING Calcite cleanses the organs of elimination. It encourages calcium uptake in bones but dissolves calcifications, strengthening the skeleton and joints. It alleviates intestinal and skin conditions. Calcite stimulates blood clotting and tissue healing. It fortifies the immune system and can encourage growth in small children. Calcite works quickly as an elixir and can be applied to the skin, ulcers, warts, and suppurating wounds. At a subtle level, Calcite cleans and reenergizes the chakras*.

POSITION Hold or place as appropriate. Wear as a pendant. Can be used to grid around a bed. Use as gem essence.

SPECIFIC COLORS
In addition to the generic attributes, the following colors have additional properties:

Black Calcite is a record-keeper stone for regression and regaining memories so that the past can be released. It returns the soul to the body after trauma or stress, alleviates depression, and is a useful companion during a dark night of the soul.

Black Calcite (raw)

Blue Calcite is a gentle stone for recuperation and relaxation. It lowers blood pressure and dissolves pain on all levels. Gently soothing the nerves and lifting anxieties, it releases negative emotions. Used on the throat chakra* it aids clear communication, especially where there is dissent. Blue Calcite can absorb energy, filter it, and return it to benefit the sender.

Blue Calcite

Clear Calcite is a "cure-all," especially as an elixir. It is a powerful detoxifier. At a physical level it acts as an antiseptic and at the subtle levels it cleanses and aligns all the chakras*, higher and lower. A clear Calcite with rainbows brings about

Clear Calcite

major change—it is a stone of new beginnings. Clear Calcite brings the gift of deep soul healing and revitalization of the subtle bodies*. It opens and clears the inner and outer eyes.

Gold Calcite is excellent for meditation and for attuning to the higher mental planes. It instills mental alertness as it grounds the higher mental energies into the physical realm. Place on the navel or crown chakras.

Gold Calcite (raw)

Green Calcite is a mental healer, dissolving rigid beliefs and old programs and restoring balance to the mind. It helps in letting go of what is familiar and comforting but which no longer serves, and aids communication and the transition from a stagnant to a positive situation. Green Calcite helps children to hold their own in debates. It is a powerful stimulator for the immune system and is especially useful in grids*. This stone absorbs negativity and rids the body of bacterial infections. It ameliorates arthritis and constrictions of the ligaments or muscles and is helpful in bone adjustments. Its green ray cools fevers, burns, and inflammation, calms the adrenals, and soothes anger-generated dis-ease*.

Green Calcite

91

Green Calcite placed regularly on the body absorbs dis-ease* and should be cleansed thoroughly after use.

Iceland Spar (Optical Calcite) amplifies images and heals the eyes. It can aid in seeing the double meaning hidden behind words. It reduces the tension that causes migraines. This form of Calcite is an excellent cleanser of the subtle bodies*.

Icelandic Calcite

Orange Calcite is a highly energizing and cleansing stone, especially for the lower chakras*. Orange Calcite balances the emotions, removes fear, and overcomes depression. It dissolves problems and maximizes potential. This stone heals the reproductive system, gallbladder, and intestinal disorders such as irritable bowel syndrome (IBS), and removes mucus from the system.

Orange Calcite

Pink Calcite (Mangano Calcite) is a heart crystal in contact with the angelic realm*. A stone of forgiveness, it releases fear and grief that keep the heart trapped in the past, bringing in unconditional love. It aids self-worth and self-acceptance, heals nervous conditions, and lifts tension and anxiety. This stone prevents nightmares. Pink Calcite's loving energy gently dissolves resistance. It is helpful for anyone who has suffered trauma or assault.

Red Calcite

Red Calcite increases energy, uplifts emotions, aids willpower, and opens the heart chakra. It removes stagnant energy, including constipation, and dissolves blockages. It resonates to the base chakras, which it energizes and heals. It alleviates fear, bringing understanding of the source. Red Calcite's vitality energizes a party. At a physical level, it heals hip and lower limb problems, loosening up joints, and on a subtle level it removes the blockages that prevent you from stepping forward in your life.

Rhomboid Calcite closes off mind chatter, bringing mental stillness. It is a powerful healer of the past.

Yellow Calcite

Yellow or Golden Calcite is a great eliminator and stimulates the will. Its energy, especially as an elixir, is uplifting. It enhances meditation, inducing a deep state of relaxation and spirituality and linking to the highest source of spiritual guidance. It stimulates the higher mind. Use at the crown and solar plexus chakras. Golden Calcite has an extremely expansive energy.

Green Calcite that has been acid-treated to enhance its color and texture

93

CARNELIAN

*Natural
formation*

COLOR	Red, orange, pink, brown
APPEARANCE	Small, translucent pebble, often water-worn or tumbled
RARITY	Common
SOURCE	Britain, India, Czech Republic, Slovakia, Peru, Iceland, Romania

ATTRIBUTES Carnelian grounds and anchors you in the present reality. A stabilizing stone with high energy, it is excellent for restoring vitality and motivation, and for stimulating creativity. It is useful for dramatic pursuits. Carnelian has the ability to cleanse other stones.

Psychologically, Carnelian imparts an acceptance of the cycle of life and removes fear of death. In ancient times it was used to protect the dead on their journey to the afterlife. It gives courage, promotes positive life choices, dispels apathy, and motivates for success in business and other matters. Carnelian is useful for overcoming abuse of any kind. This stone helps you to trust yourself and your perceptions. It gets to the bottom of what makes you tick, overcomes negative conditioning, and encourages steadfastness.

Mentally, Carnelian improves analytic abilities and clarifies perception. It removes extraneous thoughts in meditation and tunes daydreamers into everyday reality. It sharpens concentration and dispels mental lethargy. Emotionally, this stone is a powerful protector against envy, rage, and resentment, yours or other people's. It calms anger and banishes emotional negativity, replacing it with a love of life.

HEALING Carnelian is full of the life force and vitality. It stimulates the metabolism. Carnelian activates the base chakra*, influences the female reproductive organs, and increases fertility. This stone overcomes frigidity and impotence, heals lower back problems, rheumatism, arthritis, neuralgia, and depression, especially in those of advanced years. It regulates bodily fluids and the kidneys, accelerates healing in bones and ligaments, and stanches blood. Carnelian improves the absorption of vitamins and minerals and ensures a good supply of blood to organs and tissues.

POSITION Use as a pendant or belt buckle, or place in contact with the skin as appropriate. Carnelian near the front door invokes protection and invites abundance into the home.

SPECIFIC COLORS
In addition to the generic attributes, the following colors have additional properties:

Pink Carnelian

Pink Carnelian improves the parent–child relationship. It helps to restore love and trust after abuse or manipulation.

*Orange
Carnelian*

Red Carnelian warms and energizes. It is particularly useful for combating sluggishness and for invigorating the mind and body.

95

CELESTITE

Blue geode

Blue point

COLOR	Blue, yellow, red, white
APPEARANCE	Transparent, pyramidal crystals as medium to large cluster or geode, or platelike piece
RARITY	Easily obtained but quite expensive
SOURCE	Britain, Egypt, Mexico, Peru, Poland, Libya, Madagascar

ATTRIBUTES Celestite has a high vibration and is a teacher for the New Age. It is imbued with divine energies. It takes you into the infinite peace of the spiritual and contacts the angelic realms*. It jump-starts spiritual development and urges you toward enlightenment. It is a useful stone for stimulating clairvoyant* communication, dream recall, and journeys out of the body*. This beautiful crystal promotes purity of the heart and attracts good fortune. It heals the aura* and reveals truth. It is a stone that brings balance and alignment. The deep peace it holds assists in conflict resolution and in maintaining a harmonious atmosphere in times of stress. Celestite can improve dysfunctional relationships by opening a space for peaceful negotiation.

Celestite is a creative stone, especially useful for the arts.

Psychologically, Celestite imparts gentle strength and enormous inner peace despite urging toward greater openness to new experiences. It is a teacher of trust in the infinite wisdom of the divine. With its calming effect, Celestite can cool fiery emotions.

Mentally, Celestite calms and sharpens the mind, dispersing worries and promoting mental clarity and fluent communication. It aids the analysis of complex ideas. This stone synthesizes intellect with instinct and promotes mental balance.

Placed on the third eye*, Celestite opens a connection to the universal energies. It brings a vision of peaceful coexistence with the whole of creation and holds the possibility of total harmony.

HEALING Celestite is an excellent healing stone, dissolving pain and bringing in love. It treats disorders of the eyes and ears, eliminates toxins, and brings cellular order. Its soothing influence relaxes muscle tension and calms mental torment. As with all blue crystals, Celestite is an effective opener and healer of the throat chakra* and its associated physical conditions.

POSITION Place as appropriate or use for meditation and scrying*. A large piece of Celestite placed within a room heightens the vibrations in that room. Do not place in direct sunlight as color will fade.

CERUSSITE

*Record-keeper
(note chevrons)*

COLOR	White, gray, gray-black, yellow
APPEARANCE	White and yellow translucent crystals, or gray and black granular, usually on a matrix
RARITY	Can be obtained from specialist stores
SOURCE	Namibia

ATTRIBUTES Cerussite is an excellent grounding stone that assists in feeling comfortable in the environment. It is extremely useful for people who feel that the earth is not their natural home, as it ameliorates "homesickness" and makes the soul feel at home wherever it finds itself. Cerussite may also form a star-shaped or record-keeper crystal. These precious stones attune to higher wisdom and karmic purpose*. Meditating reveals the unique secrets they hold for you. The star is said to assist in extraterrestrial contact. Cerussite helps to explore past lives that were not on earth and in recognizing people from past lives and the place they hold in the present. It explains why you chose to come to earth, the lessons you are learning, the task you have to do, and the gifts you bring to advance the evolution of humanity. This stone assists in letting go of the past and its effects.

Cerussite is beneficial for travel, whether on business or for pleasure, reducing jet lag and helping you to adjust to a different culture. This is a useful stone for making short-term compromises and adjusting to situations to which inner resistance is strong.

Cerussite is a pragmatic stone that promotes decision-making and stimulates growth. Teaching how to become flexible and how to take responsibility, it relieves tension and anxiety and shows how to adapt to necessary change. It instills the ability to be tactful in any situation and helps to promote extroversion rather than withdrawal.

Enhancing communication, Cerussite makes correspondence easy and imparts the ability to listen attentively. It balances the right- and left-brain hemispheres and encourages creativity. It is an excellent stone for anyone engaged in the arts.

Cerussite elixir has a useful insecticidal property. It can be sprayed onto house plants or into a room to protect from pests and diseases.

ATTRIBUTES Cerussite is a wonderful stone for imparting vitality and energy, especially where an illness has persisted for some time. It aligns the nervous system, treating involuntary movements, and strengthens muscles and bones. It is helpful for Parkinson's and Tourette's Syndrome. It overcomes insomnia and nightmares.

POSITION Place or hold as appropriate. Use as an elixir for pest control and for house plants.

CHALCEDONY

White geode

Blue (tumbled)

COLOR	White, pink, blue, red, grayish
APPEARANCE	Transparent or opaque, sometimes banded, all sizes, often seen as geode or small tumbled stone
RARITY	Common
SOURCE	United States, Austria, Czech Republic, Slovakia, Iceland, Mexico, Britain, Mexico, New Zealand, Turkey, Russia, Brazil, Morocco

ATTRIBUTES Chalcedony is a nurturing stone that promotes brotherhood and good will and enhances group stability. It can be used to assist thought transmission and telepathy. This stone absorbs negative energy and then dissipates it to prevent onward transmission.

In ancient times, chalices would be formed out of Chalcedony and lined with silver. They were said to prevent poisoning.

Chalcedony brings the mind, body, emotions, and spirit into harmony.

Instilling feelings of benevolence and generosity, Chalcedony removes hostility and transforms melancholy into joy. Psychologically, Chalcedony eases self-doubt and facilitates constructive inward reflection. It creates an open and enthusiastic persona. It absorbs and dissipates negative thoughts, emotions, and bad dreams.

HEALING Chalcedony is a powerful cleanser, including open sores. It fosters the maternal instinct and increases lactation, improves mineral assimilation, and combats mineral buildup in veins. Chalcedony lessens the effects of dementia and senility. This stone increases physical energy. It balances body, emotions, mind, and spirit and heals the eyes, gallbladder, bones, spleen, blood, and circulatory system.

POSITION Wear on fingers, around neck, on belt buckle, or place as appropriate, especially over organs and in contact with the skin.

SPECIFIC COLORS
In addition to the generic attributes, the following colors and forms have additional properties:

Blue Chalcedony (raw)

Blue Chalcedony is a creative stone. It opens the mind to assimilate new ideas and helps acceptance of new situations. Blue Chalcedony imparts mental flexibility and verbal dexterity, enhancing listening skills and communication. It stimulates the ability to learn new languages and improves memory. Blue Chalcedony gives a feeling of light-heartedness and the ability to look forward optimistically. It improves self-perception. This stone was traditionally used in weather magic and for clearing illnesses associated with changes in the weather.

Physically, Blue Chalcedony aids regeneration of mucus membranes and ameliorates dis-ease* caused by weather sensitivity or pressure, such as glaucoma. Blue Chalcedony enhances the immune system. It stimulates the flow of lymph and banishes edema, has an anti-inflammatory effect, and lowers temperature and blood pressure. It heals the lungs and clears the respiratory system of the effects of smoking.

Dendritic Chalcedony promotes clear and precise thought. This stone is useful when you are under pressure or attack as it facilitates calm communication while remaining relaxed. It encourages living in the present moment and helps you to face up to unpleasant matters. Dendritic Chalcedony helps in processing memories and brings joy to life. This stone supports an easy, friendly approach to other people. It promotes tolerant interaction without judgment.

Dendritic Chalcedony is a useful stone for chronic illness, for which it should be worn for long periods, and problems associated with smoking, strengthening the immune system. It enhances the assimilation of copper into the body, detoxifies the liver, removes inflammations of the female sexual organs, and treats thrush.

Pink Chalcedony encourages kindness and all good qualities. It brings out a sense of childlike wonder and

Pink Chalcedony (raw)

willingness to learn new things. It encourages storytelling as a form of creativity. This is a spiritual stone that encourages empathy and inner peace. It creates a deep sense of trust.

This stone is particularly useful for treating psychosomatic dis-eases*. Pink Chalcedony fortifies the heart and supports the immune system. It eases breastfeeding problems and the flow of lymphatic fluids.

Red Chalcedony bestows strength and persistence in reaching goals. It advises when to fight and when to give in gracefully. A confident stone, it helps to manifest dreams, devising strategies to bring these into being in the most positive way. As a healing stone, Red Chalcedony stimulates the circulation without raising blood pressure and encourages clotting of the blood. It reduces hunger pangs but should not be used for long periods, as it inhibits the absorption of nutrients and may cause temporary nausea.

NOTE Chalcedony geodes that have been painted silver or various colors are sold in Morocco and other places. The paint runs when wet to reveal white or gray Chalcedony underneath. The attributes are as generic Chalcedony.

CHAROITE

Polished

COLOR	Purple
APPEARANCE	Mottled, swirled and veined, often small to medium, tumbled or polished
RARITY	Becoming more easily obtainable
SOURCE	Russia

ATTRIBUTES Charoite is a stone of transformation. It is the soul stone that overcomes fear. Charoite stimulates inner vision and spiritual insight and aids in coping with enormous change at a spiritual level. To facilitate this, it synthesizes the heart and crown chakras*, cleanses the aura*, and stimulates unconditional love. Charoite encourages vibrational change and links to higher realities. At the same time, it provides deep physical and emotional healing. It helps you to accept the present moment as perfect.

Psychologically, Charoite integrates "negative qualities" and facilitates acceptance of others. It releases deep fears and is particularly useful for overcoming resistance or putting things into perspective. It bestows drive, vigor, and spontaneity and is able to reduce stress and worry, bringing about a relaxed attitude. Charoite can be used to overcome compulsions and obsessions. By balancing the crown chakra, it assists in overcoming a sense of alienation or frustration.

Mentally, Charoite stimulates perceptive observations and analysis and applies these to facilitate a fast decision. It helps anyone who is driven by other people's thoughts and programs rather than their own.

Spiritually, Charoite grounds the spiritual self into everyday reality. It encourages a path of service to humanity. This stone opens and balances the crown chakra. It can bring insightful visions of past lives and suggests ways to redress karma on a personal and collective level.

HEALING Charoite transmutes negative energy into healing and converts dis-ease into wellness. It reenergizes the body when exhausted, heals and integrates dualities, and regulates blood pressure. Charoite treats the eyes, heart, liver, and pancreas. It reverses liver damage due to alcohol, and alleviates cramps, aches, and pains. Charoite bestows deep sleep with powerful dreams, overcomes insomnia, and gives children calm sleep. It is helpful where dysfunction of the autonomic nervous system is affecting the heart. Charoite heals autism and bipolar disorders.

POSITION Over heart or placed as appropriate in contact with the skin. Gridding with Charoite is highly effective. Gem elixir is an excellent cleanser for the physical body and stabilizer for emotional turmoil.

CHIASTOLITE

ALSO KNOWN AS CROSS STONE, ANDALUSITE

Andalusite

Green

Brown

COLOR	Brown-gray, rose, gray, reddish-brown, olive green
APPEARANCE	Distinctive cross in center of stone, often small and tumbled
RARITY	Easily obtained
SOURCE	Chile, Russia, Spain

ATTRIBUTES Chiastolite is a powerfully protective stone. In ancient times it was used to ward off ill wishing and curses. It has the property of transmuting dissension into harmony. This is a creative stone with the power to dispel negative thoughts and feelings. It transmutes conflict into harmony and aids problem-solving and change.

Chiastolite is a gateway into mysteries and facilitates journeys out of the body. It facilitates understanding and exploration of immortality. Linked to death and rebirth, it is helpful for those making the transition beyond death. This stone can provide the answer to mysterious events.

Psychologically, Chiastolite dissolves illusions and calms fears, enabling you to face reality, and is particularly helpful in overcoming the fear of going mad. It aids in the transition between one situation and another, especially at the psychological level, and releases worn-out patterns and conditioning.

Mentally, Chiastolite aids problem-solving by strengthening analytic capabilities. Emotionally, Chiastolite clears feelings of guilt and stabilizes the emotions. Chiastolite maintains spirituality during illness or trauma, invoking protective forces. It assists in attuning to the soul's purpose.

HEALING Chiastolite lessens fevers, stanches blood flow, and alleviates overacidification, healing rheumatism and gout. It stimulates lactation in nursing mothers. This stone repairs chromosome damage and balances the immune system. It can cure paralysis and is a nerve fortifier.

POSITION Place as appropriate or wear around neck.

Green Andalusite is a heart cleanser and balancing stone. It releases emotional and chakra* blockages caused by pent-up anger and old emotional trauma, and is very helpful in psycho- or crystal therapy.

CHLORITE

Chlorite Phantom

COLOR	Green
APPEARANCE	Several forms, usually opaque, may be occluded in Quartz (generic name for a group)
RARITY	Easily obtained
SOURCE	Russia, Germany, United States

ATTRIBUTES A powerful, positive healing stone, beneficial for the environment or personal energy field. With Amethyst, it removes energy implants* and wards off psychic attack*. With Carnelian and Ruby, it protects against psychic attack and assists earthbound spirits to move on.

HEALING Chlorite assists in the elimination of toxins and the assimilation of Vitamins A and E, iron, magnesium, and calcium. It is a useful painkiller and removes skin growths and liver spots. This stone encourages the proliferation of helpful bacteria.

POSITION Hold or place as appropriate. Grid* an area against negative energies or entities.

(*See also* Chlorite Phantom, pages 233–234, and Seraphinite, page 262.)

CHRYSANTHEMUM STONE

Natural

COLOR	Brown, gray with white
APPEARANCE	Resembles the flower of a chrysanthemum, medium stone
RARITY	Readily available
SOURCE	China, Japan, Canada, United States

ATTRIBUTES Chrysanthemum Stone drifts gently through time, facilitating time travel. It exudes calm confidence and enhances any environment with its gentle presence. Radiating harmony, it synthesizes change with equilibrium and shows how the two can work together. This stone helps you to enjoy being centered in the present moment and encourages the self to bloom. It inspires and energizes, and brings endeavors to fruition. Chrysanthemum Stone teaches how to remain childlike, fun-loving, and innocent while on the spiritual path, and provides an impetuousity to self-development. Strengthening character, it overcomes bigotry, ignorance, narrow-mindedness, self-righteousness, and jealousy and encourages showing more love to the world, which in turn brings more love into your life.

Mentally, Chrysanthemum Stone counteracts superficiality. It adds depth to thought and guards against distractions. With Chrysanthemum Stone, the bigger picture can be perceived. Emotionally, Chrysanthemum Stone brings stability and trust, eliminating resentment and animosity.

HEALING Chrysanthemum Stone promotes physical maturation and transition. It treats the skin, skeleton, and eyes. It is a useful stone for dispersing toxins and dissolving growths.

POSITION Wear, carry, or place in the environment. Use as an elixir, but make by the indirect method of placing the stone in a glass bowl within the bowl of water as otherwise the "flower" is affected.

CHRYSOCOLLA

Raw

Polished

COLOR	Green, blue, turquoise
APPEARANCE	Opaque, often bands or inclusions, all sizes, frequently tumbled or polished
RARITY	Common
SOURCE	United States, Britain, Mexico, Chile, Peru, Zaire, Russia

ATTRIBUTES Chrysocolla is a tranquil and sustaining stone. It helps meditation and communication. Within the home, Chrysocolla draws off negative energies of all kinds. It can help you to accept with serenity situations that are constantly changing, invoking great inner strength. It is beneficial to relationships that have become rocky, stabilizing and healing both the home and personal interaction.

Chrysocolla calms, cleanses, and reenergizes all the chakras* and aligns them with the divine. At the solar plexus chakra, it draws out negative

111

emotions such as guilt, and reverses destructive emotional programming. At the heart chakra, it heals heartache and increases the capacity to love. At the throat, it improves communication but helps you to discern when to keep silent. At the third eye*, it opens psychic vision.

Psychologically, Chrysocolla encourages self-awareness and inner balance, and imparts confidence and sensitivity. It enhances personal power and inspires creativity. Overcoming phobias, it draws out negativity and supplies motivation for those who lack it.

Mentally, Chrysocolla reduces mental tensions and helps you to keep a cool head. It promotes truth-telling and impartiality. Emotionally, Chrysocolla alleviates guilt and brings in joy.

HEALING Chrysocolla treats arthritis, bone disease, muscle spasms, the digestive tract, ulcers, blood disorders, and lung problems. It detoxifies the liver, kidneys, and intestines. It reoxygenates the blood and the cellular structure of the lungs, giving greater lung and breathing capacity, and regenerates the pancreas, regulates insulin, and balances blood. This stone strengthens muscles and alleviates muscle cramps. With its cooling action, it heals infections, especially in the throat and tonsils, lowers blood pressure, and soothes burns. It relieves arthritic

pain, strengthens the thyroid and is beneficial to the metabolism. An excellent stone for women, Chrysocolla treats PMS and menstrual cramps. On a subtle level, Chrysocolla dissolves miasms*.

POSITION Place as appropriate on skin or third eye.

COMBINATION STONE

Drusy Chrysocolla

Drusy Chrysocolla combines the properties of Chrysocolla with those of Quartz. This stone has great clarity and works extremely fast.

112

CHRYSOPRASE

Lemon
(tumbled)

Tumbled

Raw

COLOR	Apple green, lemon
APPEARANCE	Opaque, flecked, often small and tumbled
RARITY	Common
SOURCE	United States, Russia, Brazil, Australia, Poland, Tanzania

ATTRIBUTES Chrysoprase imparts a sense of being a part of the divine whole. It induces deep meditative states. Said by the ancients to promote love of truth, Chrysoprase also promotes hope and gives personal insights. It draws out talents and stimulates creativity. It encourages fidelity in business and personal relationships. This crystal energizes the heart and sacral chakras* and brings universal energy into the physical body.

Psychologically, Chrysoprase is calming and nonegotistical, creating openness to new situations. It assists in looking at egotistical motives in the past and the effect they have had on your development, and it aligns your ideals with your behavior. Overcoming compulsive or impulsive thoughts and actions, it turns your attention to positive events. This stone opposes judgmentalism, stimulating acceptance of oneself and others. It is useful for forgiveness and compassion.

Mentally, Chrysoprase stimulates fluent speech and mental dexterity. It prevents you from speaking out unthinkingly in anger. It lifts oppressive and recurrent images, preventing nightmares, especially in children. Emotionally, Chrysoprase brings a sense of security and trust. It is useful in healing codependence, supporting independence and yet encouraging commitment.

Physically, Chyrosprase has a strong detoxifying action. It can mobilize heavy metals out of the body, and it stimulates liver function.

HEALING Chrysoprase is excellent for relaxation and peaceful sleep. Resonating with the sacral chakra*, it enhances fertility, reverses infertility caused by infection, and guards against sexually transmitted diseases. This stone aids gout, eye problems, and mental illness. It treats skin diseases, heart problems, and goiters, balances the hormones, and soothes the digestive system. Chrysoprase ameliorates infirmity and brings universal energy into the body. It increases absorption of Vitamin C. Combined with Smoky Quartz, it treats fungal infections. The elixir calms stomach problems caused by stress. Chrysoprase heals the inner child*, releasing emotions locked in since childhood. It reduces claustrophobia and nightmares.

POSITION Wear or place as appropriate. In acute cases, use as an elixir. Carrying Chrysoprase for long periods attunes to the devic realm*.

CINNABAR

ALSO KNOWN AS DRAGON'S BLOOD

*Raw crystals
on matrix*

COLOR	Red, brown-red, gray
APPEARANCE	Small, crystalline or granular mass on matrix
RARITY	Readily available but expensive
SOURCE	China, United States

ATTRIBUTES Cinnabar attracts abundance. It increases persuasiveness and assertiveness in selling, and aids in prospering in one's endeavors without inciting aggression. It also assists organization and community work, business, and finance. Cinnabar is helpful when you want to enhance your persona or change your image as it invests a person with dignity and power. It makes the outward demeanor aesthetically pleasing and elegant. Mentally, Cinnabar imparts fluency to the mind and to speech. At a spiritual level, it connects to the acceptance of everything being perfect exactly as it is. It releases energy blockages and aligns the energy centers.

HEALING Cinnabar heals and purifies blood. It imparts strength and flexibility to the physical body, stabilizes weight, and enhances fertility.

POSITION Hold or place as appropriate. Keep in cash box.

115

CITRINE

ALSO KNOWN AS CAIRNGORM

Point

Geode

COLOR	Yellow to yellowish brown or smoky gray-brown
APPEARANCE	Transparent crystals, all sizes, often as geode, point, or cluster
RARITY	Natural Citrine is comparatively rare; heat-treated Amethyst is often sold as Citrine
SOURCE	Brazil, Russia, France, Madagascar, Britain, United States

Cluster

ATTRIBUTES Citrine is a powerful cleanser and regenerator. Carrying the power of the sun, this is an exceedingly beneficial stone. It is warming, energizing, and highly creative. This is one of the crystals that never needs cleansing. It absorbs, transmutes, dissipates, and grounds negative energy and is therefore extremely protective for the environment. Citrine energizes every level of life. As an aura* protector, it acts as an early warning system so that action can be taken to protect oneself. It has the ability to cleanse the chakras*, especially the solar plexus and navel chakras. It activates the crown chakra and opens the intuition. Citrine cleanses and balances the subtle bodies*, aligning them with the physical.

Citrine is one of the stones of abundance. This dynamic stone teaches how to manifest and attracts wealth and prosperity, success, and all good things. Citrine is a happy, generous stone and encourages sharing what you have and yet helps you to hold on to your wealth. It has the power to impart joy to all who behold it. Gloom and negativity have no place around Citrine. It is a useful stone for smoothing group or family discord.

Psychologically, Citrine raises self-esteem and self-confidence, and removes destructive tendencies. It enhances individuality, improves motivation, activates creativity, and encourages self-expression. It makes you less sensitive, especially to criticism, and encourages acting on constructive criticism. It helps you develop a positive attitude and to look forward optimistically, going with the flow instead of hanging on to the past. This stone promotes enjoyment of new experiences and encourages exploring every possible avenue until you find the best solution.

Mentally, Citrine enhances concentration and revitalizes the mind. It is excellent for overcoming depression, fears, and phobias. Citrine promotes inner calm so that wisdom can emerge. It helps in digesting information, analyzing situations and steering them in a positive direction. This stone awakens the higher mind. Wearing a Citrine pendant overcomes difficulty in verbalizing thoughts and feelings.

Emotionally, Citrine promotes joy in life. It releases negative traits, fears, and feelings at the deepest of levels. It overcomes fear of responsibility and stops anger. This stone helps you move into the flow of feelings and become emotionally balanced.

Physically, Citrine imparts energy and invigoration to the physical body. It is useful for people who are particularly sensitive to environmental and other outside influences.

HEALING Citrine is an excellent stone for energizing and recharging. It is highly beneficial for CFS* and reverses degenerative disease. Citrine stimulates digestion, the spleen, and the pancreas. It negates infections in the kidney and bladder, helps eye problems, increases blood circulation, detoxifies the blood, activates the thymus, and balances the thyroid. It has a warming effect and fortifies the nerves. Citrine is an eliminator—it relieves constipation and removes cellulite. As an elixir, it is helpful for menstrual problems and menopausal symptoms such as hot flashes, balancing the hormones and alleviating fatigue.

POSITION Wear on fingers or throat in contact with the skin. Wearing a Citrine pointdown brings the golden ray of spirit into the physical realm. Position as appropriate for healing. Use a sphere for meditation. Place in the wealth corner of your home or business, or in your cash box. Citrine fades in sunlight.

Wealth corner

House viewed from above

Front door

The wealth corner is the farthest back left point from your front door or the door into an individual room

DANBURITE

Pink

COLOR	Pink, yellow, white, lilac
APPEARANCE	Clear with striations, all sizes
RARITY	Readily available
SOURCE	United States, Czech Republic, Russia, Switzerland, Japan, Mexico, Myanmar

ATTRIBUTES Danburite is a highly spiritual stone carrying a very pure vibration and working on the heart energy. It activates both the intellect and higher consciousness, linking into the angelic realms*. Its brilliance comes from cosmic light and Danburite is sometimes found with a Buddha formation within the crystal that draws enlightenment and spiritual light. It smoothes the path ahead.

Wearing Danburite provides a link to serenity and eternal wisdom. Used in meditation, it takes you to a high state of consciousness and accesses inner guidance.

Danburite is an excellent stone for facilitating deep change and for leaving the past behind. It can act as a karmic cleanser, releasing miasms* and mental imperatives that have been carried forward. It starts the soul off on a new direction. Placed by the bedside, this crystal can accompany the dying on their journey beyond death, enabling a conscious spiritual transition to take place.

Spiritually, Danburite stimulates the third eye*, the crown, and the higher crown chakras*, opening these up to the fourteenth level. It aligns the heart chakra to these higher crown chakras (see pages 364–365, Crystals and the Chakras). Danburite clarifies the aura*. It promotes lucid dreaming.

Psychologically, Danburite promotes ease and changes recalcitrant attitudes, bringing patience and peace of mind.

HEALING Danburite is a very powerful healing stone. It clears allergies and chronic conditions and has a strong detoxifying action. It treats the liver and gallbladder. It adds weight to the body where required. It aids muscular and motor function.

POSITION Place as appropriate, especially over heart. Place Danburite under the pillow to promote lucid dreams.

SPECIFIC COLOR

In addition to the generic attributes, the following color has additional properties:

Pink Danburite opens the heart and encourages loving oneself.

Lilac Danburite

DIAMOND

Faceted

Raw

COLOR	Clear white, yellow, blue, brown, pink
APPEARANCE	Small, clear, transparent gemstone when cut and polished
RARITY	Expensive
SOURCE	Africa, Australia, Brazil, India, Russia, United States

ATTRIBUTES The Diamond is a symbol of purity. Its pure white light can help you to bring your life into a cohesive whole. It bonds relationships, bringing love and clarity into a partnership. Said to enhance the love of a husband for his wife, it is seen as a sign of commitment and fidelity. Diamond has been a symbol of wealth for thousands of years and is one of the stones of manifestation, attracting abundance. The larger the Diamond, the more abundance there is. A large Diamond is also excellent for blocking geopathic* or electromagnetic stress* and for protection against cell phones.

Diamond is an amplifier of energy. It is one of the few stones that never needs recharging. It increases the energy of whatever it comes into contact with and is very effective when used with other crystals for healing as it enhances their power. However, it can increase negative energy as well as positive. On a subtle level, it fills "holes" in the aura*, reenergizing it.

Psychologically, the qualities that Diamond imparts include fearlessness, invincibility, and fortitude. However, the merciless light of Diamond will pinpoint anything that is negative and requires transformation. Diamond clears emotional and mental pain, reduces fear, and brings about new beginnings. It is a highly creative stone, stimulating imagination and inventiveness.

Mentally, Diamond provides a link between the intellect and the higher mind. It brings clarity of mind and aids enlightenment.

At a spiritual level, Diamond cleanses the aura of anything shrouding a person's inner light, allowing the soul light to shine out. It reminds you of your soul's aspirations and aids spiritual evolution. It activates the crown chakra*, linking it to divine light.

HEALING Diamond treats glaucoma, clears sight, and benefits the brain. It treats allergies and chronic conditions and rebalances the metabolism. Traditionally, it was used to counteract poisons.

POSITION Wear next to the skin, hold, or place on the appropriate place. Particularly effective worn as earrings, especially against cell phone emanations.

DIOPTASE

*Blue-Green
(non-crystalline)*

Crystalline

COLOR	Deep blue-green or emerald green
APPEARANCE	Brilliant small crystals, usually on a matrix, or non-crystalline mass
RARITY	Quite rare and expensive
SOURCE	Iran, Russia, Namibia, Democratic Republic of the Congo, North Africa, Chile, Peru

ATTRIBUTES Dioptase is a powerful healer for the heart and opener for the higher heart chakra*. Its wonderful blue-green color brings all the chakras up to a greater level of functioning and facilitates spiritual attunement, reaching the highest levels of consciousness. It has a dramatic effect on the human energy field.

Psychologically, Dioptase promotes living in the present moment and, paradoxically, activates past-life memories. It supports a positive attitude to life and instills the ability to tune into one's own resources. Working in all areas of life to turn negative into positive, it overcomes any sense of lack and enables fulfilling potential. It is especially helpful when you do not know what to do next, as it indicates your direction.

Mentally, Dioptase is a strong mental cleanser and detoxifier. It releases the need to control others. Emotionally, Dioptase can act as a bridge to emotional healing, especially for the child within. Its green ray reaches deep within the heart to absorb festering wounds and forgotten hurts. It dissolves grief, betrayal, and sorrow and is extremely effective for healing heartache and the pain of abandonment.

Dioptase teaches that ultimately pain and difficulty in a relationship is a mirroring of an inner separation from the self. Repairing that link and drawing in love at all levels, it can heal an emotional black hole that is desperate for love. This stone clears away perceptions as to how love ought to be and brings in a new vibration of love.

Spiritually, Dioptase placed on the third eye* activates spiritual attunement and psychic vision*. It brings awareness of inner riches.

HEALING Dioptase regulates cell disorders, activates T-cells and the thymus, relieves Ménière's disease, eases high blood pressure, and alleviates pain and migraines. It prevents heart attacks and heals heart conditions. Dioptase lessens fatigue and overcomes shock. It is a detoxifier, lessening nausea and regenerating the liver. It is particularly effective for overcoming addictions and stress. Use as an elixir for headaches and pain.

POSITION Over the higher heart chakra. Excellent as a gem essence.

EMERALD

Raw

COLOR	Green
APPEARANCE	Small bright gemstone or larger cloudy crystal
RARITY	Gem quality is expensive but unpolished emerald readily available
SOURCE	India, Zimbabwe, Tanzania, Brazil, Egypt, Austria

ATTRIBUTES Emerald is a stone of inspiration and infinite patience. It is a life-affirming stone with great integrity. Known as the "stone of successful love," it brings domestic bliss and loyalty. It enhances unity, unconditional love, and partnership and promotes friendship. Emerald keeps a partnership in balance. If it changes color, it is said to signal

126

unfaithfulness. Emerald opens the heart chakra* and has a calming effect on the emotions.

This stone ensures physical, emotional, and mental equilibrium. It eliminates negativity and brings in positive actions. Focusing intention and raising consciousness, it brings about positive action. It enhances psychic abilities, opens clairvoyance*, and stimulates gathering wisdom from the mental planes. Traditionally, emerald was said to protect from enchantment and the ploys of magicians, and to foretell the future.

Psychologically, Emerald gives the strength of character to overcome the misfortunes of life. It is a stone of regeneration and recovery and can heal negative emotions. It enhances the ability to enjoy life to the fullest. It is helpful in cases of claustrophobia.

Emerald imparts mental clarity, strengthens memory, inspires a deep inner knowing, and broadens vision. It is a wisdom stone, promoting discernment and truth, and aiding eloquent expression. It helps bring to the surface what is unconsciously known. Emerald is extremely beneficial to mutual understanding within a group of people, stimulating cooperation.

HEALING Emerald aids recovery after infectious illness. It treats sinuses, lungs, heart, spine, and muscles, and soothes the eyes. It improves vision and has a detoxifying effect on the liver. Emerald alleviates rheumatism and diabetes. It has been used as an antidote to poisons. Worn around the neck, Emerald was believed to ward off epilepsy. Its green ray can assist healing of malignant conditions.

POSITION Wear on the little finger, ring finger, over the heart, or on the right arm. Position as appropriate for healing. Do not wear constantly as it can trigger negative emotions. Opaque Emeralds are not suitable for mental attunement.

FLUORITE

Clear

Green

Brown

Purple

Purple

COLOR	Clear, blue, green, purple, yellow, brown
APPEARANCE	Transparent, cubic or octahedral crystals, all sizes
RARITY	Common
SOURCE	United States, Britain, Australia, Germany, Norway, China, Peru, Mexico, Brazil

ATTRIBUTES Fluorite is highly protective, especially on a psychic level. It helps you to discern when outside influences are at work within yourself and shuts off psychic manipulation and undue mental influence. This stone cleanses and stabilizes the aura*. It is extremely effective against computer and electromagnetic stress. Appropriately positioned, it blocks geopathic stress*. Used in healing, Fluorite draws off negative energies and stress of all kinds. It cleanses, purifies, dispels, and reorganizes anything within the body that is not in perfect order. This is the best crystal to use to overcome any form of disorganization.

Fluorite grounds and integrates spiritual energies. It promotes unbiased impartiality and heightens intuitive powers; makes you more aware of higher spiritual realities and can quicken spiritual awakening; and focuses the mind and links it into the universal mind. Fluorite brings stability to groups, linking them into a common purpose.

Fluorite is associated with progress on many levels, incorporating structure into daily life. This stone can overcome chaos and reorganize the physical, emotional, and mental bodies.

Psychologically, Fluorite dissolves fixed patterns of behavior and gently opens the door to the subconscious, bringing suppressed feelings to the surface for resolution. It increases self-confidence and dexterity.

Fluorite improves physical and mental coordination and counteracts mental disorders. Dissolving fixed ideas, it helps to move beyond narrow-mindedness to the bigger picture. This stone dissolves illusions and reveals truth. It is very helpful when you need to act impartially and objectively.

Fluorite is an excellent learning aid—it organizes and processes information, linking what is already known into what is being learned, and increases concentration. It helps you to absorb new information and promotes quick thinking.

Emotionally, Fluorite has a stabilizing effect. It helps you to understand the effect of the mind and emotions on the body. In relationships, it teaches the importance of balance. Physically, Fluorite assists balance and coordination.

HEALING Fluorite is a powerful healing tool, dealing with infections and disorders. It benefits teeth, cells, and bones and repairs DNA damage. It is powerful against viruses, especially as an elixir. Fluorite regenerates the skin and mucus membranes, particularly in the respiratory tract, and heals ulcers and wounds. It is beneficial for colds, flu, and sinusitis. Dissolving adhesions and mobilizing joints, Fluorite alleviates arthritis, rheumatism, and spinal injuries. Stroked across the body toward the heart, Fluorite provides pain relief. It ameliorates the discomfort of shingles and other nerve-related pain, and heals the skin, removing blemishes and wrinkles. It can be used during dental work. Fluorite rekindles sexual libido.

POSITION Wear at earlobes or place in your environment. Position as appropriate for healing. Fluorite draws off negative energy and stress and needs cleansing after each application. Place on computer or between yourself and source of electromagnetic smog*. Spray the gem essence into the environment. Palm stones are useful soothers.

SPECIFIC COLORS
In addition to the generic attributes, the following colors have additional properties:

Blue Fluorite enhances creative, orderly thought and clear communication. A dual-action stone, it calms or revitalizes energy as needed for the physical or the biomagnetic bodies*. Blue Fluorite is effective for eye, nose, ear, and throat problems. It amplifies your healing potential by tightly focusing brain activity, and can invoke spiritual awakening.

Blue Fluorite

130

Clear Fluorite stimulates the crown chakra*, energizes the aura*, and harmonizes the intellect with the spirit. It aligns all the chakras, bringing universal energy into the physical body. This stone enhances the effect of other crystals during healing and can clear obscured vision.

*Clear Fluorite
on matrix*

Green Fluorite grounds excess energy, dissipates emotional trauma, and clears infections. It is particularly effective at absorbing negative energies within the environment. It brings information up from the subconscious mind and accesses intuition. It is an effective auric, chakra, and mental cleanser, dissipating obsolete conditioning. It relieves stomach disorders and cramp in the intestines.

Violet and Purple Fluorite stimulates the third eye and imparts common sense to psychic communication. It is an excellent meditation stone. It is useful in the treatment of bones and bone marrow disorders.

Green Fluorite

Violet Fluorite

Yellow Fluorite enhances creativity and stabilizes group energy. It is particularly helpful for cooperative endeavors. It supports intellectual activities. At a physical level, it releases toxins. It treats cholesterol and aids the liver.

Yttrian Fluorite takes a slightly different form from other Fluorites and does not correct disorganization. It is, nevertheless, an effective healer of other conditions associated with Fluorite. This is a service-orientated stone. It attracts wealth and abundance, teaching the principles of manifestation. It heightens mental activity.

Yellow Fluorite

131

FUCHSITE

ALSO KNOWN AS GREEN MUSCOVITE

Raw

COLOR	Green
APPEARANCE	Plate-like and layered (form of mica), all sizes
RARITY	Available from specialist stores
SOURCE	Brazil

ATTRIBUTES Fuchsite accesses knowledge with great practical value. It can channel information regarding herbal treatment and holistic remedies. It suggests the most holistic action to take and receives guidance on health matters and well-being. Fuchsite helps you to understand your interaction with other people and relates to basic concerns about life.

Psychologically, Fuchsite deals with issues of servitude from past or present lives. It reverses a tendency toward martyrdom. It is excellent for those who instantly fall into savior or rescuer mode, whether it be to save one person or a group, and who then quickly become victims. It shows how to be of service without becoming embroiled in power struggles or false humility. Many people who serve do so out of a feeling of "not being good enough," and Fuchsite teaches true self-worth.

Fuchsite shows you how to do only what is appropriate and necessary for someone else's soul growth and assists you to stand by placidly while they learn their own lessons. It combines unconditional love with the tough love that says "no more." It is useful for combating a situation in which you appear to be "helping" and yet are actually gaining great psychological satisfaction from keeping the other person dependent. Fuchsite releases both souls to their own unique pathway.

It is particularly helpful for "the identified patient" within a family or group situation on whom dis-ease and tension is projected. The identified patient becomes ill or addicted on behalf of the family. When they want to become well, the family often puts pressure on the patient to remain "ill" or dependent. Fuchsite gives the identified patient the strength to find wellness and to withdraw from the family conflict. Fuchsite overcomes codependency and emotional blackmail. It imparts resilience after trauma or emotional tension.

HEALING Fuchsite amplifies the energy of crystals and facilitates their transfer. It moves energy to the lowest point, redressing the balance. It releases blockages caused by excess energy, shifting the energy into positive channels. It balances the red and white blood cell ratio, treats carpal tunnel syndrome and repetitive strain injury, and realigns the spine. Fuchsite increases flexibility in the musculoskeletal system.

POSITION Place as appropriate or hold during meditation.

(*See also* Muscovite, page 192.)

GALENA

Raw

COLOR	Metallic gray-lilac
APPEARANCE	Small shiny mass or larger granular and knobbly
RARITY	Available from specialist outlets
SOURCE	United States, Britain, Russia

ATTRIBUTES Galena is a "stone of harmony," bringing balance on all levels and harmonizing the physical, etheric, and spiritual planes. It is a grounding stone, anchoring and centering. It aids holistic healing. It is excellent for doctors, homeopaths, and herbalists. It encourages further investigation and experimental trials. Galena opens up the mind, expanding ideas and dissolving self-limiting assumptions from the past.

HEALING Galena reduces inflammation and eruptions, stimulates circulation and benefits veins, and increases assimilation of selenium and zinc. It is beneficial for the hair.

POSITION Place as appropriate. As Galena is lead-based, elixirs should be made by the indirect method only (see page 371) and applied externally to unbroken skin.

GARNET

Raw

Polished

Garnet crystal

Garnet pebble

COLOR	Red, pink, green, orange, yellow, brown, black
APPEARANCE	Transparent or translucent crystal, often small and faceted or larger opaque piece
RARITY	Common
SOURCE	Worldwide

135

ATTRIBUTES Garnet is a powerfully energizing and regenerating stone. It cleanses and reenergizes the chakras*. It revitalizes, purifies, and balances energy, bringing serenity or passion as appropriate. It is said to be able to warn of approaching danger and was long ago carried as a protective talisman. Garnet is one of the most plentiful stones. It has several forms according to its mineral base, each of which have different properties in addition to the generic attributes.

Garnet inspires love and devotion. It balances the sex drive and alleviates emotional disharmony. Red Garnet in particular stimulates the controlled rise of kundalini* energy and aids sexual potency. This is a stone of commitment.

Garnet is a useful crystal to have in a crisis. It is particularly helpful in situations where there seems to be no way out or where life has fragmented or is traumatic. It fortifies, activates, and strengthens the survival instinct, bringing courage and hope into seemingly hopeless situations. Crisis is turned into challenge under Garnet's influence. It also promotes mutual assistance in times of trouble.

Garnet has a strong link with the pituitary gland and can stimulate expanded awareness and past-life recall. Garnet activates other crystals, amplifying their effect. It clears negative chakra energy.

Square-cut garnets are said to bring success in business matters.

Psychologically, Garnets sharpen your perceptions of yourself and other people. It dissolves ingrained behavior patterns that are no longer serving you and bypasses resistance or self-induced unconscious sabotage. Mentally, Garnet helps you to let go of useless or old or obsolete ideas. Emotionally, Garnet removes inhibitions and taboos. It opens up the heart and bestows self-confidence.

HEALING Garnet regenerates the body. It stimulates the metabolism. Garnet treats spinal and cellular disorders, purifies and reenergizes the blood, heart, and lungs, and regenerates DNA. It assists assimilation of minerals and vitamins.

POSITION Earlobes, finger, or over heart. Wear in contact with the skin. Place on the skin as appropriate in healing. Past-life recall: place on the third eye*.

VARIETIES OF GARNET

In addition to the generic attributes, the following forms and colors have additional properties:

Almandine Garnet is a strongly regenerative healing stone bringing strength and stamina. It is supportive in taking time for yourself, bringing deep love, and aids in integrating truth and an affinity with the higher self. It opens the higher mind and initiates charity and compassion. Almandine opens the pathway between the base and crown chakras, channeling and grounding spiritual energies into the physical body, and anchoring the subtle body into physical incarnation. Almandine helps you to absorb iron in the intestines. It stimulates the eyes, and treats the liver and pancreas.

Almandine Garnet

Andradite is dynamic and flexible. It stimulates creativity and attracts into your relationships what you most need for your development. It dissolves feelings of isolation or alienation and attracts intimate encounters with others. Andradite supports male qualities such as courage, stamina, and strength. It realigns the magnetic fields of the body. It cleanses and expands the aura*, opening psychic vision. Andradite encourages the formation of blood and energizes the liver. It aids assimilation of calcium, magnesium, and iron.

Grossularite is a useful stone to have during challenges and lawsuits. It teaches relaxation and going with the flow, and inspires service and cooperation. This stone enhances fertility and aids assimilation of Vitamin A. It is excellent for arthritis and rheumatism and fortifies the kidneys. It is beneficial for the mucus membranes and skin.

Hessonite imparts self-respect, eliminating feelings of guilt and inferiority, and encourages service. It supports in seeking out new challenges. This stone opens the intuition and psychic abilities. Used for out-of-body journeys*, it carries you to your destination. It regulates hormone production; reduces infertility and impotence; heals the olfactory system, and draws off negative influences that cause ill health.

Melanite strengthens resistance and promotes honesty. It releases blockages from the heart and throat chakras*, enabling the speaking of truth. It overcomes lack of love in any situation, dispelling anger, envy, jealousy, and mistrust. It moves a partnership on to the next stage, no matter what that might be. Melanite strengthens bones and helps the body to adjust to medication. It treats cancer, strokes, rheumatism, and arthritis.

Pyrope bestows vitality and charisma and promotes an excellent quality of life. It unites the creative forces within oneself. This stone protects the base and crown chakras, aligning them with the subtle bodies, and linking the groundedness of the base with the wisdom of the crown. Pyrope is a stabilizing stone. It fortifies circulation and treats the digestive tract. It neutralizes heartburn and soothes a sore throat.

Rhodolite is a warm, trusting, and sincere stone. It stimulates contemplation, intuition, and inspiration. Rhodolite protects the base

chakra and enhances healthy sexuality, overcoming frigidity.
It stimulates the metabolism and treats heart, lungs, and hips.

Spessartite vibrates at a high rate. It imparts a willingness to help
others and strengthens the heart. It enhances analytical processes and
the rational mind. It is an antidepressant and it suppresses nightmares.
Spessartite relieves sexual problems and treats lactose intolerance and
calcium imbalances.

Uvarovite promotes individuality without egocentricity, and at the
same time links the soul into its universal nature. It stimulates the
heart chakra and enhances spiritual relationships. This is a calm and
peaceful stone, helpful in experiencing solitude without loneliness.
It is a detoxifier, reduces inflammation, and lowers fever. It treats
acidosis, leukemia, and frigidity.

Red Garnet represents love. Attuned to the heart energy, it revitalizes
feelings and enhances sexuality. Red Garnet controls anger, especially
toward the self.

HEMATITE

Raw (crystalline)

Tumbled   *Raw*

COLOR	Silver, red
APPEARANCE	"Brain-like," red or gray when unpolished. Shiny when polished. Heavy. All sizes
RARITY	Common
SOURCE	Britain, Italy, Brazil, Sweden, Canada, Switzerland

ATTRIBUTES Hematite is particularly effective at grounding and protecting. It harmonizes mind, body, and spirit. Used during out-of-body journeying, it protects the soul and grounds it back into the body. This stone has a strong yang element and balances the meridians*, redressing yin imbalances. It dissolves negativity and prevents negative energies from entering the aura*, restoring peace and harmony to the body.

Hematite is said to be beneficial for legal situations.

Psychologically, Hematite is strong. It supports timid women, boosts self-esteem and survivability, enhances willpower and reliability, and imparts confidence. This stone removes self-limitations and aids expansion. It is a useful stone for overcoming compulsions and addictions. Hematite brings attention to the unfulfilled desires that are driving life. It treats overeating, smoking, and any form of overindulgence. Hematite helps you to come to terms with mistakes and to accept them as learning experiences rather than disasters.

Mentally, Hematite stimulates concentration and focus. It enhances memory and original thought. It brings the mind's attention to basic survival needs and helps to sort out problems of all kinds. This is a useful stone for the study of mathematics and technical subjects.

Physically, Hematite has a powerful connection with blood. It restores, strengthens, and regulates the blood supply. It can draw heat from the body.

HEALING Hematite aids circulatory problems such as Reynaud's Disease and blood conditions such as anemia. It supports the kidneys in cleansing blood and it regenerates tissue. Hematite stimulates the absorption of iron and the formation of red blood cells. It treats leg cramps, anxiety, and insomnia, and aids spinal alignment and fractures. Use as an elixir for fevers.

POSITION Base and top of spine to facilitate spinal manipulation. Hold or place as appropriate for healing or calming. Hematite should not be used where inflammation is present or for long periods of time.

HERKIMER DIAMOND

| Small | Large, with smoky occlusions |

COLOR	Clear
APPEARANCE	Clear, oily, inner rainbows, usually double terminated, small to large
RARITY	Expensive but readily available
SOURCE	United States, Mexico, Spain, Tanzania

ATTRIBUTES This stone energizes, enlivens, and promotes creativity. A powerful attunement crystal, especially the smaller, exceptionally clear stone. It stimulates psychic abilities, such as clairvoyance*, spiritual vision, and telepathy, linking into guidance from higher dimensions, and promotes dream recall and understanding. This stone stimulates conscious attunement to the highest spiritual levels and to your own potential. It clears the chakras* and opens channels for spiritual energy to flow. It can be used to access past-life information so that you recognize blockages or resistance to your spiritual growth. Herkimer then facilitates gentle release and transformation, bringing your soul's purpose forward. It activates the light body*.

142

Herkimer attunes people and links them together when they have to be parted: each person should retain one stone. It enhances telepathy, especially in the initial practice stages and attunes healer and patient. Herkimer has a crystal memory into which can be poured information for later retrieval. It can be programmed for other people to draw on. Herkimer Diamonds are one of the strongest crystals for clearing electromagnetic pollution or radioactivity. They block geopathic stress* and are excellent when gridded around a house or bed, for which the larger stones should be used.

HEALING Herkimer Diamond is a detoxificant. It protects against radioactivity and treats disease caused by contact; relieves insomnia caused by geopathic stress or electromagnetic pollution; corrects DNA, cellular disorders, and metabolic imbalances; and eliminates stress and tension from the body. It promotes past-life recall of injuries and disease that still affect the present life. Herkimer Diamond makes an excellent environmental spray or gem elixir.

POSITION Wear as pendant or earrings (short periods only). Place at base of spine or as appropriate. Position between yourself and source of electromagnetic smog*, or spray a room.

Smoky Herkimer has a particularly strong grounding energy that heals the earth chakra and the environment, clearing electromagnetic pollution and geopathic stress. It can be gridded* around a bed to help you overcome feeling wired.

Herkimer with Citrine is an excellent antidote to fatigue caused by negative energies.

HOWLITE

Tumbled

COLOR	Green, white, blue—often artificially colored
APPEARANCE	Marbled stone, often tumbled. All sizes
RARITY	Easily obtained
SOURCE	United States

ATTRIBUTES Howlite is an extremely calming stone. Placed under the pillow, it is an excellent antidote to insomnia, especially when this is caused by an overactive mind. It can also be used as an elixir and sipped for an hour or so before going to bed.

Howlite links into the spiritual dimensions, opening attunement and preparing the mind to receive wisdom and insights. It assists journeys out of the body and accessing past lives. Focusing your sight into a piece of Howlite can transport you to another time or dimension. Placed on the third eye*, it opens memories of other lives, including those in the "between-life"* state and the spiritual dimensions.

Howlite formulates ambitions, both spiritual and material, and aids in achieving them.

144

Psychologically, Howlite teaches patience and helps to eliminate rage and uncontrolled anger. A piece placed in the pocket absorbs your own anger and any that is directed toward you. It also helps to overcome a tendency to criticalness and selfishness, strengthening positive character traits.

Howlite stills the mind and is excellent for sleep or meditation. It allows for calm and reasoned communication to take place. This stone strengthens memory and stimulates a desire for knowledge.

Howlite can calm turbulent emotions, especially those that have past-life causes. It releases the strings that tie old emotions to present-life triggers.

HEALING Howlite relieves insomnia. It balances the calcium levels within the body and aids teeth, bones, and soft tissue. Howlite makes a useful gem essence.

POSITION Place as appropriate or hold during meditation or to mitigate anger. Grid* around bed to aid insomnia. Keep in pocket to absorb negativity.

SPECIFIC COLOR

In addition to the generic attributes, the following color has additional properties:

Blue Howlite aids dream recall, accessing the insights dreams bring.

Blue Howlite (artificially colored)

IDOCRASE

Tumbled

COLOR	Green, brown, yellow, pale blue, red
APPEARANCE	Resinous, small transparent crystal with flecks
RARITY	Available from specialist shops
SOURCE	United States

ATTRIBUTES Idocrase provides a link to the higher self and the information it offers to the soul in incarnation. Psychologically, it releases feelings of imprisonment and restraint. It is helpful for healing past-life experiences of being a prisoner, of extreme danger, or of mental or emotional restraint; it gently dissolves anger and alleviates fear, creating inner security. Idocrase has powerful mental connections. It opens the mind and clears negative thought patterns so that the mind can function more clearly. It stimulates inventiveness and the urge to discover, linking this into creativity.

HEALING Idocrase strengthens the enamel on teeth and restores the sense of smell. It assists in assimilating nutrients from food. Idocrase banishes depression.

POSITION as appropriate.

IOLITE

Raw

COLOR	Gray, violet, blue, yellow
APPEARANCE	Small, translucent, color changes with angle of view
RARITY	Obtainable from specialist shops
SOURCE	United States

ATTRIBUTES Iolite is a vision stone. It activates the third eye* and facilitates visualization and intuitive insight when all the chakras* are in alignment. It stimulates connection to inner knowing. It is used in shamanic ceremonies and assists in journeys out of the body. In contact with the auric field, Iolite gives off an electrical charge that reenergizes the field and aligns with the subtle bodies*.

Psychologically, Iolite aids in understanding and releasing the causes of addiction and helps you to express your true self, freed from the expectations of those around you. At a mental level, Iolite clears thought forms*.

147

Emotionally, Iolite releases discord within relationships. As it encourages taking responsibility for yourself, it can overcome codependency within your partnership.

HEALING Iolite creates a strong constitution. It reduces fatty deposits in the body, mitigates the effect of alcohol, and supports detoxification and regeneration of the liver. This stone treats malaria and fevers, aids the pituitary, the sinuses, and the respiratory system, and alleviates migraine headaches. It also kills bacteria.

POSITION As appropriate, and on the third eye* if all chakras* are already aligned.

IRON PYRITE

ALSO KNOWN AS FOOL'S GOLD

Pyrite flower   *Cubic Pyrite*

COLOR	Gold or brownish
APPEARANCE	Metallic, may be cubic, small to medium
RARITY	Readily available
SOURCE	Britain, North America, Chile, Peru

ATTRIBUTES Iron Pyrite is an excellent energy shield. It blocks out negative energy and pollutants at all levels including infectious diseases. Worn around the neck, it protects all the subtle* and physical bodies*, deflecting harm and danger.

Iron Pyrite is a very positive stone. It overcomes inertia and feelings of inadequacy. It facilitates tapping into abilities and potential, stimulating the flow of ideas. A piece of Iron Pyrite placed on a desk energizes the area around it. It is helpful when planning large business concepts. This stone teaches how to see behind a façade to what is, and promotes diplomacy.

149

Psychologically, Iron Pyrite relieves anxiety and frustration and boosts self-worth and confidence. It is helpful for men who feel inferior as it strengthens confidence in themselves and their masculinity, but it may be too powerful for "macho" men, initiating aggression. It helps women to overcome servitude and inferiority complexes.

Mental activity is accelerated by Iron Pyrite as it increases blood flow to the brain. It improves memory and recall. Cubic Pyrite in particular expands and structures mental capabilities, balancing instinct with intuition, creativity with analysis.

Emotionally, Iron Pyrite is helpful for melancholy and deep despair. Physically, Iron Pyrite increases energy and overcomes fatigue. It blocks energy leaks from the physical body and the aura*. Iron Pyrite increases the oxygen supply to the blood and strengthens the circulatory system. It is a stone that holds the ideal of perfect health and well-being. In healing it is extremely fast acting, bringing up the cause of the dis-ease* to be examined. It is particularly helpful for getting to the root of karmic and psychosomatic dis-ease.

HEALING Iron Pyrite treats bones and stimulates cellular formation, repairs DNA damage, aligns the meridians, and aids sleep disturbed by gastric upset. It strengthens the digestive tract and neutralizes ingested toxins, benefits the circulatory and respiratory systems, and boosts oxygen in the bloodstream. Iron Pyrite is beneficial for the lungs, alleviating asthma and bronchitis.

POSITION Place at throat in a pouch, or under pillow.

JADE

ALSO KNOWN AS JADEITE, NEPHRITE

Green (tumbled)

Green (polished)

Blue

COLOR	Green, orange, brown, blue, blue-green, cream, lavender, red, white
APPEARANCE	Translucent (Jadeite) or creamy (Nephrite), somewhat soapy feel. All sizes
RARITY	Most colors are available but some are rare. Nephrite is more easily obtained than Jadeite
SOURCE	United States, China, Italy, Myanmar, Russia, Middle East

ATTRIBUTES Jade is a symbol of purity and serenity. Much prized in the East, it signifies wisdom gathered in tranquility. Jade is associated with the heart chakra* and increases love and nurturing. It is a protective stone, which keeps the wearer from harm and brings harmony. It is believed to attract good luck and friendship.

Psychologically, Jade stabilizes the personality and integrates the mind with the body. It promotes self-sufficiency. Mentally, Jade releases negative thoughts and soothes the mind. It stimulates ideas and makes tasks seem less complex so that they can be acted upon immediately.

Emotionally, Jade is a "dream stone." Placed on the forehead, it brings insightful dreams. It aids emotional release, especially of irritability.

Spiritually, Jade encourages you to become who you really are. It assists in recognizing yourself as a spiritual being on a human journey and awakens hidden knowledge.

Physically, Jade is a cleansing stone, aiding the body's filtration and elimination organs. It is the stone par excellence for the kidneys. Jadeite and Nephrite have the same healing properties but individual colors have specific attributes.

HEALING Jade treats the kidneys and supra-adrenal glands, removes toxins, rebinds cellular and skeletal systems, and heals stitches. It assists fertility and childbirth. It works on the hips and spleen. Jade balances the fluids within the body and the water–salt/acid–alkaline ratios.

POSITION Place or wear as appropriate. The Chinese believe that holding Jade transfers its virtues into the body.

SPECIFIC COLORS
In addition to the generic attributes, the following colors have additional properties:

Blue/Blue-Green Jade symbolizes peace and reflection. It brings inner serenity and patience. It is the stone for slow but steady progress. It helps people who feel overwhelmed by situations beyond their control.

Blue-Green Jade

Brown Jade is strongly grounding. It connects to the earth and brings comfort and reliability. It aids in adjusting to a new environment.

Green Jade is the most common Jade. It calms the nervous system and channels passion in constructive ways. Green Jade can be used to harmonize dysfunctional relationships.

Lavender Jade alleviates emotional hurt and trauma and bestows inner peace. It teaches subtlety and restraint in emotional matters and sets clear boundaries.

Lavender Jade

Orange Jade is energetic and quietly stimulating. It brings joy and teaches the interconnectedness of all beings.

Red Jade is the most passionate and stimulating Jade. It is associated with love and letting off steam. It accesses anger, releasing tension in such a way that it can be constructive.

Multicolored Jade

White Jade directs energy in the most constructive way. It filters distractions, emphasizing the best possible result, and aids decision-making as it pulls in relevant information.

Yellow Jade is energetic and stimulating but with a mellowness to it, bringing joy and happiness. It teaches the interconnectedness of all beings. It aids the digestive and elimination systems of the body.

JASPER

Tumbled

Red, raw

Brecciated, raw

COLOR	Red, brown, yellow, green, blue, purple
APPEARANCE	Opaque, patterned, often water-worn or small and tumbled
RARITY	Common
SOURCE	Worldwide

ATTRIBUTES Jasper is known as the "supreme nurturer." It sustains and supports during times of stress, and brings tranquility and wholeness. Used in healing, it unifies all aspects of your life. Jasper reminds people to help each other.

Jasper aligns the chakras and can be used in chakra* layouts. Each color is appropriate to a specific chakra. This stone facilitates shamanic journeys and dream recall. It provides protection and grounds energies and the body. It absorbs negative energy and cleanses and aligns the chakras and the aura*. Jasper balances yin and yang and aligns the physical, emotional, and mental bodies with the etheric realm. It clears electromagnetic and environmental pollution, including radiation, and aids dowsing.

Psychologically, Jasper imparts determination to all pursuits. It brings the courage to get to grips with problems assertively, and encourages honesty with yourself. It supports during necessary conflict.

Mentally, Jasper aids quick thinking, and promotes organizational abilities and seeing projects through. It stimulates the imagination and transforms ideas into action.

Physically, Jasper prolongs sexual pleasure. It supports during prolonged illness or hospitalization and reenergizes the body.

HEALING Jasper supports the circulatory, digestive, and sexual organs. It balances the mineral content of the body. It is particularly useful as a gem elixir because it does not overstimulate the body.

POSITION As appropriate in contact with the skin. Specific placements are shown under each color. Use for long periods of time as Jasper works slowly. Place a large piece of decorative Brown Jasper in a room to absorb negative energy.

SPECIFIC COLORS AND FORMS
In addition to the generic attributes, the following colors have additional properties:

*Blue Jasper
(tumbled)*

Blue Jasper connects you to the spiritual world. It stimulates the throat chakra*, balances yin–yang energy, and stabilizes the aura*. This stone sustains energy during a fast, heals degenerative diseases, and balances mineral deficiency. *Position* Navel and heart chakras for astral travel.

Brown Jasper (including Picture Jasper) is connected to the earth and encourages ecological awareness. As a result, it brings stability and balance. It is particularly useful for alleviating geopathic* and environmental stress*. It facilitates deep meditation, centering, and regression to past lives, revealing karmic causes. This stone improves night vision, encourages astral travel*, and stimulates the earth chakra. It boosts the immune system, clears pollutants and toxins from the body, and stimulates the cleansing organs. It heals the skin. Brown Jasper strengthens the resolve to give up smoking. *Position* Forehead, or as appropriate.

Green Jasper heals and releases dis-ease* and obsession. It balances out parts of your life that have become all-important to the detriment of others. This stone stimulates the heart chakra. Green Jasper treats skin disorders and dispels bloating. It heals ailments of the upper torso, the digestive tract, and the purifying organs. It reduces toxicity and inflammation.

*Green Jasper
(raw)*

Purple Jasper stimulates the crown chakra. It eliminates contradictions. *Position* Crown.

Red Jasper (including Brecciated Jasper) is gently stimulating. It grounds energy and rectifies unjust situations. Red Jasper brings problems to light before they become too big and provides insights into the most difficult situations. It makes an excellent "worry bead," calming the emotions when played with. Placed under the pillow, it helps dream recall. Red Jasper stimulates the base chakras and assists rebirthing. It cleans and stabilizes the aura, and strengthens your boundaries. This is a stone of health, strengthening and detoxifying the circulatory system, the blood, and liver. It dissolves blockages in the liver or bile ducts. *Position* Base chakra or as appropriate.

Yellow Jasper protects during spiritual work and physical travel. It channels positive energy, making you feel physically better, and energizes the endocrine system. Yellow Jasper stimulates the solar plexus chakra. It releases toxins and heals digestion and the stomach. *Position* Forehead, chest, throat, wrist, or place over pain until it eases.

Yellow Jasper (tumbled)

Basanite (Black Jasper) is a useful scrying* stone. It takes you deep into an altered state of consciousness and brings prophetic dreams and visions.

Mookaite (Australian Jasper) provides a useful balance between inner and outer experiences*. It imparts both a desire for new experiences and a deep calm with which to face them. Flexible Mookaite encourages versatility. It points out all possibilities and assists in choosing the right one. Mookaite is a physically stabilizing stone that fortifies the immune system, heals wounds, and purifies the blood.

Mookaite (tumbled)

Picture Jasper (see Brown Jasper) is said to be the Earth Mother speaking to her children. It contains a message from the past within its pictures for those who can read it. It brings to the surface hidden feelings of guilt, envy, hatred, and love, and thoughts that are normally pushed aside, whether from the present or past lives. Once the repression is released, they are seen as lessons along the way. This stone

Tiger Iron (raw)

instills a sense of proportion and harmony. Picture Jasper brings comfort and alleviates fear. It stimulates the immune system and cleanses the kidneys.

Orbicular Jasper supports service, assists in accepting responsibility and instilling patience. Its circular markings resonate with circular breathing, which it facilitates. It eliminates the toxins that cause unpleasant body odor.

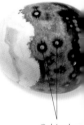

Orbicular Jasper

Royal Plume Jasper opens the crown chakra* and aligns the spiritual energies to personal purpose, bringing status and power. This stone eliminates contradictions and supports preserving one's dignity. It brings emotional and mental stability.

Brecciated Jasper (Jasper veined with Hematite) is an excellent aid to keeping your feet on the ground and attaining emotional stability. It draws excess energy away from the head, promoting mental clarity.

(*See also* Rhyolite, pages 248–249.)

COMBINATION STONE

Tiger Iron is a combination of Jasper, Hematite, and Tiger's Eye. It promotes vitality and helps in passing through change, pointing to a place of refuge when danger threatens. It is extremely helpful for people who are deeply exhausted at any level, especially those suffering from emotional or mental burn-out or family stress. It promotes change by opening a space to contemplate what is needed and then supplying the energy necessary for action. Tiger Iron's solutions are usually pragmatic and simple. Tiger Iron is a creative and artistic stone that brings out inherent talents.

*Tiger Iron
(tumbled)*

Tiger Iron works on the blood, balancing the red-white cell count, eliminates toxins, and heals the hips, lower limbs, and feet, strengthening muscles. It aids assimilation of B vitamins and produces natural steroids. Keep Tiger Iron in contact with the skin.

JET

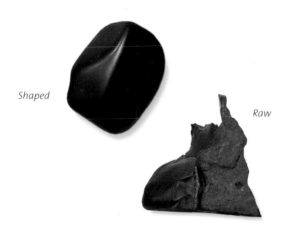

Shaped

Raw

COLOR	Black
APPEARANCE	Coal-like, usually polished and small
RARITY	Readily available
SOURCE	Worldwide, especially United States

ATTRIBUTES Jet is actually formed from fossilized wood but looks like coal. It has been used as a talisman since Stone Age times. Jet draws out negative energy and alleviates unreasonable fears. Worn around the neck, it is a stone of protection. It guards against violence and illness and provides protection during spiritual journeying. It was used in olden times to protect from "entities of darkness."

It is said that those who are attracted to this stone are "old souls" who have a long experience of being incarnated on the earth.

Jet can also be used to open to psychic experiences and to assist the quest for spiritual enlightenment.

Traditionally, Jet jewelry was said to become part of the body of the wearer. This suggests that Jet jewelry that is inherited or purchased should be cleansed with particular care. Jet used in healing should be thoroughly cleansed after each application.

Jet is said to stabilize finances and to protect businesses. It can be placed in a cash box or the wealth corner of the house (far left rear corner) or business premises.

Psychologically, Jet promotes taking control of life. It balances mood swings and alleviates depression, bringing stability and balance.

Jet cleanses the base chakra* and stimulates the rise of the kundalini* force. Placed at the chest, it directs the kundalini force toward the crown chakra.

HEALING Jet treats migraines, epilepsy, and colds. It diminishes glandular and lymphatic swellings and heals stomach pain. It was traditionally used for menstrual cramps.

POSITION Anywhere. As jewelry, Jet should be set in silver.

KUNZITE

Green (Hiddenite)

Pink

COLOR	Pink, green, yellow, lilac, clear
APPEARANCE	Transparent or translucent, striated crystal, all sizes
RARITY	Becoming more readily available
SOURCE	United States, Madagascar, Brazil, Myanmar, Afghanistan

ATTRIBUTES Tranquil Kunzite is an extremely spiritual stone with a high vibration. It awakens the heart center and unconditional love, producing loving thoughts and communication. It radiates peace and connects you to universal love. Kunzite induces a deep and centered meditative state and is beneficial for those who find it hard to enter into meditation. It also enhances creativity. Kunzite encourages humility and the willingness to serve.

Kunzite is a protective stone, working on the individual and the environment. It has the power to dispel negativity. This stone shields the aura* from unwanted energies, providing a protective sheath around it, and dispelling attached entities* and mental influences* from it. It imparts the ability to be self-contained, even within a crowd. Kunzite strengthens the energy field around the body.

Psychologically, Kunzite encourages self-expression and allows free expression of feelings. It removes obstacles from your path and helps you to adjust to the pressure of life. It can aid in recovering memories that have been blocked. It is a useful healer for people who had to grow up too fast, bringing back lost trust and innocence. It promotes the quality of tolerance for the self and others. Kunzite is helpful in reducing stress-related anxiety.

Mentally, Kunzite facilitates introspection and the ability to act on constructive criticism. It has the power to combine intellect, intuition, and inspiration.

Kunzite can be used to clear emotional debris and to free up the emotions, healing heartache, especially that carried forward from other lives. It clears resistance and assists in effecting compromises between personal needs and those of others. Kunzite's mood-lifting effect is helpful in depression arising from emotional causes. It is excellent for alleviating panic attacks.

Spiritually, Kunzite activates the heart chakra* and aligns it with the throat and third eye.

Physically, Kunzite can be used to block geopathic stress*. It is most effective when worn as a pendant or taped to a cell phone or other electromagnetic device.

HEALING This stone strengthens the circulatory system and the heart muscle. It is helpful for conditions affecting the nerves of the body, such as neuralgia. It calms epilepsy and soothes joint pain. It neutralizes the effects of anesthesia and stimulates the immune system. Kunzite contains lithium and is beneficial for psychiatric disorders and depression, especially when taken as an elixir. Kunzite helps the physical body to recover from the effects of emotional stress. It can be used by radionic* practitioners to represent the patient during treatment given at a distance.

POSITION Hold or place as appropriate or use as an elixir. (Sunlight causes Kunzite to fade.) Wear as a pendant or tape to a mobile phone or computer. Holding Kunzite or placing on solar plexus alleviates panic.

SPECIFIC COLORS
In addition to the generic attributes, the following colors have additional properties:

Clear Kunzite assists soul retrieval* work. It facilitates the journey back to the site of the soul loss and can be used as the receptacle for the soul until it is reintegrated into the body.

Clear Kunzite

Yellow Kunzite clears environmental smog* and deflects radiation and microwaves from the auric field. It aligns the chakras*, restructures DNA, stabilizes the cellular blueprint and the calcium–magnesium balance in the body.

Lilac Kunzite is a Celestial Doorway* and a symbol of infinity. It facilitates transition for the dying, imparting the knowledge that the departing soul requires, helping it to move over into enlightenment. Lilac Kunzite breaks through the barriers of time into the infinite.

Lilac Kunz

Hiddenite (Green Kunzite) varies in color from yellow to emerald green. It connects to other worlds to assist the transfer of knowledge from the higher realms. Hiddenite benefits intellectual and emotional experiences. It will gently release feelings of failure and helps people who "put a brave face" on things to accept comfort and support from other people and the universe. It has the power to link the intellect with love to give birth to the unknown. Green Kunzite grounds spiritual love. This is a stone that supports new beginnings. In healing, Hiddenite facilitates diagnosis when gently "combed" over the body, showing areas of weakness, coldness, and dis-ease*. It supports the thymus and the chest area of the body. To stimulate spiritual insight, it is best placed on the third eye*.

Hiddenite

KYANITE

ALSO KNOWN AS DISTHENE

*Blue
(pearlized blades)*

COLOR	Blue-white, pink, green, yellow, gray, black
APPEARANCE	Striated, bladed crystal, may be transparent or opaque and "pearlized," all sizes
RARITY	Readily available
SOURCE	Brazil

ATTRIBUTES Kyanite is excellent for attunement and meditation. It is tranquilizing and a powerful transmitter and amplifier of high frequency energies, stimulating psychic abilities and the intuition. With its ability to tune into the causal level, this stone can help spiritual energy to manifest in thought. This crystal connects to spirit guides* and instills compassion. Grounding spiritual vibrations, it brings spiritual integrity and maturation. It facilitates dream recall and promotes healing dreams. Kyanite is helpful for those making the transition through death.

Kyanite instantly aligns the chakras* and subtle bodies*, clearing the pathways and meridians. It restores Qi* to the physical body and its organs. In healing, it stabilizes the biomagnetic field* after clearing and transformation.

As Kyanite does not hold negativity, it never requires cleaning.

Psychologically, Kyanite encourages speaking one's truth, cutting through fears and blockages. Opening the throat chakra, this stone encourages self-expression and communication. It cuts through ignorance and opens to spiritual and psychological truth.

Kyanite slices through confusion and dispels blockages, illusion, anger, frustration, and stress. It increases the capacity for logical and linear thought, stimulates the higher mind, and links into the causal level.

Spiritually, Kyanite assists in detaching from the idea of blind fate or implacable karma*. It shows the part played by the self in creating causes and the measures required to balance the past. Kyanite facilitates the ascension process by drawing the light body* down into the physical realm and connecting the higher mind to the highest frequencies.

HEALING Kyanite treats muscular disorders, fevers, the urogenital system, thyroid and parathyroid, adrenal glands, throat, and brain. A natural pain reliever, it lowers blood pressure and heals infections.

It releases excess weight, supports the cerebellum and the motor responses of the body. Kyanite helps to balance yin–yang energy.

POSITION As appropriate, particularly between navel and heart. Wear as pendant.

SPECIFIC COLORS
In addition to the generic attributes, the following colors have additional properties:

Blue Kyanite strengthens the voice and heals the throat and the larynx. Useful for performers and public speakers.

Black Kyanite grounds the body when aligning the chakras* and during or after meditation.

LABRADORITE

ALSO KNOWN AS SPECTROLITE

Polished

COLOR	Grayish to black with blue, yellow
APPEARANCE	All sizes, usually polished: dark until catches light, then iridescent blue or gold flashes. Yellow form is transparent, usually small and tumbled
RARITY	Readily available
SOURCE	Italy, Greenland, Finland, Russia, Canada, Scandinavia

ATTRIBUTES Iridescent Labradorite is a highly mystical and protective stone, a bringer of light. It raises consciousness and connects with universal energies. Labradorite deflects unwanted energies from the aura and prevents energy leakage. It forms a barrier to negative

169

energies shed during therapy. It can take you into another world or into other lives. A stone of esoteric knowledge, it facilitates initiation into the mysteries.

Labradorite aligns the physical and etheric bodies* and accesses spiritual purpose. It raises consciousness and grounds spiritual energies into the physical body. This stone stimulates intuition and psychic gifts, including the art of "right timing," bringing messages from the unconscious mind to the surface and facilitating their understanding.

Psychologically, Labradorite banishes fears and insecurities and the psychic debris from previous disappointments, including those experienced in past lives. It strengthens faith in the self and trust in the universe. It removes other people's projections, including thought forms that have hooked into the aura*.

Labradorite calms an overactive mind and energizes the imagination, bringing up new ideas. Analysis and rationality are balanced with the inner sight. Labradorite brings contemplation and introspection. Synthesizing intellectual thought with intuitive wisdom, it is an excellent dispeller of illusions, going to the root of a matter and showing the real intention behind thoughts and actions. This stone brings up suppressed memories from the past.

Labradorite is a useful companion through change, imparting strength and perseverance. A stone of transformation, it prepares body and soul for the ascension process.

HEALING Labradorite treats disorders of the eyes and brain, relieves stress, and regulates metabolism. It treats colds, gout, and rheumatism, balances hormones and relieves menstrual tension, and lowers blood pressure. Labradorite can be used as a witness during radionic* treatment, pinpointing the cause of the dis-ease*.

POSITION Wear over the higher heart chakra*, hold or place as appropriate.

SPECIFIC COLOR

In addition to the generic attributes, the following color has additional properties:

Yellow Labradorite accesses the highest levels of consciousness, enhances visualization, trance, clairvoyance*, and channeling*. It is beneficial for the solar plexus chakra and expands the mental body, bringing in higher wisdom. It heals the stomach, spleen, liver, gallbladder, and adrenal glands.

Yellow Labradorite

Position: Place on third eye*, solar plexus, or hold.

LAPIS LAZULI

Raw   Polished

COLOR	Deep blue flecked with gold
APPEARANCE	Dense, veined, Lapis Lazuli looks like the night sky. All sizes, sometimes tumbled
RARITY	Easily obtained but expensive
SOURCE	Russia, Afghanistan, Chile, Italy, United States, Egypt, Middle East

ATTRIBUTES Lapis Lazuli opens the third eye* and balances the throat chakra*. It stimulates enlightenment and enhances dream work and psychic abilities, facilitating spiritual journeying and stimulating personal and spiritual power. This stone quickly releases stress, bringing deep peace. It possesses enormous serenity and is the key to spiritual attainment.

Lapis Lazuli is a protective stone that contacts spirit guardians. This stone recognizes psychic attack*, blocks it, and returns the energy to its source. It teaches the power of the spoken word, and can reverse curses or dis-ease caused by not speaking out in the past.

This stone harmonizes the physical, emotional, mental, and spiritual levels. Imbalances between these levels can result in depression, dis-ease*, and lack of purpose. In balance, the harmony brings deep inner self-knowledge.

Lapis Lazuli encourages taking charge of life. It reveals inner truth, encourages self-awareness, and allows self-expression without holding back or compromising. If repressed anger is causing difficulties in the throat or in communication, Lapis Lazuli releases these. This stone brings the enduring qualities of honesty, compassion, and uprightness to the personality.

Lapis Lazuli is a powerful thought amplifier. It stimulates the higher faculties of the mind, bringing objectivity and clarity. It encourages creativity through attunement to the source. Lapis Lazuli helps you to confront truth, wherever you find it, and to accept what it teaches. It aids in expressing your own opinions and harmonizes conflict. It teaches the value of active listening.

Lapis Lazuli bonds relationships in love and friendship and aids expressing feelings and emotions. It dissolves martyrdom, cruelty, and suffering. As a gem essence, it dissolves emotional bondage.

HEALING Lapis Lazuli alleviates pain, especially that of migraine headaches. It overcomes depression, benefits the respiratory and nervous systems and the throat, larynx, and thyroid, cleanses organs, bone marrow, thymus, and the immune system. Lapis Lazuli overcomes hearing loss, purifies blood, and boosts the immune system. It alleviates insomnia and vertigo, and lowers blood pressure.

POSITION Wear or place at the throat or third eye*. Lapis Lazuli should be positioned above the diaphragm, anywhere between the sternum and the top of the head.

LARIMAR

ALSO KNOWN AS DOLPHIN STONE, BLUE PECTOLITE

Tumbled

COLOR	Blue, blue-green, gray, or red, with white
APPEARANCE	Translucent, smooth, with whorls of color or white veins showing through the base color. Often small to medium, tumbled
RARITY	Easily obtained
SOURCE	Dominican Republic, Bahamas

ATTRIBUTES Recently discovered, ethereal Larimar is one of the "spiritual stones" that open to new dimensions, stimulating evolution of the earth. It radiates love and peace and promotes tranquility. Larimar effortlessly induces a deeply meditative state. It naturally raises consciousness and harmonizes body and soul to new vibrations. Spiritually, it is empowering, dissolving spurious boundaries that constrain the spiritual self, and guiding the soul onto its true pathway in life. Larimar facilitates angelic contact and communication with other realms. It is an excellent stone for those seeking a soulmate, and it facilitates the healing of past-life relationships or heart trauma.

Psychologically, Larimar removes self-imposed blockages and constraints. It dissolves self-sabotaging behavior, especially a tendency

174

toward martyrdom, and assists taking control of life. It is particularly useful for alleviating guilt and removing fear. When moving through periods of stress and inevitable change, it enables challenges to be met with equanimity.

Mentally, Larimar brings serenity and clarity, and constructive thought. It stimulates creativity and encourages "going with the flow."

Emotionally, Larimar brings calmness and equilibrium. It is an antidote to emotional extremes and ameliorates bipolar disorders. It heals trauma to the heart and reconnects to natural playfulness and joyful childlike energy.

An earth-healing stone, Larimar connects to the energy of the earth goddess, helping women to reattune to their innate femininity and restoring their connection with nature. Placed on the earth, it will counteract earth energy imbalances and geopathic stress*.

HEALING Positioned over the heart, third eye*, or solar plexus, or gently stroked over the body, Larimar removes attached entities*. It stimulates third eye, heart, crown, and throat chakras*, and promotes self-healing. It is particularly helpful for cartilage and throat conditions, dissolving energy blockages in the chest, head, and neck. It can also be laid on constricted joints or blocked arteries. Placed on a painful spot, it will quietly draw out the pain. Used as a reflexology tool, Larimar pinpoints the site of dis-ease* and clears the meridians* of the body.

POSITION Hold or wear for prolonged periods; use on feet.

LEPIDOLITE

Raw (mica form)   *Polished*

COLOR	Purple, pink
APPEARANCE	Plate-like layers, slightly shiny, or grainy mass, all sizes
RARITY	Easily obtained
SOURCE	United States, Czech Republic, Brazil, Madagascar, Dominican Republic

ATTRIBUTES Lepidolite clears electromagnetic pollution and should be placed on computers to absorb their emanations. When Lepidolite takes mica-like form its properties are greatly amplified, and this is the most efficient "mopping up" tool. Lepidolite insists on being used for the highest good. It dissipates negativity. It activates and opens the throat, heart, third eye*, and crown chakras*, clearing blockages and bringing cosmic awareness. This stone aids in shamanic or spiritual journeying and accesses the Akashic Record*. It tunes you in to thoughts and feelings from other lives that are creating a blockage in your life now. It can take you forward into the future.

Lepidolite is extremely useful in the reduction of stress and depression. It halts obsessive thoughts, relieves despondency, and overcomes insomnia. Lepidolite contains lithium and is helpful in stabilizing mood swings and bipolar disorders. It is excellent for overcoming any kind of emotional or mental dependency, supportive in releasing from addictions and complaints of all kinds, including anorexia. As a "stone of transition," it releases and reorganizes old psychological and behavioral patterns, inducing change. Lepidolite encourages independence and achieving goals without outside help.

Mentally, Lepidolite stimulates the intellect and analytic qualities. With its power of objectivity and concentration, it speeds up decision-making. Lepidolite focuses on what is important, filtering out extraneous distractions.

Emotionally, Lepidolite enhances standing in your own space, free from the influences of others. It is a calming stone that soothes sleep disturbances and emotional stress, bringing deep emotional healing.

HEALING Lepidolite locates the site of dis-ease*. Placed on the body over an area of dis-ease, it vibrates gently. Lepidolite relieves allergies, strengthens the immune system, restructures DNA, and enhances the generation of negative ions. It relieves exhaustion, epilepsy, and Alzheimers. It numbs sciatica and neuralgia, and overcomes joint problems. It is a detoxifier for the skin and connective tissue. Lepidolite is excellent for the menopause, especially as a gem elixir. It treats illnesses caused by "sick-building syndrome"* or computer stress.

POSITION Place or wear as appropriate. Place under pillow for relief from sleep disturbances.

MAGNESITE

"Brain-like" form (raw)

Marbled form (tumbled)

COLOR	White, gray, brown, yellow
APPEARANCE	Size and form varies widely, may be "brain-like," chalky and marbled, or crystalline
RARITY	Readily available, crystalline is rare
SOURCE	Brazil, United States

ATTRIBUTES Magnesite brings a deep peace to meditation and relaxation. Placed on the third eye*, this stone enhances visualization and imagery. It opens the heart chakra* and stimulates heartfelt love, including love for the self, which is necessary before you can embrace love from other people.

Magnesite can be very helpful in the practice of unconditional love in situations where relationships with other people are difficult because of their behavior or addictions. It helps you to feel centered, standing by placidly and allowing the other person to be totally who they are without requiring them to change or being affected yourself in any way by their difficulties.

Psychologically, Magnesite brings to the surface all forms of self-deceit. It helps to recognize unconscious thoughts and feelings and to explore the reason for these, taking you back into the past if necessary. It induces a positive attitude to life. Magnesite helps egotistical people to take a back seat and teaches how to listen attentively to others.

The brain-like form of Magnesite has a powerful effect on the mind, bringing the hemispheres into harmony and stimulating ideas and their application.

Magnesite brings a calming effect to the emotions, promoting tolerance for emotional stress. It supports people who are nervous and fearful and helps them to overcome irritability and intolerance.

HEALING Magnesite contains a high level of magnesium and aids its absorption in the body. It detoxifies and neutralizes body odor, acts as an antispasmodic and muscle relaxant, and treats menstrual, stomach, intestinal, and vascular cramps and the pain from gallbladder and kidney stones. Magnesite treats bone and teeth disorders and prevents epilepsy. It relieves headaches, especially migraines, and slows blood clotting. Magnesite speeds up fat metabolism and disperses cholesterol, preventing arteriosclerosis and angina. It is a useful preventative for heart disease. It balances body temperature, lessening fevers and chills.

POSITION Place as appropriate in contact with the skin. Can be used as a gem essence for internal or external application.

MAGNETITE

ALSO KNOWN AS LODESTONE

Raw

COLOR	Black, brownish-gray
APPEARANCE	Dark and grainy, magnetic (iron ore), all sizes
RARITY	Easily obtained
SOURCE	United States, Canada, India, Mexico, Romania, Italy, Finland, Austria

ATTRIBUTES Magnetite is magnetic and has a powerful positive–negative polarity. It can be used as magnetic therapy, working with the body's own biomagnetic field* and meridians*, and with that of the planet in earth healing. It acts as a grounding stone. When used by an experienced healer, it realigns reversed and retroverted energy flows in the body or the earth.

Magnetite will attract and repel, energize and sedate. There are times when the body tries too hard to heal itself, in which case a meridian is overenergized. If an organ or meridian is overactive, then Magnetite will calm it with its negative charge. If it is sluggish, Magnetite will activate it with its positive charge. It is extremely useful for sports injuries as it relieves aches and pains in muscles.

Magnetite temporarily aligns the chakras* and the meridians of the subtle* and etheric bodies*. It connects the base and earth chakras* to the nurturing energies of the earth, which sustains the life force and vitality in the physical body.

Magnetite aids telepathy, meditation, and visualization. It provides for a balanced perspective and trust in your own intuitions.

As Magnetite is magnetic, it attracts love, commitment, and loyalty.

Psychologically, Magnetite can be used to alleviate negative emotions such as fear, anger, grief, and overattachment, and bring in positive qualities such as tenacity and endurance. It points out how to remove yourself from detrimental situations and promotes objectivity. This stone balances the intellect with the emotions to bring inner stability.

HEALING Magnetite provides the healing energy necessary for recovery. It is beneficial for asthma, blood and the circulatory system, skin, and hair. It stimulates sluggish organs and sedates overactive ones. It is anti-inflammatory, healing muscle strains and cramps. It is useful for stopping nosebleeds.

POSITION Place on back of neck and base of spine, or on an aching joint. Put at the end of the bed to end night cramps.

MALACHITE

Tumbled

Raw

COLOR	Green
APPEARANCE	Concentric light and dark bands and rosettes. All sizes, often tumbled or polished
RARITY	Easily obtained
SOURCE	Romania, Zambia, Democratic Republic of the Congo, Russia, Middle East

ATTRIBUTES Malachite is a powerful stone but one that needs to be handled with caution. It is best used under the supervision of a qualified crystal therapist. It is toxic and should be used only in its polished form. Avoid breathing its dust. If used as a gem elixir, apply externally only or make by the indirect method of placing the stone in a glass container and standing this within spring water so that the stone does not touch the water.

Malachite amplifies both positive and negative energies. It grounds spiritual energies onto the planet. It is believed by some people that Malachite is still evolving and will be one of the most important healing stones of the new millennium.

Malachite is already an important protection stone. It absorbs negative energies and pollutants easily, picking them up from the atmosphere and from the body. It should be cleansed before and after use by placing it on a quartz cluster in the sun (do not use salt, which will damage the surface).

Malachite soaks up plutonium pollution, and guards against radiation of all kinds. It should be placed in the home of anyone who lives near a nuclear or natural radiation source. It also clears electromagnetic pollution and heals earth energies. It has a strong affinity with nature and with the devic* forces.

This stone clears and activates the chakras and attunes to spiritual guidance. Placed on the third eye*, it activates visualization and psychic vision. On the heart, it brings balance and harmony. It opens the heart to unconditional love.

Malachite can be used for scrying* or to access other worlds, inner or outer*. Journeying through its convoluted patterns releases the mind and stimulates pictures. It can assist in receiving insights from the subconscious or messages from the future.

Psychologically, Malachite is a stone of transformation. Life is lived more intensely under the influence of this adventurous stone, which encourages risk-taking and change. It mercilessly shows what is blocking your spiritual growth. Malachite draws out deep feelings and psychosomatic causes, breaks unwanted ties and outworn patterns, and teaches how to take responsibility for one's actions, thoughts, and feelings. It releases inhibitions and encourages expressing feeling. This stone develops empathy with other people, showing how it would feel to be in their place. It alleviates shyness, and supports friendships. Malachite is useful for psycho-sexual problems, especially when these have been caused by traumatic past-life sexual experiences. It assists the rebirthing process.

Mentally, Malachite goes to the core of a problem, enhancing intuition and insight. It helps alleviate mental disturbances, including psychiatric illness, and combats dyslexia. It strengthens the ability to absorb and process information, makes you more observant, and helps in understanding difficult concepts.

Placed on the solar plexus, Malachite facilitates deep emotional healing. It releases negative experiences and old traumas, bringing suppressed feelings to the surface and restoring the ability to breathe deeply. At this point, it balances the heart and navel chakras*, revealing insights. At an emotional level, it may make moods more intense but quick to change. Malachite can be used for inner exploration. It stimulates dreams and brings memories vividly to life. However, Malachite may need to be supported in the healing and transformation process by other stones.

HEALING Malachite is an extremely versatile healing stone. It is particularly useful for cramps, including menstrual cramps, and facilitates childbirth—it has been called the midwife stone. It resonates with the female sexual organs and treats any sexual dis-ease*. This stone lowers blood pressure, treats asthma, arthritis, epilepsy, fractures, swollen joints, growths, travel sickness, vertigo, tumors, the optic nerve, pancreas, spleen, and the parathyroid. It aligns DNA and cellular structure, and enhances the immune system. Malachite stimulates the liver to release toxins, reducing acidification of tissues. It treats diabetes when worn around the waist.

POSITION Wear on left hand or place on third eye. Position as appropriate for healing. Place on solar plexus to absorb negative emotions. Use polished malachite and indirect method for elixir preparation. Apply externally.

Note: Malachite may cause slight heart palpitations, in which case remove immediately and replace with Rose Quartz or Rhodonite.

COMBINATION STONE

Malachite with Chrysocolla may manifest as a clear, gem crystal with a very high healing vibration. This combination symbolizes wholeness and peace. Placed on an area of imbalance, it gently restores equilibrium. If one stone is placed on the third eye and another on the solar plexus, mind, body, and emotions are balanced.

(*See also* Azurite with Malachite, page 78.)

Malachite with Chrysocolla (raw)

Malachite with Chrysocolla (polished)

MERLINITE

Shaped and polished

COLOR	Black and white
APPEARANCE	Two distinct opaque colors, usually small
RARITY	Becoming more readily available
SOURCE	New Mexico

ATTRIBUTES Merlinite is a magical stone that holds the imprint of the combined knowledge of shamans, alchemists, magician–priests, and other workers of magic. Its dual coloring blends the spiritual and earthly vibrations together, giving access to the spiritual and shamanic realms. This stone supports shamanic practices or magical ritual. It facilitates reading the Akashic Record*, inducing travel into past or future lives to gain insight on how to live life in the future. Merlinite can bring magic into your life.

HEALING Merlinite can be used for past-life healing and to bring harmony into the present life. It balances yin–yang and masculine and feminine energies, conscious and subconscious, intellect and intuition.

POSITION Wear around the neck or place behind the ears to access past lives.

186

MOLDAVITE

Crystalline

COLOR	Dark green
APPEARANCE	Small, transparent, folded mass, often glassy
RARITY	Rare but readily available, although increasingly expensive as source is used up
SOURCE	Czech Republic, Germany, Moldova

ATTRIBUTES Moldavite is another of the stones for the New Age. It is a form of Tektite, said to have extraterrestrial origin, formed when a giant meteorite struck the earth. The heat of impact metamorphosed surrounding rocks, creating a "strew field" by flinging the resulting crystals over a vast area. Moldavite is therefore a fusion of extraterrestrial energies with mother earth. This is a rare stone. It is now found along the banks of the river Moldau and is unlikely to be discovered anywhere else in the world. The crystal will become extinct.

Moldavite has been used since Stone Age times as a talisman and amulet for good fortune and fertility. Many people believe that it came to aid in earth's transition and healing and that the time has come to use Moldavite's energies wisely. It can greatly enhance the effect of other crystals, taking them to their highest vibration.

Moldavite brings you into communication with the higher self and with extraterrestrials. Moldavite has its own cosmic oversoul*, which can put you in touch with the Ascended Masters* and cosmic messengers. Holding the stone up to the light and gazing into it shifts your consciousness. This stone takes you into the highest spiritual dimensions and facilitates the ascension process. It needs to be grounded or else it can leave you spaced-out and rootless. Holding a pair of Boji Stones gently grounds after spiritual experiences with Moldavite, and the energies of clear Quartz stabilize its effects.

Moldavite has an extremely high vibration, which opens, clears blockages from, and aligns the chakras*. It integrates the divine blueprint and accelerates spiritual growth. Moldavite resonates with the crown chakra, opening it to receive the highest spiritual guidance. Placed on the throat, Moldavite communicates interplanetary messages especially with regard to the state of the ecology of the earth and its need for healing.

This is a stone that transcends time. Placed on the third eye*, Moldavite can enable you to go forward into the future or back into the past. It facilitates journeys to other lives if this is appropriate. Rather than going back into the past to relive a life, except to regain spiritual wisdom, or journeying to the before-incarnation state to access purpose, Moldavite shows you future potentials. Under the influence of Moldavite you can go forward to a future life to see the results of actions taken in the present life, or to learn what is needed in the present life in order to prevent destruction in the future.

Moldavite is a useful stone for sensitive people who find it difficult being in incarnation on the earth and who cannot adjust to suffering and deep emotions. Many such people are star children* who have come to aid the earth in its time of transition to a new vibration. They are unused to the heavy energies of earth and find it difficult to integrate the spiritual bodies into the physical, and need to ground. Moldavite, used in conjunction with grounding stones such as Hematite and Smoky Quartz, aids this process. Placed on the heart, Moldavite eases "homesickness" for those whose origin is not Earth. Moldavite has no crystalline structure and so it takes you way beyond your limits and boundaries. Psychologically, it assists in developing detachment from mundane, earthbound security issues such as money and worries for the future. Moldavite provides an overview of reasons for incarnating and contacts your spiritual purpose, integrating this into earthly life. It supports qualities such as empathy and compassion.

At a mental level, Moldavite is unconventional and inspiring, bringing the unexpected solution forward. It can awaken latent memories and access spiritual information through the intellect. It releases fixed ideas and archaic belief systems and can neutralize hypnotic commands*.

Physically, holding Moldavite may trigger a huge rush of energy through the body that has powerful metaphysical effects. It "downloads" information from the Akashic Record* and the light body*, which then has to be processed and made conscious. This process may take some time but the process accelerates spiritual growth and the raising of personal vibrations.

HEALING Rather than healing individual conditions, Moldavite makes one aware of the cause and source of dis-ease* and then supports the releasing and healing process. It also brings the gift contained within the illness to your attention. Moldavite can be used as a tool for diagnosis. People who dislike its deep green color often have an aversion to emotion and need to experience unconditional love and wholeness. They may also have hidden emotional trauma that needs to surface and heal, for which other crystals are required.

POSITION Place on forehead, throat, or crown. Note: Moldavite is fragile and should not be cleaned with salt as it scratches the surface.

MOONSTONE

Cream (natural state)   White   Clear (polished)

COLOR	White, cream, yellow, blue, green
APPEARANCE	Milky, translucent, all sizes
RARITY	Easily obtained
SOURCE	India, Sri Lanka, Australia

ATTRIBUTES Moonstone is a "stone of new beginnings." As its name suggests, it is strongly connected to moon and to the intuition. Like the moon, the stone is reflective and reminds us that, as the moon waxes and wanes, so everything is part of a cycle of change. Its most powerful effect is that of calming the emotions.

Moonstone makes conscious the unconscious and promotes intuition and empathy. It encourages lucid dreaming, especially at the time of the full moon.

Moonstone has traditionally been used to enhance psychic abilities and to develop clairvoyance*. It can be worn as a pendant to encourage acceptance of your psychic gifts.

190

Psychologically, Moonstone calms overreactions to situations and to emotional triggers. Moonstone is filled with receptive, passive, feminine energy. It balances male–female energies and aids men who want to get in touch with their feminine side. It is the perfect antidote for the excessively macho man or overly aggressive female.

Mentally, Moonstone opens the mind to sudden and irrational impulses, serendipity, and synchronicity. Care has to be taken that it does not induce illusions in response to wishful thinking.

Emotionally, Moonstone soothes emotional instability and stress, and stabilizes the emotions. It improves emotional intelligence. Placed on the solar plexus, it draws out old emotional patterning so that it can be understood and then dissolved. Moonstone provides deep emotional healing and heals disorders of the upper digestive tract that are related to emotional stress.

Physically, Moonstone powerfully affects the female reproductive cycle and alleviates menstrual-related dis-ease* and tension. It is linked to the pineal gland and balances the hormonal system, stabilizes fluid imbalances, and attunes to the biorhythmic clock. It is helpful in cases of shock and can be used to calm hyperactive children.

HEALING Moonstone helps the digestive and reproductive systems, assimilates nutrients, eliminates toxins and fluid retention, and alleviates degenerative conditions of skin, hair, eyes, and fleshy organs such as the liver and pancreas. It is excellent for PMS, conception, pregnancy, childbirth, and breast-feeding. A Moonstone elixir was traditionally used for insomnia and the stone can prevent sleepwalking.

POSITION Wear as a ring or place on the appropriate body part— forehead for spiritual experiences, and solar plexus or heart for emotions. Women may need to remove Moonstone at full moon.

MUSCOVITE

ALSO KNOWN AS MICA

Raw

COLOR	Pink, gray, brown, green, violet, yellow, red, white
APPEARANCE	Pearl-like mica in layers, all sizes
RARITY	Easily obtained
SOURCE	Switzerland, Russia, Austria, Czech Republic, Brazil, New Mexico, United States

ATTRIBUTES Muscovite is the commonest form of mica. It is a mystical stone with a strong angelic contact, stimulating awareness of the higher self. Used in scrying*, this visionary stone links to the highest spiritual realms. Muscovite stimulates the heart chakra*, facilitates astral travel*, and opens the intuition and psychic vision.

Muscovite has the ability to allow recognition of the flaws in humanity and at the same time stimulates unconditional love and acceptance. It is a reflective stone, mirroring back and allowing you to recognize your projections—the parts of yourself that you do not recognize and therefore see "out there." It helps you to see that the things you do not like in another are really the characteristics you cannot accept in yourself. Muscovite then aids in the integration and transformation of these qualities.

Muscovite can be used to grid* earthquake areas as it gently and safely relieves tensions within the earth. It also releases tension within the physical body and aligns the subtle bodies* and meridians* with the physical body, bringing about balance.

Psychologically, Muscovite disperses insecurity, self-doubt, and clumsiness. It is useful for those who suffer from dyspraxia* and left–right confusion. Muscovite eliminates anger and nervous stress, to bring flexibility at all levels of being. It assists in looking forward joyfully to the future and back to the past to appreciate all the lessons that have been learned. By allowing you to see yourself as others see you, Muscovite aids in changing the image presented to the outside world. It supports during the exploration of painful feelings.

Mentally, Muscovite aids problem-solving and stimulates quick-wittedness. It facilitates the clear expression of thoughts and feelings. Physically, Muscovite improves your appearance. It imparts sheen to the hair and a sparkle to the eyes. It helps the body to achieve its most appropriate weight.

HEALING Muscovite controls blood sugar, balances pancreatic secretions, alleviates dehydration, and prevents hunger while fasting. It regulates the kidneys. Muscovite relieves insomnia and allergies and heals any condition resulting from dis-ease* or distress.

POSITION Carry or hold. Stroke over the skin.

SPECIFIC COLORS
In addition to the generic attributes, the following colors have additional properties:

Pink Muscovite is the most effective color for making angelic contact.

Violet Muscovite opens the higher crown chakras* and facilitates raising consciousness to a very fine vibration.

(*See also* Fuchsite [Green Muscovite], page 132.)

NEBULA STONE

Polished

COLOR	Black with green spots
APPEARANCE	Dense stone with distinct patches, usually small and tumbled
RARITY	A new stone recently appearing on the market
SOURCE	Southwestern United States, Mexico

ATTRIBUTES Composed of four minerals, Nebula Stone is said to have unique metaphysical properties, which are still being explored. It is known to blend the vibration of light carried in its Quartz component into the physical body, enlightening the cells and activating their consciousness. This raises overall conscious-awareness, bringing remembrance of the soul's spiritual roots.

Gazing into a Nebula Stone takes you outward into infinity and inward into the smallest particle of being. Ultimately, the two become one. This is a stone of nonduality and oneness.

HEALING Nebula Stone can bring about profound healing at the cellular level of being.

POSITION Hold in the hands or place on the third eye*.

195

OBSIDIAN

Raw

COLOR	Brown, black, blue, green, rainbow, red-black, silver, gold-sheen
APPEARANCE	Shiny, opaque, glass-like, all sizes, sometimes tumbled
RARITY	Some colors are readily available, others are rare, and some blue-green colors are manufactured glass
SOURCE	Mexico and worldwide

ATTRIBUTES Obsidian is molten lava that cooled so quickly it had no time to crystallize. Obsidian is a stone without boundaries or limitations. As a result, it works extremely fast and with great power. Its truth-enhancing, reflective qualities are merciless in exposing flaws, weaknesses, and blockages. Nothing can be hidden from Obsidian. Pointing out how to ameliorate all destructive and disempowering conditions, Obsidian impels us to grow and lends solid support while we do so. It needs careful handling and is best used under the guidance

196

of a qualified therapist as it can bring negative emotions and unpleasant truths rushing to the surface. Under skilled guidance, its cathartic qualities are exceedingly valuable. It provides deep soul healing. Obsidian can facilitate in going back to past lives to heal festering emotions or trauma that has carried forward into the present.

Obsidian is a strongly protective stone, forming a shield against negativity. It provides a grounding cord* from the base chakra* to the center of the earth, absorbs negative energies from the environment, and strengthens in times of need. It is helpful for highly sensitive people. It blocks psychic attack* and removes negative spiritual influences.

A large piece of Obsidian can be extremely efficient at blocking geopathic stress* or soaking up environmental pollution, but its propensity for exploding the truth into the open has to be taken into account. Many people find its powerful effects overwhelming and prefer to choose a gentler stone for this task. But it is extremely helpful for therapists and counselors as it not only facilitates getting to the core of the problem, but also mops up energies released as a result. Black or Mahogany Obsidian are the most suitable types for this purpose, Mahogany being the gentler.

In the same way, placing Obsidian by the bed or under the pillow can draw out mental stress and tension, and may have a calming effect, but it can also bring up the reasons for that stress. These reasons then have to be confronted before peace can return; this resolves the problem permanently rather than having a palliative effect. One of the gentler forms of Obsidian, such as an Apache Tear or Snowflake, would be best for this. As Obsidian is so effective in soaking up negative energies, it is essential to clean the stone under running water each time it has been used in this way.

Spiritually, Obsidian vitalizes soul purpose. It eliminates energy blockages and relieves tension, integrating the psychological shadow into the whole to bring spiritual integrity. It anchors the spirit into the body. This stone stimulates growth on all levels. It urges exploration of the unknown, opening new horizons.

Mentally, Obsidian brings clarity to the mind and clears confusion and constricting beliefs. However, it may well do this by making it absolutely clear what lies behind mental distress or dis-ease*. Once this has been cleared, Obsidian expands consciousness, entering the realm of the unknown with confidence and ease.

Psychologically, Obsidian helps you to know who you truly are. It brings you face to face with your shadow side and teaches you how to integrate it. This stone also helps you to identify behavioral patterning that is now outdated. Obsidian dissolves emotional blockages and ancient traumas, bringing a depth and clarity to emotions. It promotes qualities of compassion and strength.

HEALING Obsidian's greatest gift is insight into the cause of dis-ease. It aids the digestion of anything that is hard to accept and promotes physical digestion. It detoxifies, dissolving blockages and tension in the physical and subtle bodies*, including hardened arteries. It reduces the pain of arthritis, joint problems, cramps, and injuries. An elixir is beneficial for shock. It alleviates pain and stanches bleeding, benefiting the circulation. This stone warms the extremities. It can be used to shrink an enlarged prostate.

POSITION Place as appropriate. Use as a ball or mirror for scrying*.

SPECIFIC COLORS
In addition to the generic attributes, the following colors have additional properties:

Black Obsidian is a very powerful and creative stone. It grounds the soul and spiritual forces into the physical plane, bringing them under the direction of the conscious will and making it possible to manifest spiritual energies on earth. Self-control is increased by the use of this stone.

Black Obsidian (raw)

Black Obsidian forces facing up to one's true self, taking you deep into the subconscious mind in the process. It brings imbalances and shadow qualities to the surface for release, highlighting hidden factors. It magnifies all negative energies so that they can be fully experienced and then released. This healing effect goes back into past lives, and can work on the ancestral and family line*. Black Obsidian composts the past to make fertile energy for growth of the soul. It reverses previous misuse of power and addresses power issues on all levels, teaching that to be empowered is not to wield personal power but rather to channel power for the good of all.

Black Obsidian is protective. It repels negativity and disperses unloving thoughts. It facilitates the release of old loves and provides support during change.

Used in shamanic ceremonies to remove physical disorders, Black Obsidian also has the gift of prophesy. Black Obsidian balls are powerful meditation and scrying aids but should be used only by those who can consciously process what they see and use it for the highest good of all. Clear Quartz helps to ground and articulate what is revealed.

In healing, a Black Obsidian placed on the navel grounds spiritual energy into the body. Held briefly above the third eye* it breaks through mental barriers and dissolves mental conditioning. Used with care, it can draw together scattered energy and promote emotional release.

Blue Obsidian aids astral travel, facilitates divination, and enhances telepathy. It activates the throat chakra* and supports communication skills. In healing, Blue Obsidian opens the aura* to receive healing energy. It treats speech defects, eye disorders, Alzheimer's, schizophrenia, and multiple personality disorder. Placed over the spot, it alleviates pain.

Blue-Green Obsidian opens the heart and throat chakras, facilitates speaking one's truth and understanding from the heart. It aids Reiki* healing; balances the mind, body, and spirit. Blue-Green Obsidian improves the assimilation of Vitamins A and E, and enhances night vision.

Electric-Blue Obsidian is an intuitive stone. It facilitates divination, trance states, shamanic journeying, psychic communication, and past-life regression. This stone opens the third eye, and assists inner journeys. As with all obsidians, it accesses the roots of difficulties, and balances energy fields. The stone enhances radionic* treatment and is effective as a pendulum for dowsing. It makes a patient more receptive. It treats spinal misalignment and impacted vertebrae, circulatory disorders, growths, and spasmodic conditions. As an elixir, it heals the eyes.

Gold-Sheen Obsidian

Gold-Sheen Obsidian is particularly effective for scrying. It takes you into the future and the past and deep into the core of a problem. It shows what is needed for healing, but other crystals will be needed to achieve healing. Psychologically, Gold-Sheen Obsidian eliminates any sense of futility or ego conflict. Releasing ego involvement, it imparts knowledge of spiritual direction. Used in healing, Gold-Sheen Obsidian balances energy fields.

Green Obsidian opens and purifies the heart and throat chakras. It removes hooks and ties from other people and protects against repetition. In healing, it treats the gallbladder and the heart. Ensure that the crystal you have is actually Obsidian and not glass

Mahogany Obsidian has a gentler energy than black. Resonating with the earth, it grounds and protects, gives strength in times of need, vitalizes purpose, eliminates energy blockages, and stimulates growth on all levels. It is a stabilizing stone that strengthens a weak aura and restores the correct spin to the sacral and solar plexus chakras. Worn on the body, Mahogany Obsidian relieves pain and improves circulation.

Mahogany Obsidian

Rainbow Obsidian is one of the gentler obsidians but with strong protective properties. It teaches you about your spiritual nature. This stone cuts the cords of old love and gently releases hooks that others have left in the heart, replenishing the heart energy. Worn as a pendant, Rainbow Obsidian absorbs negative energy from the aura and draws off stress from the body.

Rainbow Obsidian

Red-Black Obsidian raises the kundalini* energy. It promotes vitality, virility, and brotherhood. In healing, Red-Black Obsidian treats fevers and chills.

Silver-Sheen Obsidian enhances meditation and is the perfect crystal for crystal gazing. As with all Obsidians, it provides a mirror of inner being. It brings advantages throughout life and imparts patience and perseverance when required. It is helpful stone when journeying out of the body, as it connects the astral body with the physical body and so brings the soul back into physical incarnation.

Red-Black Obsidian

OBSIDIAN: **APACHE TEAR**

Natural formation

COLOR	Black
APPEARANCE	Small, often smooth and water-worn. Translucent when held to the light
RARITY	Common
SOURCE	United States

ADDITIONAL PROPERTIES Apache Tear is a form of Black Obsidian but it is much gentler in its effect. It still brings up negativity but does so slowly so that it can be transmuted. An Apache Tear is excellent for absorbing negative energy and for protecting the aura*. It grounds and cleanses the earth chakra*. Apache Tear is so named because it is believed to shed tears in times of sorrow. It comforts grief, provides insight into the source of distress, and relieves long-held grievances. This stone stimulates analytical capabilities and promotes forgiveness. An Apache Tear will remove self-limitations and increase spontaneity.

HEALING It enhances assimilation of Vitamins C and D, removes toxins from the body, and calms muscle spasms.

POSITION Men at abdomen, women at breast.

OBSIDIAN: **SNOWFLAKE OBSIDIAN**

Tumbled

COLOR	Black and white
APPEARANCE	Mottled black-white, as though snowflakes were on the surface, often small and tumbled
RARITY	Easily obtained
SOURCE	Worldwide

ADDITIONAL PROPERTIES Placed on the sacral chakra, Snowflake Obsidian calms and soothes, putting you in the right frame of mind to be receptive before bringing to your attention ingrained patterns of behavior. It teaches you to value mistakes as well as successes.

It is a stone of purity, providing balance for body, mind, and spirit. Snowflake Obsidian helps you to recognize and release "wrong thinking" and stressful mental patterns. It promotes dispassion and inner centering. With the aid of Snowflake Obsidian, isolation and loneliness become empowering, aiding surrender in meditation.

HEALING Snowflake Obsidian treats veins and the skeleton, and improves circulation. The elixir is good for the skin and eyes.

POSITION Place as appropriate or use as elixir.

OKENITE

*Okenite ball
on matrix*

COLOR	White
APPEARANCE	Long and fibrous, looks like a small furry snowball
RARITY	Easily obtained from specialist shops
SOURCE	India

ATTRIBUTES Okenite has a soft and furry energy and is one of the stones for the New Age. People usually want to stroke it but this mats the fibers together or breaks them. Okenite links to the higher self and supports the conscious manifestation of its energies on the earth plane. Okenite clears obstacles from your path and promotes the stamina to finish your life tasks.

This crystal helps you to come to terms with being in incarnation and brings your attention to the reasons for your current experiences.

It pinpoints karmic* debts and opportunities that help you to grow. Assisting in understanding how the karmic past has produced the present, and how the present will create the future, Okenite facilitates deep karmic healing on all levels.

Okenite can be used to prepare for channeling*. It purifies the chakras* and the physical and subtle bodies*, uniting their energies.

This crystal has a dual action. A stone of truth, it instills truthfulness in yourself and others, and protects from the harshness that can arise when others speak their truth. It helps you to accept with love the verbal jibes of other people, showing whether there is any truth there to be accepted.

Psychologically, Okenite brings deep self-forgiveness. It promotes completion of karmic cycles, going back into past lives to forgive yourself for your mistakes and easing karmic guilt. This is a stone of karmic grace. It teaches that everything is part of the cycle of learning the soul's lessons and, growing from that knowledge, that nothing has to be endured forever. When you have done all you can, you can step out of a situation without incurring further karmic debt.

Mentally, Okenite facilitates in changing your mental set. It releases old patterns and brings in new, more appropriate beliefs. It is helpful for anyone suffering from prudishness, especially where this is linked to past-life vows of chastity.

HEALING Okenite encourages the flow of blood and milk, a boon for nursing mothers, and stimulates the circulation in the upper body. It lowers fevers and relieves nervous disorders. As an elixir, it treats skin eruptions.

POSITION As appropriate.

ONYX

Polished

COLOR	Black, gray, white, blue, brown, yellow, red
APPEARANCE	Banded, marble-like, often polished. All sizes
RARITY	Readily available
SOURCE	Italy, Mexico, United States, Russia, Brazil, South Africa

ATTRIBUTES Onyx is strength-giving. It provides support in difficult or confusing circumstances and during times of enormous mental or physical stress. Centering your energy and aligning it with a higher power, accessing higher guidance, is facilitated by Onyx as is connection with the whole. It can take you forward to view the future and, with its capacity to impart personal strength, facilitates being master of one's destiny. This stone promotes vigor, steadfastness, and stamina. It aids learning lessons, imparting self-confidence and helping you to be at ease in your surroundings.

Onyx is a secretive stone that assists in keeping your own counsel. However, Onyx is said to hold the memories of things that have happened to the wearer. It can be used for psychometry, telling the story to those who are sensitive to its vibrations.

This property of holding physical memories makes Onyx useful in past-life work for healing old injuries and physical trauma that are affecting the present life. Holding a piece of Onyx takes your attention to the site of the previous injury, which can then be released through body work, reframing*, or crystal therapy. Onyx can also be used to heal old grief and sorrows.

Psychologically, Onyx recognizes and integrates dualities within the self. It anchors the flighty into a more stable way of life and generally imparts self-control. Onyx is a mental tonic that alleviates overwhelming fears and worries. Onyx conveys the invaluable gift of wise decisions.

Physically, Onyx assists in absorbing from the universe energies that are required for healing or other purposes. It balances the yin and yang energies within the body.

HEALING Onyx is beneficial for teeth, bones, bone marrow, blood disorders, and the feet.

POSITION Wear on left side of body. Place or hold as appropriate. Traditionally, Onyx worn around the neck was said to cool lust and support chastity.

OPAL

Polished

Raw

Common Opal

Dark Opal

COLOR	White, pink, black, beige, blue, yellow, brown, orange, red, green, purple
APPEARANCE	Clear or milky, iridescent and fiery, or vitreous without fire, often small and polished
RARITY	Easily obtained, although gem Opals are expensive
SOURCE	Australia, Mexico, Peru, South America, Britain, Canada, United States, Honduras, Slovakia

ATTRIBUTES Opal is a delicate stone with a fine vibration. It enhances cosmic consciousness and induces psychic and mystical visions. Stimulating originality and dynamic creativity, it aids in accessing and expressing one's true self. Opal is absorbent and reflective. It picks up thoughts and feelings, amplifies them, and returns them to source. It is a karmic* stone, teaching that what you put out comes back. Opal is a protective stone in that, when properly programmed, it makes you unnoticeable or invisible. It can be used when venturing into dangerous places, and in shamanic work where stealth is required.

Psychologically, Opal amplifies traits and brings characteristics to the surface for transformation. Enhancing self-worth, it helps you to understand your full potential. Mentally, Opal brings lightness and spontaneity. It encourages an interest in the arts.

Emotionally, Opal has always been associated with love and passion, desire and eroticism. It is a seductive stone that intensifies emotional states and releases inhibitions. It can act as an emotional stabilizer, but the stone may scatter energy and the user needs to be well-centered before using Opal to explore or induce feelings, or to have other stones standing by to aid integration. Opal shows you what your emotional state has been in the past, especially in other lives, and teaches how to take responsibility for how you feel. It encourages putting out positive emotions. Wearing Opal is said to bring loyalty, faithfulness, and spontaneity, but may amplify fickleness where the propensity is already present. Opals can be used to send healing to the earth's energy field, repairing depletions and reenergizing and stabilizing the grid.

HEALING Opal strengthens the will to live. It treats Parkinson's disease, infections, and fevers and strengthens memory. Purifying the blood and kidneys, Opal regulates insulin, eases childbirth, and alleviates PMS (use dark colors). This stone is beneficial to the eyes, especially as an elixir.

POSITION Place as appropriate, especially on the heart and solar plexus. Wear on little finger.

SPECIFIC TYPES AND COLORS
In addition to the generic attributes, the following colors have additional properties:

Black-Brown-Gray Opal resonates with the sacral chakra* and the reproductive organs. It is particularly useful for releasing sexual tension that arises from an emotional cause, and for processing and integrating newly released emotions.

Blue Opal is an emotional soother that realigns to spiritual purpose. It resonates with the throat chakra and can enhance communication, especially of that which has been suppressed through lack of confidence. It is useful when past-life experiences or injuries are affecting the present life, as these can be healed through the etheric blueprint*.

Cherry Opal aids in cleansing and activating the base and sacral chakras. It promotes a feeling of being centered. At a spiritual level, this stone activates clairvoyance* and clairsentience*. It is particularly helpful for healing headaches that arise from a blocked and unopened third eye. It promotes tissue regeneration and heals blood disorders, muscle tension, and spinal disorders, and ameliorates menopausal symptoms.

Cherry Opal

Chrysopal (Blue-Green) opens to new impressions and encourages openness to others. It helps you to observe the world with new eyes. A mood-enhancing stone, it alleviates emotional burdens, often through crying, and liberates feelings. It detoxifies and regenerates the liver and relieves feelings of constriction from heart and chest.

Fire Opal (Orange-Red) is an enhancer of personal power, awakening inner fire, and a protector against danger. It is a symbol of hope, excellent for business, and an energy amplifier. This stone facilitates change and progress. Used in situations of injustice and mistreatment, Fire Opal supports through the resulting emotional turmoil. Fire Opal is said to magnify thoughts and feelings, returning them threefold, and can release deep-seated feelings of grief even when these stem from other lives. It is a wonderful stone for letting go of the past, although it can be explosive in its action when bottled-up emotions are suddenly released.

Fire Opal

Fire Opal resonates with the abdomen and lower back and the triple burner meridian. It heals the intestines and the kidneys, balancing the adrenal glands and preventing burn-out, and stimulates the sexual organs. This is an excellent stone for reenergizing and warming.

Green Opal is a cleansing and rejuvenating stone that promotes emotional recovery and aids relationships. With the ability to filter information and reorient the mind, it gives meaning to everyday life and brings about a spiritual perspective. In healing, Green Opal strengthens the immune system and alleviates colds and flu.

Hyalite (Water Opal) is a wonderful stone for scrying. Its watery depths stimulate connection with the spiritual realms. A mood stabilizer, it connects the base chakras with the crown, enhancing meditative experience. Hyalite helps those making the transition out of the body. It teaches that the body is a temporary vehicle for the soul.

Green Hyalite

PERIDOT

ALSO KNOWN AS CHYRYSOLITE, OLIVINE

Raw

Faceted

Polished

COLOR	Olive green, yellowish-green, honey, red, brownish
APPEARANCE	Opaque. Clear crystal when faceted and polished. Usually quite small
RARITY	Easily obtained but good crystals rare
SOURCE	United States, Brazil, Egypt, Ireland, Russia, Sri Lanka, Canary Islands

ATTRIBUTES In ancient times, Peridot was believed to keep away evil spirits. It is still a protective stone for the aura*.

This stone is a powerful cleanser. Releasing and neutralizing toxins on all levels, it purifies the subtle and physical bodies, and the mind. It opens, cleanses, and activates the heart and solar plexus chakras* and releases "old baggage." Burdens, guilt, or obsessions are cleared. Peridot teaches that holding on to people, or the past, is counterproductive. Peridot shows you how to detach yourself from outside influences and to look to your own higher energies for guidance.

This stone releases negative patterns and old vibrations so that a new frequency can be accessed. If you have done the psychological work, Peridot assists you to move forward rapidly. This visionary crystal helps you to understand your destiny and your spiritual purpose. It is particularly helpful to healers.

Psychologically, Peridot alleviates jealousy, resentment, spite and anger, and reduces stress. It enhances confidence and assertion without aggression. Motivating growth, Peridot helps to bring about necessary change. It assists in looking back to the past to find the gift in your experiences, and shows how to forgive yourself. This stone promotes psychological clarity and well-being. It is attuned to the attainment of spiritual truth, and regulates the cycles of life.

Mentally, Peridot sharpens the mind and opens it to new levels of awareness. It banishes lethargy, bringing to your attention all the things you have neglected consciously or unconsciously. With Peridot's aid, you can admit mistakes and move on. It helps you to take responsibility for your own life, especially when you believe it is all "someone else's fault." The influence of Peridot can greatly improve difficult relationships.

HEALING Peridot has a tonic effect. It heals and regenerates tissues. It strengthens the metabolism and benefits the skin. Peridot aids the heart, thymus, lungs, gallbladder, spleen, intestinal tract, and ulcers, and strengthens eyes. Placed on the abdomen, it aids giving birth by strengthening the muscle contractions but lessening pain. Its energy balances bipolar disorders and overcomes hypochondria.

POSITION Wear at the throat. Place as appropriate, especially over the liver in contact with the skin.

PETALITE

Raw

COLOR	Clear, white, pink, gray, reddish-white, greenish-white
APPEARANCE	Quartz-like, striated, slightly iridescent, usually small
RARITY	Rare and expensive
SOURCE	Brazil, Madagascar

ATTRIBUTES Petalite is another stone for the New Age. It is sometimes known as the Angel Stone because it enhances angelic connection. With a high, pure vibration, Petalite opens to cosmic consciousness. It aids in spiritual purification. This is a protective stone that enhances meditation and attunement. It takes you to a very calm and clear spiritual dimension from which causes can be ascertained and transmuted. It is particularly useful for ancestral and family healing, as it reaches back to a time before the dysfunction arose.

Petalite is a shamanic stone. It provides a safe environment for spiritual contact or for a vision quest*. It activates and energizes the process, and at the same time grounds during spiritual activity.

This stone calms the aura* and opens the throat and higher crown

214

chakras*, linking to high spiritual vibrations. It moves you beyond your present metaphysical abilities, linking you to the highest levels of spiritual knowing, and facilitates speaking of what you see during spiritual visions.

Even a small piece of Petalite is extremely potent as an elixir. It can be used to release negative karma and to clear entities from the aura or the mental body. It is extremely helpful during tie-cutting as it brings the higher selves of each person into the process and neutralizes manipulation at any level.

Carried on the body, Petalite constantly energizes and activates all the energy centers of the body at every level. It enhances and energizes the environment in which it finds itself.

HEALING Petalite harmonizes the endocrine system and activates the triple-burner meridian. This stone is useful in the treatment of AIDS and cancer. It benefits cells, eyes, lungs, muscular spasms, and the intestines.

POSITION Wear as pendant or earrings, or place as appropriate, especially on the third eye.

SPECIFIC COLORS

In addition to the generic attributes, the following colors have additional properties:

Pink Petalite clears the heart meridian and emotional baggage. It strengthens the emotional body, and releases fear and worry. A stone of compassion, it promotes flexibility while maintaining gentle strength.

Clear Petalite renders negative energies impotent. It clears implants, miasms*, and negative karma at any level.

215

PHENACITE

Raw

COLOR	Colorless, may be tinted yellow, yellow-red, red, pink, brown
APPEARANCE	Glassy, quartz-like, with small crystals
RARITY	Fairly rare and usually expensive
SOURCE	Madagascar, Russia, Zimbabwe, Colorado, Brazil

ATTRIBUTES Phenacite has one of the highest crystal vibrations yet discovered. It connects personal consciousness to a high frequency, enabling information from that space to be translated to the earth. It contacts the angelic realms* and the Ascended Masters*.

Phenacite is purifying and integrating, bringing the spiritual vibrations down to earth. It resonates with the etheric body, activates the light body*, and aids the ascension process. This crystal heals the soul and purifies the subtle* and physical bodies* to provide a suitable vehicle for it. Its energies are only available to those who have prepared themselves by shifting their personal vibration to a higher level.

Phenacite has a strong connection with all the chakras* and imparts knowledge on how to heal and activate them all. It stimulates the third eye* and activates the higher crown chakra, enhancing inner knowing.

This crystal appears to have different properties, depending on where it was mined. Madagascan Phenacite is interdimensional and has been experienced as intergalactic. Phenacite from Brazil often has its own "crystal guardian."

HEALING Phenacite works at a subtle level, purifying the body and clearing energy pathways. It downloads information from the Akashic Record* via the etheric blueprint* so that dis-ease* from any source can be identified and released. Phenacite activates healing from the etheric body* to the physical, healing the etheric blueprint when necessary as a prerequisite for physical healing. Phenacite has the power to amplify the energy of other healing crystals.

POSITION Wear as faceted stone or place as appropriate, especially above head.

SPECIFIC COLORS
In addition to the generic attributes, the following colors have additional properties:

Clear Phenacite aids interdimensional travel. It facilitates moving through vibratory spiritual states that would not normally be accessed from earth. It activates memories of earlier spiritual initiations and teaches that "like attracts like," urging you to raise your vibrations, purify your thoughts, and put out only positive energy.

Yellow Phenacite has a particular aptitude for extraterrestrial contact. This is a stone of manifestation, bringing what is desired into being on the physical plane provided it is for the highest good of all.

PIETERSITE

ALSO KNOWN AS TEMPEST STONE

Tumbled

COLOR	Golden-brown to gray-blue
APPEARANCE	Mottled, iridescent, often small, tumbled
RARITY	Easily obtained
SOURCE	Namibia

ATTRIBUTES Known as the Tempest Stone because of its connection to the storm element, Pietersite is a fairly recent discovery. It is said to hold "the keys to the kingdom of heaven." It links everyday consciousness to the spiritual, reminding you that you are a spiritual being on a human journey. Centering in the spiritual being, Pietersite has the ability to ground you not to the earth but to the etheric body*. This facilitates spiritual journeying, especially to read the Akashic Record* and the insights on your incarnations that are to be found there.

Pietersite is a stone of vision and can be used for a vision quest* or shamanic journey. It works strongly with the body during moving meditations, quickly accessing a very high state of altered awareness.

218

It stimulates the third eye* and the pineal gland, accessing the intuition and promoting profound spiritual visions and precognition. It links into a very loving level of guidance.

Pietersite is said to dispel the illusion of separateness and to remove beliefs and conditioning imposed by other people. It links you to the source of your own inner guidance and helps you to recognize the truth or falsehood of other people's words. It dissolves stubborn blockages and clears confusion. Used in past-life healing, Pietersite removes dis-ease* caused by not following your own truth. It releases mental and verbal conditioning—beliefs imposed in the past by authority figures such as parents and rule-makers—and dispels spiritual illusions. It can release you from vows and promises made in other lives that have carried over into the present life, and supports your own willpower.

Psychologically, Pietersite promotes walking your own truth. It is an extremely supportive and strengthening stone, aiding in speaking out and exploring anything that is blocking your access to truth. It assists in processing ancient conflicts and suppressed feelings.

HEALING Pietersite stimulates the pituitary gland, balancing the endocrine system and the production of hormones that govern metabolism, blood pressure, growth, sex, and temperature. It helps the lungs, liver, intestines, feet, and legs and promotes absorption of nutrients from food. At a subtle level, it clears and energizes the meridian* pathways of the body. This stone clears dis-ease* caused by exhaustion in those who have no time to rest.

POSITION Place or hold as appropriate.

PREHNITE

Raw

COLOR	Green, yellow, white, brown
APPEARANCE	Bubbles on matrix, small to medium pieces
RARITY	Easily obtained from specialist stores
SOURCE	South Africa

ATTRIBUTES Serene Prehnite is a stone of unconditional love and the crystal to heal the healer. It enhances the visualization process and induces deep meditation in which the higher self is contacted. When meditating with this crystal, you are put in touch with the universe's energy grid. It is said to connect to the archangel Raphael and to other spiritual and extraterrestrial beings. Prehnite enhances precognition and inner knowing. It is a stone that enables you always to be prepared, no matter what. Attuning to divine energies, Prehnite enhances prophecy and shows you the way forward for your spiritual growth.

This crystal seals the auric field in a protective shield of divine energy. It is a useful stone for gridding* as it calms the environment and brings peace and protection. It is an excellent stone for placing in the garden and Prehnite helps you to make your home into a healing sanctuary for yourself. This stone teaches how to be in harmony with nature and the elemental forces, revitalizing and renewing your surroundings.

A good Feng Shui stone, Prehnite is helpful for "decluttering," helping you to let go of possessions you no longer need, and to organize what you keep in an appropriate way. It aids those who hoard possessions, or love, because of an inner lack. This may well come from past-life experiences of deprivation and poverty or lack of love. With Prehnite's assistance, trust in the universe is restored and the soul once again believes in divine manifestation.

Psychologically, Prehnite alleviates nightmares, phobias, and deep fears, uncovering and healing the dis-ease* that creates them. It is beneficial for hyperactive children and the karmic* causes that underlie the condition.

HEALING Prehnite is useful for diagnosis, going to the root cause. It is healing for the kidneys and bladder, thymus gland, shoulders, chest, and lungs. It treats gout and blood disorders, repairs the connective tissue in the body and can stabilize malignancy.

POSITION Place or hold as appropriate. For prophecy, visualization, and guidance, place on the third eye*.

PYROLUSITE

Natural

COLOR	Silver, black, blue, dark gray
APPEARANCE	Large, shiny, fan-like on brown matrix or granular mass
RARITY	Readily available from specialist shops
SOURCE	United States, Britain, Brazil, India

ATTRIBUTES Pyrolusite has the ability to transform and restructure energies. At its most beneficial, and when consciously directed, it can restructure life. This stone heals energetic disturbances and transmutes dis-ease* in the physical, emotional, and mental bodies.

Pyrolusite is an extremely useful stone to place in your immediate environment or meditation space. It repels negative energy and dispels psychic interference from any source, strengthening the aura* in the process. It can prevent undue mental influence from someone with a strong mind, dissolve emotional manipulation, and provide a barrier to the attentions of those who inhabit the lower astral worlds.

If you have to be in the presence of someone in authority with a specific agenda to which you do not subscribe, keep a piece of Pyrolusite close beside you. It will enable you to stay true to your own beliefs. Because of its delicate construction, some Pyrolusite is not suitable for wearing or keeping on your person, but it can be held whenever its protective energies are required.

Psychologically, Pyrolusite promotes confidence, optimism, and determination. This tenacious stone gets to the bottom of problems and offers a means of transformation. It can give support during deep emotional healing, including past-life or body work to release emotional dis-ease* and blockages in the emotional body.

Emotionally, Pyrolusite has the power to change and stabilize relationships. It can help in transmuting negative expectations into positive ones.

HEALING Pyrolusite treats bronchitis, regulates the metabolism, reinforces blood vessels, and stimulates sexuality. It is also useful for strengthening eyesight.

POSITION Place or hold as appropriate. As Pyrolusite is quite delicate and heavy to place on the body, it can be made into an elixir by the indirect method and applied topically or taken internally.

QUARTZ

Cluster with point

Pillar (shaped)

COLOR	Clear
APPEARANCE	Long, pointed crystals, transparent, milky or striated, often in clusters, all sizes
RARITY	Most types of Quartz are easily obtained
SOURCE	Worldwide

ATTRIBUTES Quartz is the most powerful healing and energy amplifier on the planet because of its unique helical spiral crystalline form. Found worldwide, it absorbs, stores, releases, and regulates energy and is excellent for unblocking it. When acupuncture needles are coated in Quartz, the effects increase by ten percent. As demonstrated by a Kirlian camera*, holding a Quartz crystal in your hand doubles your biomagnetic field. It enhances muscle testing and protects against radiation. Quartz generates electromagnetism and dispels static electricity.

This crystal works at a vibrational level attuned to the specific energy requirements of the person needing healing or undertaking spiritual work. It takes the energy to the most perfect state possible, going back to before the dis-ease set in. It cleanses and enhances the organs and subtle bodies and acts as a deep soul cleanser, connecting the physical dimension with the mind.

At a spiritual level, this crystal raises energy to the highest possible level. Containing every color possible, Clear Quartz works on all levels of being. Storing information like a natural computer, these crystals are a spiritual library waiting to be accessed. Quartz has the ability to dissolve karmic seeds*. It enhances psychic abilities and attunes you to your spiritual purpose. Used in meditation, Quartz filters out distractions. Quartz is the most efficient receptor for programming.

At a mental level, Quartz aids concentration and unlocks memory.

Quartz is a great energy saver. Attached to a fuel line in a car, a Quartz point reduces fuel consumption.

Quartz points have different facet shapes according to how fast they formed. These shapes are deeply significant. (See the Crystal Shapes section starting on page 324.)

HEALING Quartz is a master healer and can be used for any condition. It stimulates the immune system and brings the body into balance.

It is excellent for soothing burns. Quartz harmonizes all the chakras*
and aligns the subtle bodies*.

POSITION Place as appropriate.

SPECIFIC COLORS AND TYPES OF QUARTZ
In addition to the generic attributes, specific colors and types of Quartz
have additional properties:

Blue Quartz assists in reaching out to others and assuages fear.
Calming the mind, it aids in understanding your spiritual nature and
inspires hope. In healing, it is beneficial for the organs in the upper
body. Blue Quartz purifies the bloodstream and strengthens the
immune system.

Blue Quartz

Golden Healer (naturally coated, transparent yellow) facilitates spiritual
communication over a long distance, including between worlds, and
empowers healing at all levels.

Green Quartz opens and stabilizes the heart chakra. It transmutes
negative energy, inspires creativity, and balances the endocrine system.

Harlequin Quartz has strings of red dots dancing within it. It links the
base and heart chakras with the crown chakra, drawing physical and
spiritual vitality into the body. Balancing the polarities and meridians
in the body, this crystal anchors them to the etheric, harmonizing the
subtle and physical nervous systems. Harlequin Quartz aids in the
expression of universal love and acts as a bridge between the spiritual
and physical worlds. In healing, Harlequin Quartz strengthens veins,
memory, and the thyroid, and overcomes thyroid deficiencies.

*Golden
Healer
(double
terminated)*

It activates the will to recover from illness and dis-ease* and helps to relieve despondency.

Lithium Quartz (naturally coated, spotted lilac-reddish purple) is a natural antidepressant. Its powerful healing energies gently lift the conditions underlying the depression to the surface, neutralizing ancient anger and grief. It can reach back into past lives to dissolve the roots of the emotional dis-ease that is pervading the present life. Lithium Quartz is an excellent cleanser for the chakras and will purify water. It is extremely useful as a healer for plants and animals.

Lithium Quartz

Natural Titanium is "spotted" onto Quartz Crystals that have the same powers as Rainbow Aura Quartz (see page 230) and is often occluded in Quartz as Rutilated Quartz (see page 237).

Natural Rainbow, found within many Quartz crystals, stimulates an awareness of universal love, draws off negativity, and disperses healing energy to the body and to the environment.

Titanium Quartz

Tangerine Quartz (naturally coated transparent orange) is an excellent stone to use after shock or trauma, especially at the soul level. It can be used for soul retrieval* and integration, and to

Natural Rainbow in Quartz point

227

*Tibetan Quartz with black spot occlusions**

heal after psychic attack. Tangerine Quartz can be used in past-life healing and is beneficial where the soul feels it has made a mistake for which it must pay. The soul learns to find the gift in the experience. Tangerine Quartz activates and harmonizes the sacral chakra*, stimulating the flow of creative energy. Tangerine Quartz can take you beyond your limited belief system and into a more positive vibration. It demonstrates that like attracts like.

Tibetan Quartz occurs in single and double terminators and may have "black spot" occlusions within it. It carries the resonance of Tibet and the esoteric knowledge that has existed there for so long. This knowledge can be attuned to when meditating with Tibetan Quartz. This knowledge can then be used instinctively in healing and in spiritual practices. It accesses the Akashic Record*. This rarefied and yet grounded Quartz has a strongly centered energy that passes into the body and the personal self, bringing about deep healing and energizing of the subtle bodies*. Used on the physical body, it purifies and energizes all the meridians.

Natural Siberian Quartz with phantom

(*See also* pages 229–243 for more types of Quartz and pages 336–337 for the uniquely shaped Cathedral Quartz.)

QUARTZ: **AQUA AURA AND LABORATORY-MADE SPECIALIST QUARTZES**

Aqua Aura

COLOR	Blue (Siberian), red (Rose or Ruby Aura), yellow (Sunshine Aura), rainbow
APPEARANCE	Quartz crystals artificially bonded with gold, producing intense color, small points or clusters
RARITY	Readily available
SOURCE	Manufactured coating on quartz crystal

ADDITIONAL PROPERTIES Despite being artificially created, Aqua Aura has an intense energy reflecting the alchemical process that bonds gold onto pure Quartz. Aqua Aura frees you from limitation and creates space for something new. This crystal heals, cleanses, and calms the aura*, releasing any stress and healing "holes." It then activates the chakras, especially at the throat where it encourages communication from the heart. Aqua Aura releases negativity from the subtle energetic* bodies and from the connections the spiritual body makes to universal energies. The expression of soul energy is then activated, fulfilling your highest potential.

Aqua Aura stimulates channeling* and self-expression, and deepens spiritual attunement and communication. It is a protective stone that safeguards against psychic or psychological attack*. It bestows profound peace during meditation. Used in conjunction with other crystals, Aqua Aura enhances their healing properties.

HEALING Aqua Aura strengthes the thymus gland and the immune system.

POSITION Hold, wear, or place as appropriate.

SPECIFIC AURA QUARTZES
Each Aura Quartz has its own specific properties related to its color but shares many properties because of the gold alchemized onto its surface.

Rainbow Aura is formed through the bonding of gold and titanium onto pure Quartz. Activating all the energy centers in the body, this crystal clears a path for the life force to manifest through the various bodies, bringing in vibrant energy and zest for life. Rainbow Aura is beneficial for dysfunctional relationships as it shows projections and helps release negative emotions such as resentment or old grief from the past, bringing deep insights into relationships at all levels. It aids in releasing karmic* ties that are hindering relationships in the present life. The transformed relationship is vital and harmonious.

Opal Aura Quartz has a much paler rainbow color that is produced from platinum. In the same way that a rainbow in the sky stimulates hope and optimism, Opal Aura is a crystal of joy. It purifies and balances all the chakras and integrates the light body into the physical dimensions. Opal Aura opens to a deep state of meditative awareness, grounding the information received in the physical body. It brings about a state of total union with the divine through cosmic consciousness.

Rose Aura is formed through the bonding of Quartz and platinum, producing a dynamic energy that works on the pineal gland and the heart chakra, transmuting deeply held doubts about self-worth. It bestows the gift of unconditional love of the self and connection to universal love. This form of Aura Quartz imbues the whole body with love, restoring the cells to perfect balance.

Ruby Aura is also formed from Quartz and platinum, but produces a much deeper color. Ruby Aura cleanses the base chakra* of old survival issues and abuse, bringing in passion and vitality, and activates the wisdom of the heart. Spiritually uplifting, it opens to Christ consciousness*.

Ruby Aura

This is a protective crystal against aggression and violence. In healing, Ruby Aura benefits the endocrine system and is a natural antibiotic for fungal infections and parasites.

Sunshine Aura is a garish yellow crystal formed from gold and platinum. Its energies are powerful and extremely active. It activates and cleanses the solar plexus, releasing old emotional trauma and hurt. At a spiritual level, Sunshine Aura is expansive and protective. It relieves constipation on all levels and releases toxins.

Siberian Blue Quartz is a brilliant blue laboratory-regrown crystal created from Quartz and cobalt. It is a powerful antidepressant, lifting the spirit and bringing deep peace. Siberian Blue Quartz activates the throat and third eye chakras*, stimulating psychic vision and telepathy and enhancing communication. It brings about intense visionary experiences and opens to cosmic consciousness. This stone helps you to speak your truth and facilitates being heard. As an elixir it treats throat infections, stomach ulcers, and stress. Applied externally, it relieves inflammation, sunburn, and stiff neck or muscles.

QUARTZ: **PHANTOM QUARTZ**

Amethyst   *Chlorite*

COLOR	Varies according to mineral
APPEARANCE	Ghost-like crystal within main crystal
RARITY	Easily obtained
SOURCE	Worldwide

APPEARANCE Smallish white or colored "ghost" crystal encompassed within the main clear Quartz crystal.

ADDITIONAL PROPERTIES A phantom crystal symbolizes universal awareness. Its purpose is to stimulate healing for the planet and to activate healing abilities in individuals. For this purpose, it connects to a spiritual guide* and enhances meditation. A Phantom Quartz facilitates accessing the Akashic Record*, reading past lives and recovering repressed memories to put the past into context. It can also take you into the between-lives state*. In healing, a Phantom Quartz treats hearing disorders and opens clairaudience*.

Amethyst Phantom accesses the prebirth state* and the plan for the present lifetime. It aids evaluation of progress made with spiritual lessons during the current incarnation.

Chlorite Phantom (Green) helps in self-realization and the removal of energy implants but should be used for this purpose under the guidance of a qualified crystal therapist. (*See also* Chlorite, page 108.)

Smoky Phantom takes you back to a time before you left your soul group* and links you into the purpose of the group incarnation. It can also help you to identify and attract members of your soul group. If negative energies have intervened in the group purpose, a Smoky Phantom will remove these, taking the group back to the original purity of intention.

QUARTZ: ROSE QUARTZ

Raw

Polished

COLOR	Pink
APPEARANCE	Usually translucent, may be transparent, all sizes, sometimes tumbled
RARITY	Easily obtained
SOURCE	South Africa, United States, Brazil, Japan, India, Madagascar

ADDITIONAL PROPERTIES Rose Quartz is the stone of unconditional love and infinite peace. It is the most important crystal for the heart and the heart chakra*, teaching the true essence of love. It purifies and opens the heart at all levels, and brings deep inner healing and self-love. It is calming, reassuring, and excellent for use in trauma or crisis.

If you want to attract love, look no further than romantic Rose Quartz. Placed by your bed or in the relationship corner of your home, it is so

235

effective in drawing love and relationships toward you that it often needs Amethyst to calm things down. In existing relationships, it will restore trust and harmony, and encourage unconditional love.

Rose Quartz gently draws off negative energy and replaces it with loving vibes. It strengthens empathy and sensitivity and aids the acceptance of necessary change. It is an excellent stone for mid-life crisis. Holding Rose Quartz enhances positive affirmations. The stone can then remind you of your intention. This beautiful stone promotes receptivity to beauty of all kinds.

Emotionally, Rose Quartz is the finest healer. Releasing unexpressed emotions and heartache and transmuting emotional conditioning that no longer serves, it soothes internalized pain and heals deprivation. If you have never received love, Rose Quartz opens your heart so that you become receptive. If you have loved and lost, it comforts your grief. Rose Quartz teaches you how to love yourself, vital if you have thought yourself unlovable. You cannot accept love from others nor love them unless you love yourself. This stone encourages self-forgiveness and acceptance, and invokes self-trust and self-worth.

HEALING Rose Quartz strengthens the physical heart and circulatory system and releases impurities from body fluids. Placed on the thymus, Rose Quartz aids chest and lung problems. It heals the kidneys and adrenals and alleviates vertigo. Rose Quartz is said to increase fertility. The stone or elixir soothes burns and blistering and smoothes the complexion. It is helpful in Alzheimer's, Parkinson's, and senile dementia.

POSITION Wear, especially over the heart. Place on the heart, thymus, or in relationship corner of room.

QUARTZ: RUTILATED QUARTZ

ALSO KNOWN AS ANGEL HAIR

Tumbled

COLOR	Colorless or smoky with golden brown, reddish, or black strands
APPEARANCE	Long thin "threads" in clear crystal, all sizes
RARITY	Readily available
SOURCE	Worldwide

ADDITIONAL PROPERTIES Rutilated Quartz is an effective integrator of energy at any level. It heightens the energetic impulse of Quartz and is a very efficient vibrational healer.

Spiritually, Rutilated Quartz is said to have a perfect balance of cosmic light and to be an illuminator for the soul, promoting spiritual growth. It cleanses and energizes the aura*. This stone aids astral travel*, scrying*, and channeling*. It facilitates contact with the highest spiritual guidance. It draws off negative energy and breaks down the barriers to spiritual progress, letting go of the past.

237

Rutilated Quartz is helpful for therapists and counselors as it filters negative energy from a client, and at the same time supports their energy field during emotional release and confrontation with the darker aspects of the psyche. It gives protection against psychic attack*.

Rutilated Quartz can be used in past-life healing to draw off dis-ease* from the past and to promote insights into the events in past lives that affect the present. It assists in moving to a core life to access causes and to understand the results of previous actions. It connects to soul lessons and the plan for the present life.

Psychologically, Rutilated Quartz reaches the root of problems and facilitates transitions and a change of direction. Emotionally, Rutilated Quartz soothes dark moods and acts as an antidepressant. It relieves fears, phobias, and anxiety, releasing constrictions and countering self-hatred. This stone promotes forgiveness at all levels.

Rutilated Quartz opens the aura to allow healing. At a physical level, it absorbs mercury poisoning from nerves, muscles, blood, and the intestinal tract.

HEALING Rutilated Quartz has a vitality that is helpful for chronic conditions and for impotence and infertility. It is excellent for exhaustion and energy depletion. This crystal treats the respiratory tract and bronchitis, stimulates and balances the thyroid, repels parasites. It stimulates growth and regeneration in cells and repairs torn tissues. It is said to encourage an upright posture.

POSITION Neck for thyroid; heart for thymus; solar plexus for energy; ears to balance and align; sweep over aura to draw off negativity.

QUARTZ: **SMOKY QUARTZ**

Tumbled

Natural point

COLOR	Brownish to blackish hue, sometimes yellowish
APPEARANCE	Translucent, long, pointed crystals with darker ends. All sizes. (Note: very dark quartz may be artificially irradiated and is not transparent.)
RARITY	Easily obtained but ensure that it is natural Smoky Quartz
SOURCE	Worldwide

ADDITIONAL PROPERTIES Smoky Quartz is one of the most efficient grounding and anchoring stones and at the same time raises vibrations during meditation. This protective stone has a strong link with the earth and the base chakras*, promoting a concern for the environment and ecological solutions. This stone is a superb antidote to stress. It assists in tolerating difficult times with equanimity, fortifying resolve.

Grounding spiritual energy and gently neutralizing negative vibrations, Smoky Quartz blocks geopathic stress*, absorbs electromagnetic smog*, and assists elimination and detoxification on all levels. It brings in a positive vibration to fill the space. Smoky Quartz teaches you how to leave behind anything that no longer serves you. It can be used to protect the earth chakra below the feet and its grounding cord* when in an area of disturbed earth energy.

Psychologically, Smoky Quartz relieves fear, lifts depression, and brings emotional calmness. It alleviates suicidal tendencies and ambivalence about being in incarnation. Smoky Quartz aids acceptance of the physical body and the sexual nature, enhancing virility and cleansing the base chakra so that passion can flow naturally. This crystal alleviates nightmares and manifests your dreams. When it comes into contact with negative emotions, it gently dissolves them.

Mentally, Smoky Quartz promotes positive, pragmatic thought and can be used in scrying to give clear insight and to neutralize fear of failure. It dissolves contradictions, promotes concentration, and alleviates communication difficulties. Smoky Quartz facilitates moving between alpha and beta states of mind and aids clearing the mind for meditation.

Physically, because Smoky Quartz is often naturally irradiated, it is excellent for treating radiation-related illness or chemotherapy. However, care should be taken to select naturally formed stones with minuscule radiation rather than ones that have been artificially treated with radiation (these stones are usually very black and nontransparent). Tolerance of stress is much improved with the assistance of relaxing Smoky Quartz and this stone provides pain relief. In healing, a layout of slow-release Smoky Quartz pointing out from the body can prevent a healing crisis from occurring.

HEALING Smoky Quartz is particularly effective for ailments of the abdomen, hips, and legs. It relieves pain, including headaches, and benefits the reproductive system, muscle and nerve tissue, and the heart. Smoky Quartz dissolves cramps, strengthens the back, and fortifies the nerves. This stone aids assimilation of minerals and regulates liquids within the body.

POSITION Anywhere, especially base chakra. Under pillow, by a telephone, or on geopathic stress lines. Wear as a pendant for long periods. To dispel stress, place a stone in each hand and sit quietly for a few moments. Place over painful point to dissolve pain. Place point away from body to draw off negative energies, point toward to energize.

Smoky Quartz: the one on the left has been artificially irradiated

241

QUARTZ: **SNOW QUARTZ**

ALSO KNOWN AS MILK QUARTZ, QUARTZITE

Tumbled

COLOR	White
APPEARANCE	Firmly compacted, milky, often water-worn pebble or large boulder
RARITY	Easily obtained
SOURCE	Worldwide

ADDITIONAL PROPERTIES Snow Quartz supports you while learning lessons and helps you to let go of overwhelming responsibilities and limitations. It is perfect for people who feel put upon whilst actually creating that situation because they need to be needed. It can overcome martyrdom and victimhood.

Mentally, this stone enhances tact and cooperation. It helps you to think before you speak. When used in meditation, it links to deep inner wisdom previously denied in yourself and society.

HEALING Snow Quartz is appropriate wherever Clear Quartz would be used. Its effect is slower and gentler but nevertheless effective.

POSITION Use anywhere as appropriate.

QUARTZ: **TOURMALINATED QUARTZ**

Tumbled

COLOR	Clear with dark strands
APPEARANCE	Long, thick, dark "threads" in clear crystal, all sizes
RARITY	Easily obtained
SOURCE	Worldwide

ADDITIONAL PROPERTIES Tourmalinated Quartz brings together the properties of Quartz and Tourmaline. An effective grounding stone, it strengthens the body's energy field against external invasion and deflects detrimental environmental influences. It dissolves crystallized patterns and releases tensions at any level. This stone harmonizes disparate and opposite elements and polarities, and turns negative thoughts and energies into positive ones. Psychologically, it helps to integrate and heal the shadow energies, alleviating self-sabotage. It is an effective problem solver.

HEALING Tourmalinated Quartz harmonizes the meridians*, the subtle bodies*, and the chakras*.

POSITION Place as appropriate.

RHODOCHROSITE

| Polished | Raw | Tumbled |

COLOR	Pink to orange
APPEARANCE	Banded, all sizes, often polished or tumbled
RARITY	Easily obtained
SOURCE	United States, South Africa, Russia, Argentina, Uruguay

ATTRIBUTES Rhodochrosite represents selfless love and compassion. It expands consciousness and integrates the spiritual with material energies. This stone imparts a dynamic and positive attitude.

Rhodochrosite is an excellent stone for the heart and relationships, especially for people who feel unloved. It is the stone *par excellence* for healing sexual abuse. Rhodochrosite attracts a soulmate but this may not be the blissful experience you're hoping for. Soulmates are the people who help us to learn our lessons in life, and although this is not always pleasant, it is for our higher good. Rhodochrosite teaches the heart to assimilate painful feelings without shutting down, and removes denial.

This stone clears the solar plexus and base chakras*. Gently bringing painful and repressed feelings to the surface, it allows them to be acknowledged and then dissipated through emotional release. Rhodochrosite then helps to identify ongoing patterns and shows the purpose behind the experience. This is a stone that insists you face the truth, about yourself and other people, without excuses or evasion but with loving awareness.

Rhodochrosite is useful for diagnosis at the psychological level. People who have an aversion to the stone are repressing something in themselves they do not want to look at. The stone urges that they confront irrational fears and paranoia, and reveals that the emotions they have been taught to believe are unacceptable are natural. They then see things less negatively. Psychologically, Rhodochrosite improves self-worth and soothes emotional stress.

Rhodochrosite is mentally enlivening. It encourages a positive attitude and enhances dream states and creativity. This stone links you into the higher mind and helps you integrate new information.

Emotionally, Rhodochrosite encourages spontaneous expression of feelings, including passionate and erotic urges. It lifts a depressed mood and brings lightness into life.

HEALING Rhodochrosite acts as an irritant filter and relieves asthma and respiratory problems. It purifies the circulatory system and kidneys and restores poor eyesight, normalizes blood pressure and stabilizes the heartbeat, and invigorates the sexual organs. As it dilates blood vessels, it relieves migraines. The elixir relieves infections, improves the skin, and balances the thyroid.

POSITION Wear on the wrist or place over the heart or solar plexus. For migraines, place on the top part of the spine.

RHODONITE

Tumbled

Raw

COLOR	Pink or red
APPEARANCE	Mottled, often flecked with black, often small and tumbled
RARITY	Easily obtained
SOURCE	Spain, Russia, Sweden, Germany, Mexico, Brazil

ATTRIBUTES Rhodonite is an emotional balancer that nurtures love and encourages the brotherhood of humanity. It has the ability to show both sides of an issue. This stone stimulates, clears, and activates the heart and the heart chakra*. It grounds energy, balances yin–yang, and aids in achieving one's highest potential. It is said to enhance mantra-based meditation, aligning the soul more closely to the vibration.

A useful "first aid stone," Rhodonite heals emotional shock and panic, lending a supportive energy to the soul during the process. It is extremely beneficial in cases of emotional self-destruction, codependency, and abuse. Rhodonite clears away emotional wounds and scars from the past—whenever that might be—and brings up for transmutation painful emotions such as festering resentment or anger. This stone has a strong resonance with forgiveness and assists in reconciliation after long-term pain and abuse. It can be used in past-life healing to deal with betrayal and abandonment. With its ability to promote unselfish self-love and forgiveness, it helps in taking back projections that blame the partner for what is really inside the self.

Rhodonite is a useful stone to turn back insults and to prevent retaliation. It recognizes that revenge is self-destructive and promotes remaining calm in dangerous or upsetting situations.

Rhodonite balances and integrates physical and mental energies. It builds up confidence and alleviates confusion.

HEALING Rhodonite is an excellent wound healer that also relieves insect bites. It can reduce scarring. It beneficially affects bone growth and the hearing organs, fine-tuning auditory vibrations, and stimulates fertility. This stone treats emphysema, inflammation of joints and arthritis, autoimmune diseases, stomach ulcers, and multiple sclerosis. Use the elixir as a rescue remedy for shock or trauma.

POSITION As appropriate. Place over the heart for emotional wounds, on the skin for external or internal wounds.

GEM RHODONITE activates the pineal gland and brings intuitive guidance. It aligns the chakras and removes blockages to clear chakra energy flow. Its gentle pink ray is particularly appropriate for assisting emotional healing.

RHYOLITE

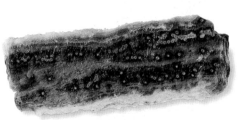

Raw

Polished and shaped

COLOR	White, green, light gray, red
APPEARANCE	Banded or spotted with crystal inclusions, all sizes, often tumbled
RARITY	Available from specialist stores, often shaped and polished
SOURCE	Australia, Mexico, United States

ATTRIBUTES Rhyolite ignites the potential and creativity of the soul. It facilitates change without enforcing it, assists in fulfilling quests and facilitates knowing from a soul level. It can access karmic* wisdom. Strengthening soul, body, and mind, Rhyolite is immensely helpful when exploring the full extent of the self.

This stone facilitates a deep state of meditation in which inner and outer journeys may be made.

A useful stone for past-life healing, Rhyolite processes the past and integrates it with the present. It brings things to a resolution, no matter where the source of difficulties may have been, and actively encourages moving forward. This is an excellent stone to keep you anchored in the present moment rather than harking back to the past.

Psychologically, Rhyolite enhances self-esteem and self-worth. It imparts a sense of self-respect and acceptance of your true self.

Mentally, Rhyolite imparts the strength to deal calmly with challenging life circumstances and brings awareness of one's own strength.

Emotionally, Rhyolite has a balancing effect, gently facilitating emotional release where this is appropriate.

HEALING Rhyolite fortifies the body's natural resistance. It treats veins, rashes, skin disorders, and infections, and improves assimilation of B vitamins. It can dissolve kidney stones and hardened tissue. As an elixir, Rhyolite gives strength and improves muscle tone.

POSITION Wear or position as appropriate. Place on the forehead for past-life regression (under the direction of a skilled therapist) and on the solar plexus for emotional release.

RUBY

Raw

Polished

COLOR	Red
APPEARANCE	Bright, transparent when polished, opaque when not. Small faceted crystal or larger cloudy piece
RARITY	Uncut Ruby is readily available, polished gemstone is expensive
SOURCE	India, Madagascar, Russia, Sri Lanka, Cambodia, Kenya, Mexico

ATTRIBUTES Ruby is an excellent stone for energy. Imparting vigor to life, it energizes and balances but may sometimes overstimulate in delicate or irritable people. Ruby encourages passion for life but never in a self-destructive way. It improves motivation and setting of realistic goals.

Ruby stimulates the heart chakra* and balances the heart. It encourages "following your bliss." This stone is a powerful shield against

250

psychic attack* and vampirism of heart energy. It promotes positive dreams and clear visualization, and stimulates the pineal gland. Ruby is one of the stones of abundance and aids retaining wealth and passion.

Psychologically, Ruby brings up anger or negative energy for transmutation and encourages removal of anything negative from your path. It promotes dynamic leadership.

Mentally, Ruby brings about a positive and courageous state of mind. Under the influence of Ruby, the mind is sharp with heightened awareness and excellent concentration. Given this stone's protective effect, it makes you stronger during disputes or controversy.

Emotionally, Ruby is dynamic. It charges up passion and fires the enthusiasm. Ruby is a sociable stone that attracts sexual activity.

Physically, Ruby overcomes exhaustion and lethargy and imparts potency and vigor. Conversely, it calms hyperactivity.

HEALING Ruby detoxifies the body, blood, and lymph, and treats fevers, infectious disease, and restricted blood flow. It is extremely beneficial for the heart and circulatory system. It stimulates the adrenals, kidneys, reproductive organs, and spleen.

POSITION Heart, finger, ankle.

COMBINATION STONE
Ruby in Zoisite (Anyolite) activates the crown chakra, creates an altered state of consciousness and facilitates access to soul memory and spiritual learning. It can be extremely helpful in soul healing and in past-life work. This stone has the unusual property of promoting individuality while at the same time retaining interconnectedness with the rest of humanity. It powerfully amplifies the biomagnetic field* around the body.

Ruby in Zoisite

SAPPHIRE

Black, polished

Black, raw

COLOR	Blue, yellow, green, black, purple
APPEARANCE	Bright, transparent when polished, often small or larger cloudy piece
RARITY	Some sapphire colors are rare but most are easily obtained as uncut stones
SOURCE	Myanmar, Czech Republic, Brazil, Kenya, India Australia, Sri Lanka

ATTRIBUTES Sapphire is known as the wisdom stone, each color having its own particular wisdom. It focuses and calms the mind and releases unwanted thoughts and mental tension. Bringing in peace of mind and serenity, Sapphire aligns the physical, mental, and spiritual planes and restores balance within the body.

This stone releases depression and spiritual confusion and stimulates concentration. It brings prosperity and attracts gifts of all kinds. Placed on the throat, Sapphire releases frustration and facilitates self-expression.

HEALING Sapphire calms overactive body systems and regulates the glands. It heals the eyes, removing impurities and stress. It treats blood disorders and alleviates excessive bleeding, strengthens veins, and improves their elasticity.

POSITION Touching the body. Wear on the finger or place as appropriate.

SPECIFIC COLORS
Each color of Sapphire has its own unique attributes in addition to the generic qualities:

Black Sapphire is protective and centering. It imparts confidence in one's own intuition. This stone heightens employment prospects and helps in retaining a job.

Blue Sapphire is a seeker after spiritual truth, traditionally associated with love and purity. It is extremely effective for earth and chakra* healing. This tranquil stone helps you to stay on the spiritual path and is used in shamanic ceremonies to transmute negative energies. It opens and heals the throat chakra and the thyroid, and facilitates self-expression and speaking your truth.

Blue Sapphire

253

*Green
Sapphire*

Green Sapphire improves vision, both inner and outer, and improves dream recall. It stimulates the heart chakra, bringing loyalty, fidelity, and integrity. This stone enhances compassion and an understanding of the frailties and unique qualities of others. It honors trust and respect for other people's belief systems.

Pink Sapphire acts as a magnet to draw into your life all that you need in order to evolve. It is a fast-acting stone that teaches you how to master emotions, clearing emotional blockages and integrating the transmuted energies.

Purple Sapphire awakens. It is helpful for meditation, stimulating the kundalini* rise and the crown chakra and opening spirituality. This stone activates the pineal gland with its link to psychic abilities, and stimulates visionary qualities. It is extremely calming for the emotionally unstable.

Royal Sapphire eliminates negative energies from chakras, and stimulates the third eye* to access information for growth. This stone teaches responsibility for your own thoughts and feelings. It treats brain disorders, including dyslexia.

Star Sapphire has a five-pointed star-shaped formation in its depths. This rare stone draws you into its depths and opens intuition. It brings about centering of your thoughts and aids in anticipating the intentions of other people. It is said to contact extraterrestrial beings.

White Sapphire has an extremely pure energy. Opening the crown chakra, it takes spiritual awareness to a very high space, opening cosmic consciousness*. This is an extremely protective stone that removes obstacles to the spiritual path. It is helpful in accessing your potential and life purpose.

Yellow Sapphire attracts wealth to the home and can be placed in cash boxes to increase prosperity and earnings. If worn, it should touch the body. Yellow Sapphire stimulates the intellect and improves overall focus so that the bigger picture is seen. As an elixir, it removes toxins from the body.

Yellow
Sapphire

SARDONYX

Black, tumbled

Black and Reddish-Brown, tumbled

COLOR	Black, red, brown, clear
APPEARANCE	Banded, opaque, may be large or small, often tumbled
RARITY	Easily obtained from specialist stores
SOURCE	Brazil, India, Russia, Asia Minor

ATTRIBUTES Sardonyx is a stone of strength and protection. It invokes the search for a meaningful existence and promotes integrity and virtuous conduct.

Bringing lasting happiness and stability to marriage and partnerships, Sardonyx attracts friends and good fortune. It can be gridded around the house and garden to prevent crime. (A stone can be placed at each corner, and at doors and windows, but it is more effective to dowse for exactly the right place (see page 374).)

Psychologically, Sardonyx supplements willpower and strengthens character. It increases stamina, vigor, and self-control. This stone alleviates depression and overcomes hesitancy. Mentally, Sardonyx improves perception and aids the process of osmosis and processing of information.

HEALING Sardonyx heals lungs and bones and resensitizes the sensory organs. It regulates fluids and cell metabolism, strengthens the immune system, and aids the absorption of nutrients and elimination of waste products.

POSITION Anywhere, especially laid on the stomach.

SPECIFIC COLORS
In addition to the generic properties, specific colors have additional attributes:

Black Sardonyx absorbs negativity.

Brown Sardonyx grounds energy.

Clear Sardonyx purifies.

Red Sardonyx stimulates.

Red Sardonyx

SELENITE

ALSO KNOWN AS SATIN SPAR, DESERT ROSE

Egg

Pillar with gateway

White Satin Spar

Orange-Brown

COLOR	Pure white, orange, blue, brown, green
APPEARANCE	Translucent with fine ribbing (Satin Spar) or coarser ribbing, fishtail, or petal-like (Desert Rose). All sizes
RARITY	Easily obtained
SOURCE	United States, Mexico, Russia, Austria, Greece, Poland, Germany, France, England

ATTRIBUTES Translucent Selenite has a very fine vibration and brings clarity of mind, opening the crown and higher crown chakras* and accessing angelic consciousness and higher guidance. Pure Selenite is a link to the light body*, helping to anchor it in the earth vibration.

Selenite is a calm stone that instills deep peace and is excellent for meditation or spiritual work. Telepathy is enhanced by each person holding a piece of pure-vibration Selenite. The purest translucent white Selenite has an ethereal quality and is said to inhabit the place between light and matter. An ancient stone, it is nevertheless one of the most powerful crystals for the new vibration on earth.

Selenite can be used to form a protective grid* around a house, creating a safe and quiet space that does not allow outside influences in—use internally in the corners of the house. A large piece of Selenite placed in the house ensures a peaceful atmosphere. Selenite wands can be used to detach entities from the aura* or for preventing anything external from influencing the mind.

Carrying the imprint of all that has happened in the world, Selenite reaches other lives and is very useful for checking on progress made and for accessing the plan for the present life from the between-lives state*. It pinpoints lessons and issues that are still being worked upon, and shows how they can best be resolved. It can be used for scrying*, to see the future or to ascertain what has happened in the past.

Psychologically, Selenite assists judgment and insight. Mentally, it clears confusion and aids in seeing the deeper picture. It brings about a conscious understanding of what has been occurring at the subconscious level. This is a powerful disperser and stabilizer for erratic emotions.

HEALING Selenite aligns the spinal column and promotes flexibility. It guards against epileptic seizures. This stone neutralizes mercury

poisoning from dental amalgam and reverses the effects of "free radicals." It is an excellent crystal for breastfeeding and nurturing a child. Its finest healing occurs at the energetic levels.

POSITION Hold, or place in or around house. (Note: Selenite dissolves when wet.)

SPECIFIC COLORS AND FORMS

In addition to the generic properties, different colored Selenites have specific properties:

Orange-Brown Selenite earths angelic energies and aids earth healing.

Blue Selenite placed on the third eye quiets the intellect, facilitates shutting off mind chatter during meditation, and quickly reveals the core of a problem.

Blue Selenite

Green Selenite assists in working toward the highest good. It makes you feel good about yourself and helps to overcome the effects of aging on the skin and skeleton.

Green Selenite

*Fishtail
Selenite*

Fishtail Selenite provides deep healing for the nerves. It is extremely calming, stabilizing emotions and defusing tension. This form of Selenite is often called Angel's Wing Selenite, as it facilitates angelic contact.

Desert Rose Selenite helps to dissolve self-imposed programs that have been running for too long. It releases the program and assists in finding an appropriate replacement. It can be used to strengthen affirmations of purpose.

*Desert Rose
Selenite*

SERAPHINITE

ALSO KNOWN AS SERAFINA

Polished slice

COLOR	Green
APPEARANCE	Silvery feathers within the darker stone, often small and polished
RARITY	Available in specialist stores
SOURCE	Siberia

ATTRIBUTES Placed on the third eye* or meditated with, Seraphinite is a stone of spiritual enlightenment and is excellent for accessing self-healing. It is one of the crystals for making angelic connection and for opening the crown and higher crown chakras*. This stone promotes

262

living from the heart and has a gently cleansing effect on the heart chakra, opening to love.

Its feathery wings whisk you up to a high spiritual vibration and it is excellent for making journeys out of the body, protecting the physical body while you are gone. It can assist with reviewing the progress of life and with identifying the changes needed to put you on the path to peace and fulfillment.

HEALING Seraphinite works best at a subtle level. It activates the spinal cord and its links to the etheric body*, especially behind the heart, and can release muscle tension up into the neck. It is useful for overcoming chills and for promoting weight loss.

POSITION Place on third eye or heart, or under pillow, or wear around the neck.

(*See also* Chlorite, page 108.)

SERPENTINE

Raw

COLOR	Red, green, brown-red, brown-yellow, black-green, white
APPEARANCE	Mottled, dual appearance, can be water-worn and often polished. All sizes
RARITY	Easily obtained from specialist stores
SOURCE	Britain (Cornwall), Norway, Russia, Zimbabwe, Italy, United States

ATTRIBUTES Serpentine is an earthing stone that aids meditation and spiritual exploration. Clearing the chakras* and stimulating the crown chakra, it opens psychic abilities and helps you to understand the spiritual basis of life. This stone opens new pathways for the kundalini* energy to rise. It assists the retrieval of wisdom, and regains memory of past lives.

Psychologically, Serpentine helps you to feel more in control of your life. It corrects mental and emotional imbalances and assists the conscious direction of healing energy toward problem areas.

Physically, Serpentine is extremely cleansing and detoxifying for the body and blood. It is said to ensure longevity.

HEALING Serpentine eliminates parasites, aids calcium and magnesium absorption, and treats hypoglycemia and diabetes.

POSITION Hold or place on appropriate spot.

INFINITE STONE (Light-Green Serpentine) is a gentle, tender-natured stone that brings you into contact with angelic guidance. It accesses and integrates the past, present, and future and is excellent for past-life exploration, as it promotes compassion and forgiveness for yourself and what you went through. Holding this stone takes you into the healing realms that exist in the between-lives state* so that healing that was not undertaken after a former life ended can be completed.

Infinite Stone

This stone heals imbalances from past lives and clears emotional baggage from previous relationships. Placed on the throat, it aids speaking of the past and resolves issues that have been carried over into the present. Use Infinite Stone if you want to confront anyone from your past, as it brings a gentle touch to the meeting.

Light Green Serpentine is excellent for pain relief, especially menstrual and muscular aches and pains.

SHATTUCKITE

Tumbled

COLOR	Dark and light blue, turquoise
APPEARANCE	Mottled, often small and tumbled
RARITY	Obtainable from specialist stores
SOURCE	United States

ATTRIBUTES Shattuckite is a highly spiritual stone that heightens vibration. It stimulates the third eye* and the throat chakra*, bringing them into harmony and alignment. It brings clear psychic vision and aids in understanding and communicating what is seen. Particularly useful in cases where past-life experience has closed down metaphysical abilities, Shattuckite removes hypnotic commands and edicts against using psychic vision. It can clear past-life curses and commands to secrecy.

Shattuckite is helpful during channeling*, as it is strongly protective, ensuring that the entity does not take over the physical body. It reaches

266

a high vibration, ensuring that the purest source is contacted. It can be used to develop pyschic abilities such as automatic writing* and telepathy and to facilitate clear communication with extraterrestrials.

HEALING Shattuckite is beneficial for all minor health complaints, bringing the body gently back into balance. The elixir is useful as a general tonic, especially in the spring. The stone treats tonsillitis, increases the clotting properties of blood, and clears blockages from intercellular structures.

POSITION Place as appropriate.

SMITHSONITE

Pink

Blue-Green

COLOR	Pink, lavender, green, blue-green, purple, brown, yellow, white-gray, blue
APPEARANCE	Pearly, lustrous, like layers of silky bubbles, all sizes
RARITY	Easily obtained
SOURCE	United States, Australia, Greece, Italy, Mexico, Namibia

ATTRIBUTES Smithsonite is a stone of tranquility, charm, kindness, and favorable outcomes. It has an extremely gentle presence and forms a buffer against life's problems. It is the perfect stone for releasing stress that is almost at breaking point and for alleviating mental breakdown.

This stone is ideal for anyone who has had a difficult childhood and who felt unloved or unwanted. Smithsonite heals the inner child* and alleviates the effects of emotional abuse and misuse. It is gentle, dissolving emotional hurt subtly. Its effects are noticed in feeling better rather than in traumatic emotional release. It may need the support of other crystals to bring things into conscious awareness. This is an excellent crystal for birth and rebirth and can treat infertility.

Smithsonite aligns the chakras* and strengthens psychic abilities. Holding Smithsonite during psychic communication makes you intuitively aware of its validity, or otherwise. Placed on the crown chakra, it connects to the angelic realm*.

Psychologically, Smithsonite supports leadership qualities, especially where tact is required. Emotionally, Smithsonite aids difficult relationships. An excellent stone for a secure and balanced life, this stone imparts harmony and diplomacy and remedies unpleasant situations. Physically, as Smithsonite is excellent for the immune system, it can be gridded around the four corners of your bed, with a piece under the pillow or on a bedside table. It is particularly effective combined with Bloodstone or Green Tourmaline taped over the thymus.

HEALING Smithsonite heals a dysfunctional immune system, sinus and digestive disorders, osteoporosis, and alcoholism. It restores elasticity to veins and muscles.

POSITION Place as appropriate or carry always. Place at crown to align chakras. Place Pink Smithsonite over the heart or thymus. Grid* around the bed or body.

SPECIFIC COLORS
In addition to the generic attributes, specific colors of Smithsonite have additional properties:

Blue-Green Smithsonite heals emotional and other wounds by bringing in universal love. Gently releasing anger, fear, and pain, it balances the energy field between the etheric and emotional bodies, and eases panic attacks, assists in attaining the heart's desire, promotes friendship, and is auspicious in midwifery and for nurturing babies.

Lavender-Violet Smithsonite has a very gentle vibration. It clears negative energy, and encourages joyful spiritual service and higher states of consciousness, giving guidance and protection. It is an excellent stone for meditation and soul retrieval* and facilitates going back into past lives to regain soul energy that did not make the transition away from a past-life death. In this respect, it can heal past-life death trauma and point the way to soul healing. Physically, it soothes neuralgia and inflammation.

Lavender-Pink Smithsonite has a very loving vibration. It heals the heart, and experiences of abandonment and abuse, rebuilding trust and security. Assisting in feeling loved and supported by the universe, it is helpful in convalescence and soothes pain. Lavender-Pink Smithsonite helps ameliorate drug and alcohol problems and the emotions that lie behind them.

Yellow Smithsonite balances the solar plexus chakra* and the mental body. It releases old hurts and outgrown emotional patterning. In healing, this stone aids digestion and assimilation of nutrients, and relieves skin problems.

SODALITE

Raw

Tumbled

COLOR	Blue
APPEARANCE	Mottled dark and light blue-white, often tumbled. All sizes
RARITY	Easily obtained
SOURCE	North America, France, Brazil, Greenland, Russia, Myanmar, Romania

ATTRIBUTES Sodalite unites logic with intuition and opens spiritual perception, bringing information from the higher mind down to the physical level. This stone stimulates the pineal gland and the third eye and deepens meditation. When in Sodalite-enhanced meditation, the mind can be used to understand the circumstances in which you find yourself. This stone instills a drive for truth and an urge toward idealism, making it possible to remain true to yourself and stand up for your beliefs.

Sodalite clears electromagnetic pollution and can be placed on computers to block their emanations. It is helpful for people who are sensitive to "sick-building syndrome"* or to electromagnetic smog*.

This is a particularly useful stone for group work, as it brings harmony and solidarity of purpose. It stimulates trust and companionship between members of the group, encouraging interdependence.

An excellent stone for the mind, Sodalite eliminates mental confusion and intellectual bondage. It encourages rational thought, objectivity, truth, and intuitive perception, together with the verbalization of feelings. As it calms the mind, it allows new information to be received. Sodalite stimulates the release of old mental conditioning and rigid mind-sets, creating space to put new insights in practice.

Psychologically, this stone brings about emotional balance and calms panic attacks. It can transform a defensive or oversensitive personality, releasing the core fears, phobias, guilt, and control mechanisms that hold you back from being who you truly are. It enhances self-esteem, self-acceptance, and self-trust. Sodalite is one of the stones that bring shadow qualities up to the surface to be accepted without being judged.

HEALING Sodalite balances the metabolism, overcomes calcium deficiencies, and cleanses the lymphatic system and organs, boosting the immune system. This stone combats radiation damage and insomnia. It treats the throat, vocal cords, and larynx and is helpful for hoarseness and digestive disorders. It cools fevers, lowers blood pressure, and stimulates absorption of fluid in the body.

POSITION Place as appropriate or wear for long periods of time.

SPINEL

Red Spinel on matrix

COLOR	Colorless, white, red, blue, violet, black, green, yellow, orange, brown
APPEARANCE	Small, crystalline with terminations, or tumbled pebbles
RARITY	Readily available
SOURCE	India, Canada, Sri Lanka, Myanmar

ATTRIBUTES Spinel is a beautiful crystal connected with energy renewal, encouragement in difficult circumstances, and rejuvenation. It opens the chakras* and facilitates movement of kundalini* energy up the spine. Different colors of Spinel relate to the whole chakras spectrum.

Psychologically, Spinel enhances positive aspects of the personality. It aids in achieving and accepting success with humility.

POSITION May be laid out on the chakras, or worn as appropriate.

SPECIFIC COLORS

In addition to the generic attributes, specific colors of Spinel have additional properties:

Black Spinel offers insights into material problems and gives you the stamina to continue. This color is protective and earths energy to balance the rise of the kundalini.

Blue Spinel stimulates communication and channeling. It calms sexual desire and opens and aligns the throat chakra*.

Brown Spinel cleanses the aura* and opens connections to the physical body. It opens the earth chakra and grounds you.

Colorless Spinel stimulates mysticism and higher communication. Linking the chakras on the physical body with the crown chakra of the etheric body, it facilitates visions and enlightenment.

Green Spinel stimulates love, compassion, and kindness. It opens and aligns the heart chakra.

Orange Spinel stimulates creativity and intuition, balances emotions, and treats infertility. It opens and aligns the navel chakra.

Red Spinel stimulates physical vitality and strength. It arouses the kundalini* and opens and aligns the base chakra.

Violet Spinel stimulates spiritual development and astral travel. It opens and aligns the crown chakra.

Yellow Spinel stimulates the intellect and personal power. It opens and aligns the solar plexus chakra.

STAUROLITE

*Natural cross removed
from matrix*

COLOR	Brown, yellow-brown, reddish-brown
APPEARANCE	Resembles Chiastolite, may crystallize as a cruciform or exhibit a cross
RARITY	Available from specialist shops
SOURCE	United States, Russia, Middle East

ATTRIBUTES Staurolite is known as the Fairy Cross. It was believed to be formed from tears the fairies shed when they heard the news of Christ's death. Traditionally, this protective stone is a talisman for good luck.

Staurolite enhances and strengthens rituals and is used in white-magic ceremonies. It is said to access the ancient wisdom of the Middle East. This stone connects the physical, etheric, and spiritual planes, promoting communication between them.

Psychologically, Staurolite is exceptionally useful in relieving stress. It alleviates depression and addictions, and negates a tendency to overwork and to overcommit energy.

Physically, Staurolite is an excellent stone for those wishing to stop smoking and to mitigate and heal its effects. It assists in understanding the hidden reasons behind the addiction to nicotine and provides a grounding energy for airy people who have used nicotine to anchor them to the earth.

HEALING Staurolite treats cellular disorders and growths, increases assimilation of carbohydrates, and reduces depression. It was traditionally used for fever.

POSITION Hold or place as appropriate.

STILLBITE

Plate form

COLOR	White, yellow, pink, orange, red, brown
APPEARANCE	Small crystalline plates or pyramids as a cluster
RARITY	Easily obtained from specialist stores
SOURCE	United States

ATTRIBUTES Stillbite is a highly creative stone that opens the intuition and carries a loving and supportive vibration in any endeavor. It is very helpful in metaphysical working at all levels. It grounds spiritual energy and helps to manifest intuitive thought into action on the physical plane.

Stillbite aids spiritual journeying, protecting and maintaining physical contact while traveling. The stone gives guidance and direction throughout the journey, no matter where the destination may lie. Used at its highest vibration, it aids traveling into the upper spiritual realms and bringing back the conscious memory of one's experiences there. Stillbite crystal clusters can be used as a scrying* tool.

HEALING Stillbite treats brain disorders, strengthens ligaments, treats laryngitis and loss of taste. It can increase pigmentation in the skin. It was used traditionally to counteract poisoning as it is a very potent detoxifier.

POSITION Hold or position as appropriate. Place on third eye* to facilitate journeying or intuition.

Pyramid form

SUGILITE

ALSO KNOWN AS LUVULITE

Polished   Tumbled

COLOR	Purple, violet-pink
APPEARANCE	Opaque, lightly banded or, rarely, translucent, all sizes, often tumbled
RARITY	Available from specialist stores
SOURCE	Japan, South Africa

ATTRIBUTES Sugilite is one of the major "love stones," bringing the purple ray energy to earth. It represents spiritual love and wisdom and opens all the chakras* to the flow of that love, bringing them into alignment. Sugilite inspires spiritual awareness and promotes channeling* ability.

Sugilite teaches you how to live from your truth and reminds the soul of its reasons for incarnating. It accompanies moving into past lives or the between-lives state* to retrieve the cause of dis-ease*. This stone finds answers to all the great questions of life such as "Why am I here?", "Where did I come from?", "Who am I?", and "What else do I need to understand?" It is a useful accompaniment to spiritual quests of all kinds. This loving stone protects the soul from shocks, trauma and disappointments and relieves spiritual tension. It helps sensitive people and light workers to adapt to the earth vibration without becoming mired or despondent. Sugulite can help to bring light and love into the darkest situations.

Aiding forgiveness and eliminating hostility, Sugilite is a useful stone for work with groups as it resolves group difficulties and encourages loving communication.

Psychologically, Sugilite is beneficial for misfits of any kind, people who do not feel the earth is their home, and those who suffer from paranoia and schizophrenia. It is excellent for autism, helping to ground the soul more into the present reality, and overcomes learning difficulties. Sugilite promotes understanding of the effect of the mind on the body and its place in dis-ease*. Emotionally, Sugilite imparts the ability to face up to unpleasant matters. It alleviates sorrow, grief, and fear, and promotes self-forgiveness.

Mentally, Sugilite encourages positive thoughts and reorganizes brain patterns that underlie learning difficulties such as dyslexia. It supports the overcoming of conflict without compromise.

Physically, Sugilite benefits cancer sufferers, as it gently releases emotional turmoil and can alleviate despair. It draws off negative energy and lends loving support, channeling healing energy into body, mind, and spirit.

HEALING An exceptionally good pain reliever, the manganese in Sugilite clears headaches and discomfort at all levels. It treats epilepsy and motor disturbances and brings the nerves and brain into alignment. Light-colored Sugilite purifies lymph and blood.

POSITION As appropriate, especially over the heart and lymph glands. Hold to the forehead for headaches. Place on third eye* to alleviate despair.

SULPHUR

Natural crystalline form

COLOR	Yellow
APPEARANCE	Powdery or smallish translucent crystals on matrix
RARITY	Obtainable from specialist shops
SOURCE	Italy, Greece, South America, volcanic regions

ATTRIBUTES Sulphur has a negative electrical charge and is extremely useful for absorbing negative energies, emanations, and emotions. Placed in the environment, it absorbs negativity of any kind and removes barriers to progress.

Volcanically produced, this is an excellent stone for anything that erupts: feelings, violence, skin conditions, and fevers. It can also be useful for bringing latent psychic abilities to the surface.

Psychologically, Sulphur ameliorates willfulness and aids in identifying negative traits within the personality. It reaches the rebellious, stubborn, or obstreperous part of a personality that willfully disobeys instructions and tends automatically to do the opposite of whatever is suggested, especially when this is "for your own good." Sulphur softens this position and assists the recognition of the effect, opening the way to conscious change.

Mentally, Sulphur blocks repetitive and distracting thought patterns. Inspiring the imagination, it aids reasoning and grounds thought processes in the practical here and now.

Physically, Sulphur is helpful in reenergizing after exhaustion or serious illness and can enhance creativity.

Sulphur is toxic and should not be taken internally. The gem elixir is best made with the crystalline form by the indirect method and applied externally only.

HEALING Sulphur is extremely useful for conditions that flare up, such as infections and fevers. Placed over the site of the swelling, it reduces fibrous and tissue growths. Placed in the bathwater, or as an essence, Sulphur alleviates painful swellings and joint problems. It can be applied externally to heal skin conditions. Powdered sulphur can be used as a natural insecticide fumigant, but it is toxic to humans and a mask should be worn to avoid breathing the fumes. Ventilate the area thoroughly afterward.

POSITION Place or hold as appropriate (the crystalline form is better for this, as the powdery form is messy and best kept for bathwater or environmental use.) It is traditional that Sulphur that has been placed over growths be buried afterward. If not, thoroughly cleanse before reusing. Burn powdered Sulphur to fumigate (wear a mask.) Make the elixir by the indirect method (see page 371) and use externally only.

SUNSTONE

Raw   *Polished*

COLOR	Yellow, orange, red-brown
APPEARANCE	Clear transparent or opaque crystal with iridescent reflections, often small, tumbled
RARITY	Easily obtained from specialist shops
SOURCE	Canada, United States, Norway, Greece, India

ATTRIBUTES Sunstone is a joyful, light-inspiring stone. It instills *joie de vivre* and good nature and heightens intuition. If life has lost its sweetness, Sunstone will restore it and help you to nurture yourself. Clearing all the chakras* and bringing in light and energy, this stone allows the real self to shine through happily. Traditionally it linked to benevolent gods and to luck and good fortune. This is an alchemical stone that brings about a profound connection to light and the regenerative power of the sun during meditation and in everyday life.

Sunstone is extremely useful for removing "hooks" from other people, whether located in the chakras or the aura*. These hooks can be at the mental or emotional level and may come from possessive parents, children, or lovers. They have the effect of draining your energy. Sunstone lovingly returns the contact to the other person and is extremely beneficial for tie-cutting. Keep Sunstone with you at all times if you have difficulty saying "No" and continually make sacrifices for others. Removing codependency, it facilitates self-empowerment, independence, and vitality. If procrastination is holding you back, Sunstone will overcome it.

Emotionally, Sunstone acts as an antidepressant and lifts dark moods. It is particularly effective for seasonal affective disorder, lightening the darkness of winter. It detaches from feelings of being discriminated against, disadvantaged, and abandoned. Removing inhibitions and hang-ups, Sunstone reverses feelings of failure and increases self-worth and confidence. Encouraging optimism and enthusiasm, Sunstone switches to a positive take on events. Even the most incorrigible pessimist responds to Sunstone. Placed on the solar plexus, Sunstone lifts out heavy or repressed emotions and transmutes them.

HEALING Sunstone stimulates self-healing powers, regulates the autonomic nervous system, and harmonizes all the organs. It treats chronic sore throats and relieves stomach ulcers. Exceptionally good for seasonal affective disorder, Sunstone lifts any depression. Sunstone can be gridded around the body and relieves cartilage problems, rheumatism, and general aches and pains.

POSITION Place, wear, or hold as appropriate. Sunstone is particularly beneficial when used in the sun.

(*See also* Yellow Labradorite, page 171.)

TEKTITE

Raw

COLOR	Black or dark brown, green (Moldavite)
APPEARANCE	Small, glassy, densely translucent
RARITY	Because Tektite is a meteorite, it is quite rare but available from specialist shops
SOURCE	Middle and Far East, Philippines, Polynesia, can occur worldwide

ATTRIBUTES Because of its extraterrestrial origin, Tektite is believed to enhance communication with other worlds and to encourage spiritual growth through absorption and retention of higher knowledge. It forms a link between the creative energy and matter. Tektite helps you to release undesirable experiences, remembering lessons learned and concentrating on those things that are conducive to spiritual growth. It takes you deep into the heart of a matter, promoting insight into the true cause and necessary action.

Placed on the chakras*, Tektite balances the energy flow and may reverse a chakra that is spinning the wrong way. Helpful for telepathy and clairvoyance*, if Tektite is placed on the third eye* it opens communication with other dimensions. This stone strengthens the biomagnetic sheath* around the body.

Traditionally, Tektites have been worn as talismans for fertility on all levels. This stone balances male–female energies within the personality.

HEALING Tektite reduces fevers, aids the capillaries and circulation. It prevents the transmission of diseases. Certain types of Tektites have been used for psychic surgery.

POSITION Place or hold as appropriate.

(*See also* Moldavite, page 187.)

THULITE

ALSO KNOWN AS PINK THULITE

Raw

COLOR	Pink, rose, white, red, gray
APPEARANCE	Granulated mass, often large
RARITY	Obtained from specialist stores
SOURCE	Norway

ATTRIBUTES A dramatic stone with a powerful link to the life force, stimulating healing and regeneration, Thulite is helpful wherever there is resistance to be overcome. It assists in bringing out the extrovert, promoting eloquence and showmanship. Mentally, it encourages curiosity and inventiveness in solving problems and explores the dualities of the human condition, combining love with logic.

Emotionally, Thulite encourages expression of passion and sexual feelings. It teaches that lust, sensuality, and sexuality are normal parts of life and encourages their constructive and positive expression.

HEALING Thulite treats calcium deficiencies and gastric upsets. It enhances fertility and treats disease of the reproductive organs. A strengthening and regenerating stone, useful in cases of extreme weakness and nervous exhaustion.

POSITION Place on skin or pubic bone as appropriate.

TIGER'S EYE

Raw

Tumbled

COLOR	Brown-yellow, pink, blue, red
APPEARANCE	Banded, slightly shiny, often small and tumbled
RARITY	Easily obtained
SOURCE	United States, Mexico, India, Australia, South Africa

ATTRIBUTES Tiger's Eye combines the earth energy with the energies of the sun to create a high vibrational state that is nevertheless grounded, drawing the spiritual energies to earth. Placed on the third eye*, it enhances psychic abilities in earthy people and balances the lower chakras*, stimulating the rise of the kundalini* energy.

Tiger's Eye is a protective stone that was traditionally carried as a talisman against ill wishing and curses. It shows the correct use of power and brings out integrity. It assists in accomplishing goals, recognizing inner resources and promoting clarity of intention. Placed on the navel chakra, Tiger's Eye is excellent for people who are spaced out or uncommitted. It grounds and facilitates manifestation of the will. Tiger's Eye anchors change into the physical body.

This stone is useful for recognizing both your needs and those of other people. It differentiates between wishful thinking about what you want and what you really need.

Mentally, Tiger's Eye integrates the hemispheres of the brain and enhances practical perception. It aids in collecting scattered information to make a coherent whole. It is helpful for resolving dilemmas and internal conflicts, especially those brought about by pride and willfulness. Tiger's Eye is particularly useful for healing mental dis-ease* and personality disorders.

Psychologically, Tiger's Eye heals issues of self-worth, self-criticism, and blocked creativity. It aids in recognizing one's talents and abilities and, conversely, faults that need to be overcome. It supports an addictive personality in making changes.

Emotionally, Tiger's Eye balances yin–yang and energizes the emotional body. It alleviates depression and lifts moods.

HEALING Tiger's Eye treats the eyes and aids night visions, heals the throat and reproductive organs, and dissolves constrictions. It is helpful for repairing broken bones.

POSITION Wear on the right arm or as a pendant for short periods. Position on the body as appropriate in healing. Place on the navel chakra for spiritual grounding.

SPECIFIC COLORS

In addition to the generic attributes, specific colors of Tiger's Eye have specific properties:

Blue Tiger's Eye is calming and releases stress. It aids the overanxious, quick-tempered, and phobic. In healing, Blue Tiger's Eye slows the metabolism, cools an overactive sex drive, and dissolves sexual frustrations.

Blue Tiger's Eye

Gold Tiger's Eye aids in paying attention to detail, warning against complacency. It assists in taking action from a place of reason rather than emotion. Gold Tiger's Eye is an excellent companion for tests and important meetings.

Red Tiger's Eye is a stimulating stone that overcomes lethargy and provides motivation. In healing it speeds up a slow metabolism and increases a low sex drive.

Red Tiger's Eye

SPECIFIC FORM

In addition to the generic properties, a type of Tiger's Eye has the following properties.

Hawk's Eye

Hawk's Eye

ADDITIONAL PROPERTIES A banded "hawk-like" form of Tiger's Eye, Hawk's Eye is an excellent stone for healing the earth's energy and for grounding energy. It stimulates and invigorates the physical body. Soaring above the world, Hawk's Eye aids vision and insight, and increases psychic abilities such as clairvoyance*. Hawk's Eye clears and energizes the base chakra*.

Placed in the wealth corner of a room, Hawk's Eye attracts abundance.

Hawk's Eye is particularly good for dissolving restrictive and negative thought patterns and ingrained behavior. It brings issues into perspective, ameliorates pessimism and the desire to blame others for problems of your own making. This stone will also bring to the surface locked-in emotions and dis-ease from the present or past lives. Placed on the third eye*, Hawk's Eye aids in traveling back to the source of an emotional blockage, whenever that might be.

HEALING Hawk's Eye improves the circulatory system, bowels, and legs. It can bring to the surface the psychosomatic reasons behind a frozen shoulder or stiff neck.

POSITION Hold or place on appropriate spot.

TOPAZ

Blue Topaz (polished)   *Golden-Yellow Topaz (raw)*

COLOR	Golden-yellow, brown, blue, clear, red-pink, green
APPEARANCE	Transparent, pointed crystals, often small and faceted or large piece
RARITY	Easily obtained from specialist stores, red-pink is rare
SOURCE	United States, Mexico, India, Australia, South Africa, Sri Lanka, Pakistan

ATTRIBUTES Topaz is a mellow, empathetic stone that directs energy to where it is needed most. It soothes, heals, stimulates, recharges, remotivates, and aligns the meridians of the body. Topaz promotes truth and forgiveness. It helps shed light on the path, highlights goals, and taps into inner resources. This crystal brings about a trust in the universe that enables you to "be" rather than to "do." It cuts through doubt and uncertainty.

Topaz's vibrant energy brings joy, generosity, abundance, and good health. It has traditionally been known as a stone of love and good fortune, bringing successful attainment of goals. It is extremely supportive for affirmations and manifestation, and for visualization. It is said that the facets and ends of a Topaz crystal have both positive and negative energies through which a request to the universe can be focused and then manifested on the earth plane.

Excellent for cleaning the aura* and for inducing relaxation, Topaz releases tension at any level and can speed up spiritual development where it has been laborious.

Psychologically, Topaz helps you to discover your own inner riches. It makes you feel confident and philanthropic, wanting to share your good fortune and spread sunshine all around. Negativity does not survive around joyful Topaz. This stone promotes openness and honesty, self-realization, self-control, and the urge to develop inner wisdom.

Mentally, Topaz aids problem-solving and is particularly useful for those engaged in the arts. It helps you to become aware of the influence you have and of the knowledge you have gained through hard work and life experiences. This stone has the capacity to see both the bigger picture and the minute detail, recognizing how they interrelate. Topaz assists in expressing ideas and confers astuteness.

Topaz is an excellent emotional support—it stabilizes the emotions and makes you receptive to love from every source.

HEALING Topaz can be used to manifest health. It aids digestion and combats anorexia, restores the sense of taste, fortifies the nerves, and stimulates the metabolism. Saint Hildegard of Bingen recommended an elixir of Topaz to correct dimness of vision.

POSITION Ring finger, solar plexus, and brow chakra*. Position or place as appropriate for healing. The elixir can be applied to the skin.

SPECIFIC COLORS

In addition to the generic properties, certain colors have additional attributes:

Blue Topaz, placed on the throat chakra or third eye*, aids those chakras and verbalization. It is an excellent color for meditation and attuning to the higher self, assisting in living according your own aspirations and views. This color attunes to the angels of truth and wisdom. It assists in seeing the scripts you have been living by and to recognize where you have strayed from your own truth.

Clear Topaz aids in becoming aware of thoughts and deeds, and the karmic* effect that these have. It assists in purifying emotions and actions, activating cosmic awareness. In healing, Clear Topaz removes stagnant or stuck energy.

Clear Topaz

Golden Topaz (Imperial Topaz) acts like a battery and recharges spiritually and physically, strengthening faith and optimism. It is an excellent stone for conscious attunement to the highest forces in the universe and can be used to store information received in this way.

Golden Topaz It reminds you of your divine origins.

Imperial Topaz assists in recognizing your own abilities, instills a drive toward recognition, and attracts helpful people. This stone is beneficial for those seeking fame as it bestows charisma and confidence with pride in your abilities while remaining generous and open-hearted. It assists in overcoming limitations and in setting great plans afoot. In healing, it regenerates cellular structures and strengthens the solar plexus, and is beneficial for nervous exhaustion and insufficient combustion of nutrients. It treats the liver, the gallbladder, and the endocrine glands.

Yellow Topaz

Pink Topaz is a stone of hope. It gently eases out old patterns of dis-ease* and dissolves resistance, opening the way to radiant health. This stone shows you the face of the divine.

COMBINATION STONE
Rutilated Topaz is rare but is extremely effective for visualization and manifestation. It is an excellent stone for scrying*, bringing deep insights when properly programmed and attracting love and light into one's life.

TOURMALINE

Blue Tourmaline

Light Blue Tourmaline

Blue Tourmaline wand

COLOR	Black, brown, green, pink, red, yellow, blue, watermelon, blue-green
APPEARANCE	Shiny, opaque, or transparent, long striated or hexagonal structure. All sizes
RARITY	Easily obtained from specialist stores
SOURCE	Sri Lanka, Brazil, Africa, United States, Western Australia, Afghanistan, Italy

ATTRIBUTES Tourmaline cleanses, purifies, and transforms dense energy into a lighter vibration. It grounds spiritual energy, clears and balances all the chakras*, and forms a protective shield around the body.

Tourmaline is a shamanic stone that brings protection during rituals. It can be used for scrying* and was traditionally used to point to the culprit or cause in times of trouble, and indicate a "good" direction in which to move.

Natural Tourmaline wands are useful healing tools. They clear the aura, remove blockages, disperse negative energy, and point to solutions for specific problems. They are excellent for balancing and connecting the chakras. At a physical level, they rebalance the meridians*.

Tourmaline has a strong affinity with the devic* energies and is extremely beneficial for the garden and plants. It can act as a natural insecticide, keeping pests at bay, and, buried in the soil, encourages the growth and health of all crops.

Psychologically, Tourmaline aids in understanding oneself and others, taking you deep into yourself, promoting self-confidence and diminishing fear. It banishes any feeling of being a victim and attracts inspiration, compassion, tolerance, and prosperity.

Tourmaline is a powerful mental healer, balancing the right–left hemispheres of the brain and transmuting negative thought patterns into positive ones. This stone brings the mental processes, the chakras, and the biomagnetic sheath* into alignment. It is helpful in treating paranoia, and for overcoming dyslexia, as it improves hand-to-eye coordination and the assimilation and translation of coded information.

Emotionally, Red, Yellow, and Brown Tourmalines are beneficial for sexuality and the emotional dysfunction that can lie behind loss of libido. Physically, Tourmaline releases tension, which makes it helpful in spinal adjustments. It balances male–female energy within the body.

HEALING The striations along the side of Tourmaline enhance energy flow, making it an excellent stone for healing, energy enhancement, and removal of blockages. Each of the different colors of Tourmaline has its own specific healing ability.

POSITION Place or wear as appropriate. To stimulate meridians*, place with the tip pointing in the same direction as the flow. Excellent for gem essences which work quickly and efficiently.

SPECIFIC COLORS AND FORMS

In addition to the generic properties, colored Tourmalines have specific additional properties:

Black Tourmaline (Schorl) protects against cell phones, electromagnetic smog*, radiation, psychic attack*, spells and ill-wishing, and negative energies of all kinds. Connecting with the base chakra*, it grounds energy and increases physical vitality, dispersing tension and stress. Clearing negative thoughts, Schorl promotes a laid-back attitude and objective neutrality with clear, rational thought processes. It encourages a positive attitude, no matter what the circumstances, and stimulates altruism and practical creativity. In healing, Black Tourmalines placed point-out from

Black Tourmaline

298

the body draw off negative energy. Black Tourmaline defends against debilitating disease, strengthens the immune system, treats dyslexia and arthritis, provides pain relief, and realigns the spinal column. Wear around your neck or place between yourself and the source of electromagnetics.

Blue Tourmaline (Indicolite) activates the throat and third eye chakra* and stimulates the urge for spiritual freedom and clarity of self-expression. This color aids psychic awareness, promotes visions, and opens the way for service to others, encouraging fidelity, ethics, tolerance, and a love of truth. It carries the ray of peace and dissolves sadness and blocked feelings, bringing them up gently to the surface to be healed and dissipated, and assists in developing an inner sense of responsibility. This stone promotes living in harmony with the environment. It is an excellent stone for healers, as it prevents negativity from sticking.

In healing, bright Blue Tourmaline is a useful diagnostic tool and helps in identifying underlying causes of dis-ease*. Blue Tourmaline benefits the pulmonary and immune systems and the brain, corrects fluid imbalances, treats kidney and bladder, thymus and thyroid, and chronic sore throat. It is helpful for insomnia, night sweats, sinusitis, and bacterial infections. It is traditionally used on the throat, larynx, lungs, esophagus, and eyes. It soothes burns and prevents scarring. Dark Blue Tourmaline is particularly helpful for the eyes and brain and can be made into an elixir. Blue Tourmaline can be placed anywhere there is dis-ease or congestion. It helps to overcome speech impediments.

Brown Tourmaline (Dravide) is an excellent grounding stone, clearing and opening the earth chakra and the grounding cord* holding the physical body in incarnation. It clears the aura, aligns the etheric body

and protects it. Encouraging community spirit and social commitment, Brown Tourmaline makes one feel comfortable in a large group. This stone heals dysfunctional family relationships and strengthens empathy. Brown Tourmaline is pragmatic and promotes creativity. In healing, Brown Tourmaline treats intestinal disorders and skin diseases, and stimulates regeneration in the whole body.

Brown Tourmaline

Colorless Tourmaline (Achroite) synthesizes all other colors and opens the crown chakra*. In healing, it aligns the meridians* of the physical* and etheric bodies*.

Green Tourmaline (Verdelite) is an excellent healer and is helpful for visualization. It opens the heart chakra, promotes compassion, tenderness, patience, and a sense of belonging. This nurturing stone brings balance and *joie de vivre*. Transforming negative to positive energy and dispelling fears, Green Tourmaline promotes openness and patience. It rejuvenates and inspires creativity. With this stone, one is able to see all possible solutions and to select the most constructive. It magnetizes the wearer to prosperity and abundance. Green Tourmaline overcomes problems with father figures. It facilitates the study of herbalism and enhances the application of remedies, and has the power to heal plants.

Colorle Tourma

In healing, as with all green stones, this color aids sleep and quiets the mind. It fortifies the nervous

Green Tourmaline

300

system and prepares it for a vibrational shift. Green Tourmaline treats eyes, heart, thymus, brain, and immune system; facilitates weight loss; and relieves CFS and exhaustion. It assists in realigning the spine and aids strained muscles. Green Tourmaline is a useful detoxifier and heels constipation and diarrhea. It can reduce claustrophobia and panic attacks. Green Tourmaline is beneficial for hyperactive children.

Multicolored Gem Tourmaline (Elbaite) contains all colors and, as a result, it brings the mind, body, spirit, and soul into wholeness. It is an excellent stone for imagery and promoting dreams, inspiring creativity and enhanced imagination. This stone provides a gateway into the inner self and the higher spiritual realms.

In healing, Multicolored Tourmaline stimulates the immune system and the metabolism.

Pink Tourmaline is an aphrodisiac that attracts love in the material and spiritual world. Providing assurance that it is safe to love, it inspires trust in love, and confirms that it is necessary to love yourself before you can hope to be loved by others. This stone assists in sharing physical pleasure. It disperses emotional pain and old destructive feelings through the heart chakra, which it cleanses, and synthesizes love with spirituality. Promoting peace and relaxation, Pink Tourmaline connects you to wisdom and compassion and stimulates receptivity to healing energies.

In healing, Pink Tourmaline balances a dysfunctional endocrine system and treats heart, lungs, and skin. Place on the heart.

Purple-Violet Tourmaline stimulates healing of the heart and produces loving consciousness.

Purple Tourmaline

It connects the base and heart chakras*, increasing devotion and loving aspiration. This stone stimulates creativity and intuition. It unblocks the third eye* chakra, stimulates the pineal gland, and strips away illusions. This is a useful stone for past-life healing, taking you to the heart of the problem and then dispersing it.

In healing, Purple Tourmaline reduces depression and releases obsessional thoughts. It treats sensitivity to pollutants, Alzheimer's, epilepsy, and CFS*.

Red Tourmaline (Rubellite) strengthens the ability to understand love, promotes tactfulness and flexibility, sociability and extroversion, balancing too much aggression or overpassivity. It heals and energizes the sacral chakra and increases creativity on all levels. This color offers stamina and endurance. In healing, Red Tourmaline gives vitality to the physical body and detoxifies. It heals the heart; it treats the digestive system, blood vessels, and the reproductive system;

Red Tourmaline in matrix

it stimulates blood circulation and spleen and liver function; and it repairs veins. It is useful for muscle spasms and chills.

Watermelon Tourmaline (pink enfolded in green) is the "super-activator" of the heart chakra, linking it to the higher self and fostering love, tenderness, and friendship. This stone instills patience and teaches tact and diplomacy. Alleviating depression and fear, it promotes inner security. Watermelon Tourmaline assists understanding of situations and expressing intentions clearly. It treats emotional dysfunction and releases old pain. Watermelon Tourmaline is beneficial for relationships and helps to find the joy in situations.

In healing, Watermelon Tourmaline dissolves any resistance to becoming whole once more. It encourages regeneration of the nerves, especially in paralysis or multiple sclerosis, and treats stress.

Watermelon Tourmaline

Yellow Tourmaline stimulates the solar plexus and enhances personal power. It opens up the spiritual pathway and benefits intellectual pursuits and business affairs.

In healing, Yellow Tourmaline treats the stomach, liver, spleen, kidneys, and gallbladder.

Yellow Tourmaline

COMBINATION STONES
Black Tourmaline with Mica
returns ill-wishing to its source
so the perpetrator learns from it.
This combination is particularly
efficient at nullifying
electromagnetic smog*.

Black Tourmaline rod in Quartz
Quartz containing chunky Black
Tourmaline rods, as opposed to the
strands in Tourmalinated Quartz,
is excellent for neutralizing
psychic or actual attack*,
strengthening the person on the

Black Tourmaline with Mica

receiving end and enhancing their well-being. It can be used to guard against terrorist attack and to heal the effects of such an attack. This stone has the ability to go beyond dualities and to integrate the shadow into the whole personality.

Tourmaline with Lepidolite on a matrix is excellent for giving up addictions of all kinds, for understanding the reasons behind addiction, and for accepting that denial has been present. It then helps you to live life without the spurious support of the addictive substance or behavior, replacing it with the love and protection of the universal energies and powerful self-healing potential.

Tourmaline rod in Quartz

(*See also* Tourmalinated Quartz, page 243.)

Tourmaline with Lepidol

TURQUOISE

Polished

Tumbled

COLOR	Turquoise, green or blue
APPEARANCE	Opaque, often veined, all sizes often polished
RARITY	Easily obtained
SOURCE	United States, Egypt, Mexico, China, Iran, Peru, Poland, Russia, France, Tibet, Egypt, Afghanistan, Arabia

ATTRIBUTES Turquoise is a most efficient healer, providing solace for the spirit and well-being for the body. It is a protective stone and has been used for amulets since time immemorial. It is believed to change color to warn of danger of infidelity. Turquoise promotes spiritual attunement and enhances communication with the physical and

305

spiritual worlds. Placed on the third eye*, it enhances intuition and meditation. On the throat chakra*, it releases old vows, inhibitions, and prohibitions, and allows the soul to express itself once more. It explores past lives and shows how the creation of your "fate" is ongoing and depends on what you do at each moment.

Turquoise is a purification stone. It dispels negative energy and clears electromagnetic smog*, providing protection against pollutants in the environment. It balances and aligns all the chakras with the subtle bodies and attunes the physical level to the spiritual. In traditional thought, Turquoise unites the earth and the sky, bringing together male and female energies. This stone is empathetic and balancing. A promoter of self-realization, it assists creative problem-solving and calms the nerves when speaking in public.

Psychologically, Turquoise is a strengthening stone. It dissolves a martyred attitude or self-sabotage. Mentally, Turquoise instills inner calm while remaining alert, and aids creative expression. Emotionally, Turquoise stabilizes mood swings and brings inner calm. It stimulates romantic love.

Physically, Turquoise is an excellent stone for exhaustion, depression, or panic attacks. One of its protective functions is against outside influences or pollutants in the atmosphere.

HEALING Turquoise strengthens the meridians of the body and the subtle energy fields. It enhances the physical and psychic immune systems and regenerates tissue, supports the assimilation of nutrients, alleviates pollution and viral infections, and heals the whole body, especially the eyes, including cataracts. It reduces excess acidity and benefits gout, rheumatism, and the stomach. This stone is anti-inflammatory and detoxifying and alleviates cramps and pain.

POSITION Anywhere but especially on the throat, third eye, and solar plexus. It makes an excellent elixir.

SPECIFIC TYPE

In addition to the generic properties, the following type has additional attributes:

Tibetan Turquoise is green and carries a slightly different vibration from the more vivid blue. It is especially useful for healing throat chakra blockages and suppressed self-expression back down the ancestral line until the source is cleared.

Tibetan Turquoise (raw)

ULEXITE

ALSO KNOWN AS TV STONE

Shaped

COLOR	Transparent
APPEARANCE	Clear, silky, squarish crystal, sometimes lightly striated. Magnifies.
RARITY	Easily obtained
SOURCE	United States

ATTRIBUTES Ulexite is best known for its ability to magnify anything placed under it. It is an extremely clear stone and brings things into focus on the inner and spiritual levels, lending much-needed objectivity and clarity. It is excellent for understanding the meaning of dreams and visions. It shows the path one should take at a spiritual level and takes you deep into the self.

At a more pragmatic level, Ulexite takes you to the core of a problem, pointing the way to resolution and activating solutions. Ulexite is a stone of revelation in the physical world. It gives you the ability to see into another's heart, knowing what they are thinking and feeling, so that decisions can be based on a complete knowing.

Ulexite's soft energy is beneficial for meditation and relaxation. Placed on the third eye*, it enhances visualization and dispels negative mental energy. Balancing the yin–yang energies, it aligns the subtle bodies*.

Mentally, Ulexite enhances the imagination and stimulates creativity, especially in business. If you are getting things out of proportion, Ulexite helps you to see them clearly.

HEALING Ulexite is used to bring clarity to the eyes. It is excellent as a skin elixir for smoothing wrinkles, but should not be left in water for too long, as it has a tendency to dissolve.

POSITION Wear or place as appropriate, especially on the eyes and third eye. Ulexite makes an excellent meditation stone if you gaze into its depths.

UNAKITE

Tumbled

Raw

COLOR	Green-pink
APPEARANCE	Mottled, often small tumbled stone
RARITY	Easily obtained
SOURCE	United States, South Africa

ATTRIBUTES Unakite is a stone of vision. It balances emotions with spirituality. Placed on the third eye*, it opens it and promotes visualization and psychic vision. This stone also provides grounding when it is needed and can be useful after meditation or psychic work.

Unakite can be used as a casting crystal for scrying*, signifying where compromise and integration are needed. The best way to use it is with ten or twelve other suitable stones (see pages 375–376). The tumbled stones should be kept together in a bag. One stone is then selected to answer a question, or a handful are cast onto a scrying wheel.

Placed in the environment, either as a large piece or as several tumbled stones in a bowl, Unakite brings a calm gentle energy and can negate the effects of electromagnetic pollution from television sets if placed on top or close by.

Unakite facilitates rebirthing, bringing to light and integrating insights from the past about the cause of blockages, and gently releasing conditions that inhibit spiritual and psychological growth. It is also helpful in past-life healing for going back to the source of a problem and reframing it. Unakite can be held or placed on the third eye for this purpose.

Whether dis-ease* arises in the far or near past, Unakite reaches the root cause of it at whatever level it occurs, bringing it to the surface so that it can be transformed.

HEALING Unakite is supportive in convalescence and recovery from a major illness. It treats the reproductive system, stimulates weight gain where required, and aids healthy pregnancy and the growth of skin tissue and hair.

POSITION Place as appropriate or apply as an elixir.

VANADINITE

Crystals on matrix

COLOR	Orange-brown, red-brown, yellow-brown, red, orange, yellow
APPEARANCE	Very small, bright transparent crystals on a matrix
RARITY	Obtainable from specialist stores
SOURCE	United States

ATTRIBUTES Vanadinite is an excellent stone for people who have problems accepting their physicality. It has a strong connection with the earth chakra* in the earth body beneath the feet. Grounding the soul into the physical body and assisting it being comfortable in the earth environment, Vanadinite guards against squandering energy and teaches you how to conserve energy at the physical level.

Vanadinite is an aid to meditation. Shutting off mind chatter, it can facilitate a state of "no mind" or be used to direct awareness consciously for psychic vision and journeying. It has the power to open an internal channel within the body to receive an inflooding of universal energy. This energy aligns the chakras and brings the higher self into the physical body, facilitating a deep inner peace.

Mentally, Vanadinite fills the gap between thought and intellect. It assists in defining and pursuing goals and shuts off mind chatter, allowing insight and rational thought to combine in an inner voice of guidance.

This stone has the useful property of curbing overspending. Place in the wealth corner of the house or put a small piece in your purse to retain your money.

Vanadinite is poisonous and elixirs should be prepared by the indirect method (see page 371).

HEALING Vanadinite is useful for breathing difficulties such as asthma and congested lungs. It facilitates the practice of circular breathing. Vanadinite treats chronic exhaustion and bladder problems. If used as an elixir, only one made by the indirect method can be taken internally.

POSITION Place as appropriate or rub the elixir externally over the chest area. If using to aid acceptance of physicality, the indirect-method elixir should be taken for several weeks.

VARISCITE

Tumbled

COLOR	Green, gray, and white
APPEARANCE	Opaque, sometimes veined, may appear as large mass or small encrustations on a matrix
RARITY	Obtainable from specialist stores
SOURCE	United States, Germany, Austria, Czech Republic, Bolivia

ATTRIBUTES Variscite is a stone of encouragement. Bringing hope and courage, it is extremely useful for illness and invalids. It supports and encourages an invalid to continue despite the illness and helps caregivers to deal with the dis-ease* an illness can create. Opening the heart chakra, it brings unconditional love into the situation.

Variscite is extremely helpful for past-life exploration. It facilitates visual images of the experience while going deeply into the feelings and experiences of appropriate lives. It stimulates insights into the cause of dis-ease or patterns that have been carried over, and aids reframing situations to bring about healing.

Psychologically, Variscite facilitates moving out of deep despair and into a position of hope and trust in the universe. This stone does away with pretence, enabling you to show yourself to the world exactly as you are. It calms nervousness and brings a peaceful heart. Variscite supports sobriety and yet has a lively energy that prevents you from becoming too serious. Placed under the pillow at night, it brings peaceful sleep and an untroubled mind.

Mentally, Variscite aids clear thinking and increases perception. It helps in self-expression and the communication of ideas.

Physically, Variscite is an energizer that helps to restore depleted energy reserves.

HEALING Variscite heals the nervous system, treats abdominal distension and constricted blood flow, and regenerates elasticity of veins and skin. It neutralizes overacidity and aids gout, gastritis, ulcers, rheumatism, and allied conditions. Helpful for male impotence, it also relieves cramps.

POSITION Place as appropriate and use for long periods of time. Position over third eye* for past-life recall. Wear as a pendant or hold in the left hand.

WULFENITE

Crystals on matrix

COLOR	Yellow, golden, orange, green, gray, yellow-gray, brown, white, colorless
APPEARANCE	Small crystals or blades on a matrix, or large transparent, squarish crystal
RARITY	Available from specialist stores
SOURCE	United States, Mexico

ATTRIBUTES Wulfenite is an extremely useful stone as it assists in accepting the less positive aspects of life and prevents despondency or inertia setting in when you're faced with negative situations or feelings. It is particularly useful for those people who have become unbalanced by focusing only on the positive, repressing negative traits and experiences so that they become "sugary sweet" and so nice that they are inauthentic and ungrounded. Wulfenite helps them to accept and integrate the shadow energies and to move beyond the duality of "positive" and "negative," accepting them as complementary and balancing forces.

At a spiritual level, Wulfenite facilitates moving easily and quickly from the physical level to the psychic, intuitive, or spiritual levels. It is said to access the past, present, and future and to aid communication with those states. It facilitates contact and communication with the spiritual world, opening a channel to bring spiritual vibrations down to earth.

If you have made an agreement with another soul that you will meet in the present life, Wulfenite facilitates recognition of that soul and attunement to the reasons why you arranged to meet. It bonds the souls together while the purpose or lesson is carried out and then releases when appropriate.

Wulfenite is a stone that can be used for white magic, supporting and enhancing ritual working and journeying, and regaining magical knowledge that one had in other lives. This knowledge can then be put into practice in the present. Such knowledge may come from the temples of ancient Egypt or Greece or from the more recent past. If someone has suffered at the hands of the Christian Church for beliefs connected with magic, then Wulfenite helps to heal the experience, making it feel safe to practice once again.

HEALING Wulfenite has the power to rejuvenate and preserve energy but has no specific healing attributes.

POSITION Hold or place as appropriate. A piece of Wulfenite can be programmed to bring you into contact with soul links* and then placed in the relationship corner of the house.

ZEOLITE

*Cluster containing
Stillbite, Apophyllite,
Prehnite, and Okenite*

COLOR	Colorless, white, blue, peach
APPEARANCE	Varied, all sizes, often as a cluster
RARITY	Available from specialist stores
SOURCE	Britain, Australia, India, Brazil, Czech Republic, Italy, United States

ATTRIBUTES Zeolite is the generic name for a group of crystals that are often found together on a matrix. They include Apophyllite, Okenite, Pectolite, Prehnite, and Stillbite (see pages 64, 204, 220, 277). The combination stone is very beautiful and can be used as a decorative feature to enhance the environment. Zeolite absorbs toxins and odors. Buried in the ground, or placed near crops, Zeolite benefits agriculture and gardening.

Zeolite is a Reiki* stone that aids attunement to the energies and enhances the response to the healing.

HEALING Zeolite can be used to treat goiters, to dispel bloating, and to release toxins from the physical body. It has a supportive effect in overcoming addictions, especially to alcohol, and can be made into an elixir for this purpose. However, cider vinegar should be used as the preservative rather than brandy or vodka.

POSITION Place as appropriate or use as an elixir.

ZINCITE

*Transparent,
reformed*

COLOR	Red, orange-yellow, green, colorless
APPEARANCE	Grainy mass, although some striking transparent crystals are available from Poland that formed as part of the smelting process at a mine
RARITY	Available from specialist stores
SOURCE	Poland, Italy, United States

ATTRIBUTES Zincite is a powerful stone that synthesizes physical energy and personal power with creativity. This fiery stone can aid the manifestation process and reenergize depleted energy systems. It removes energy blocks from the body and allows the life force to flow unhindered. This stone attracts abundance at a physical and spiritual level and Zincite can be used to anchor the light body securely into the physical realm.

320

Zincite resonates with the lower chakras*, reenergizing the whole body and stimulating creativity and fertility. It assists with the rise of the kundalini* energy and enhances gut instincts and intuition.

Zincite instills confidence and the ability to find your own strength. Psychologically, Zincite heals shock and trauma and instills the courage to deal with traumatic situations. It ameliorates depression and releases painful memories so that these can be laid to rest. If you suffer from lethargy or procrastination, Zincite has the power to push you forward into manifesting your full potential. It helps you to embrace necessary change.

Zincite is useful for phobias. It assists in getting to the root cause and gently releasing it, and then reprograms the mind into a more positive mode. It can also release hypnotic commands and mental imprints.

If you are a woman struggling with menopausal symptoms or the empty-nest syndrome, Zincite gently alleviates the symptoms and helps you to come to terms with the change of life.

Zincite promotes group activities, drawing together like-minded people and bringing them into a whole. It is also beneficial for physical relationships. If purification is required, Zincite can stimulate a healing crisis that provides catharsis and then reenergizes the system.

HEALING Zincite improves the skin and the hair. It is beneficial for the prostate gland and for menopausal symptoms, and boosts the immune system and the energy meridians* of the body. It treats CFS, AIDS and auto-immune diseases, alleviates candida, mucus conditions, and bronchitis, and helps to prevent epilepsy. Zincite stimulates the organs of elimination and assimilation and has been used to treat problems of infertility.

POSITION Place or hold as appropriate.

ZOISITE

Raw

COLOR	Colorless, white, yellow, brown, blue, green, red, pink (Thulite), lavender-blue
APPEARANCE	Solid mass, pleochroic*, all sizes
RARITY	Obtained from specialist shops, often with Ruby
SOURCE	Austria, Tanzania, India, Madagascar, Russia, Sri Lanka, Cambodia, Kenya

ATTRIBUTES Zoisite transmutes negative energies into positive ones and connects to the spiritual realms.

Psychologically, Zoisite assists in manifesting your own self rather than being influenced by others or trying to conform to the norm. It aids in realizing your own ideas and transforms destructive urges into constructive ones. This stone dispels lethargy and brings to the surface repressed feelings and emotions so that they can be expressed.

Mentally, Zoisite is a creative stone, bringing the mind back to its objectives after an interruption. Physically, Zoisite encourages recovery from severe illness or stress.

HEALING Zoisite is a detoxifier, neutralizing overacidification and reducing inflammation. It strengthens the immune system and regenerates cells and treats the heart, spleen, pancreas, and lungs. This stone stimulates fertility and heals diseases of the ovaries and testicles. When combined with Ruby, it increases potency.

POSITION Wear or place on the body in contact with the skin as appropriate. Wear for long periods of time, as it is a slow-acting stone.

ADDITIONAL COLOR
In addition to the generic properties, the following color has additional properties:

Tanzanite (Lavender-Blue Zoisite) is a heat-amended stone with a high vibration, facilitating altered states and a profoundly deep meditative state. It changes color when viewed from different directions. This shifting color facilitates raising consciousness. It links to the angelic realms*, spirit guides*, and the Ascended Masters*. Tanzanite downloads information from the Akashic Record* and facilitates inner and outer journeying. It activates a chakra* link from the base to the higher crown chakras, bringing the higher mind into contact with the physical realm. Stimulating the throat chakra, it facilitates communication of insights received from the higher levels. In healing, Tanzanite works on the head, throat, and chest. It makes an excellent gem essence and combines with stones such as Aquamarine and Moldavite. Added to Iolite and Danburite and applied during past-life healing, Tanzanite dissolves old patterns of karmic* dis-ease* and creates the space for new patterns to be integrated.

Tanzanite

(*See also* Thulite, page 287, and Ruby in Zoisite page 251.)

CRYSTAL SHAPES

Crystals come in all shapes and sizes. Some have natural facets and points, others are rounded and smooth. Some form clusters, others stand alone. There are crystals that are formed in layers and others that are formed in bubbles. Some occur naturally; others are artificially cut to a precise shape. Each shape has its own attributes and application. Knowing how to use these different shapes opens the way to magical possibilities. For example, you can use the ability of Quartz to store information rather as a computer does. Some shapes open a window into another world—past, present, or future, earthly or extraterrestrial. Others attract a soulmate or bring abundance into your life.

A geode with its cavelike center gathers and holds energy, releasing it slowly, while a cluster radiates it out rapidly in all directions. These shape-specific properties are relevant to how you choose and use your crystal. They can make all the difference between a crystal working brilliantly or not at all. A Citrine cluster attracts abundance but it may flow out again. However, the holding properties of a Citrine geode enable you to keep hold of your money, while a single point directs it in a specific direction.

CRYSTAL FORMS

Knowing the properties of different shapes of crystals, such as geodes and points, and being aware of the potential of particular facet shapes, helps you to harness the unique power of crystals, especially the myriad forms of Quartz. Certain forms are natural, while others have been cut to shape. Some of these artificial shapes mimic those found naturally—many large Clear or Smoky Quartz crystals are cut into tall pillar crystals for use as decorative items or healing tools, for instance, and special Quartz facets that occur very rarely in their natural states can be recreated so that they are more widely available.

Apophylite cluster

Crystals seldom occur as perfect balls, but for centuries Quartz, Obsidian, and Beryl have been carefully shaped by hand as scrying* tools. Seers gaze into their depths to ascertain the future. But balls have another function; they emit energy equally in all directions into the environment.

Quartz-based crystals in particular have naturally occurring facets at their tips. There are usually six facets, which equate to the six chakras* from the base to the third eye*, with the termination point representing the crown chakra and its link with the infinite.

How a crystal grows is significant in esoteric crystal lore. Quartz crystals that are cloudy at the base and become clearer as they reach the tip represent the potential for spiritual growth. A crystal pillar or large point with flaws or occlusions* can point to a traumatic or wounding period in life. The dross has to be cleared in order for consciousness to evolve. Quartz crystals that are totally clear are symbols of alignment with cosmic harmony. Keeping one of these crystals with you aligns your energies to the spiritual realm.

While specific facet shapes are most obvious on large crystals, even the smallest Quartz point may have a "window" formed out of the facets. A left-facing parallelogram window shape will take you back into the past. Facing the opposite way, the same shape will take you forward to the future. A differently contoured window will help you to channel or to transmit healing energy over long distances. There are record-keeper crystals that hold the wisdom of the ages engraved on their sides. Meditating with these venerable stones accesses universal knowledge. A soulmate crystal, on the other hand, attracts and holds on to true love.

If your crystal has rainbows in it, it is a sign of joy and happiness. Rainbows are caused by thin fractures within the stone. A rainbow crystal can be used to alleviate depression. Enhydros are crystals that contain bubbles of liquid that is millions of years old. They are a symbol of the collective unconscious that underlies and unites everything.

Each crystal shape has a specific use in healing. Wands sharply focus energy and may stimulate points on the body or draw off negativity. Crystals with terminations at both ends help to break old patterns, and can integrate spirit and matter. A crystal egg detects and corrects energy imbalances. A single point focuses energy into a beam, a square consolidates it, and a sphere emits energy in all directions. The following pages show you how different crystals, used wisely, can make excellent healing tools.

POINT

Many crystals have points, some large and some so small they can hardly be seen with the naked eye. Points may be natural or artificially shaped. A single crystal point has a definite faceted, pointed end and the other end tends to look ragged where it has been separated from a cluster base. A single crystal point is often used in healing. Pointed away from the body, it draws energy off. Pointed inward, it channels energy to the body.

Natural point

Natural poin

DOUBLE TERMINATION

Double-terminated crystals have definite points at both ends. Some are natural and others artificially shaped. A double termination radiates or absorbs energy at both ends simultaneously, channeling it in two directions at once. A stone of balance, a double termination integrates spirit and matter and can provide a bridge between two energy points.

These crystals are useful in healing as they absorb negative energy and break old patterns, which can assist in overcoming addictions. They can also be used to integrate previously blocked parts of the self. Placed on the third eye*, double terminations can enhance telepathy.

Artificially shaped double termination
(see page 350 for a natural double termination)

CLUSTER

A cluster has many points bedded, but not necessarily
fixed, into a base. The crystals may be small or large.
Clusters radiate energy out to the surrounding
environment and can also absorb detrimental
energy. They can be programmed and left in
place to do their work. They are especially useful
for cleansing a room or other crystals, in which
case the crystal should be left overnight on the cluster.

Cluster

GEODE

A geode is contained within an outer form. When opened, it is hollow
with many crystals pointing inward. Geodes hold and amplify energy
within themselves. Due to their rounded, cavelike shape and numerous
terminations, they diffuse the amplified energy, softening the energy
but not neutralizing it, allowing it to flow out slowly if required. They
are useful for protection and aid spiritual growth. Geodes
assist in breaking addictions and are beneficial for an
addictive or overindulgent personality.

Geode

NATURALLY OCCURRING LONG POINT

This crystal focuses energy in a straight line. It is often mimicked in purpose-made crystal wands. It is used extensively in healing or ritual work. It will rapidly transmit energy if pointed toward the body, or draw it off if turned away. (See Wands on pages 354–359.)

PHANTOM

A phantom crystal appears ghostlike within the body of a larger crystal. Owing to the method of its formation, a phantom has absorbed learning over eons of time. Putting the past into perspective, it points the way toward growth and evolution and is helpful in overcoming stagnation. Each has a specific meaning, depending on the type of crystal. (See page 233.)

Long point

Phantom

BALL

Balls are usually shaped from a larger piece of crystal and may well have planes or flaws within them. They emit energy in all directions equally. Used as a window to the past or future, they move energy through time and provide a glimpse of what is to come or what has been, a practice called scrying*.

Ball

SQUARE

A square crystal consolidates energy within its form. It is useful for anchoring intention and for grounding. Naturally occurring square crystals such as Fluorite can also draw off negative energy and transform it into positive.

Square

PYRAMID

A pyramid-shaped crystal has four sides on a base, but the base itself may be squared off if the crystal is natural rather than artificially shaped. Naturally occurring pyramid-shaped crystals, such as Apophyllite, amplify and then tightly focus energy through the apex and are suitable for holding manifestation programs.

Pyramid

Pyramids can also be used to draw off negative energies and blockages from the chakras, replenishing with vibrant energy. Artificially shaped pyramids are available in an abundance of materials. They enhance and focus the inherent properties of the crystal.

EGG

Egg-shaped crystals confine and shape energy and can be used to detect and rebalance blockages in the body. The more pointed end is a useful reflexology or acupressure tool. They make excellent "hand comforters" to use in times of stress.

Egg

AMORPHOUS

Amorphous crystals, such as Obsidian, have no particular shape. Energy flows rapidly through an amorphous crystal as it has no rigid internal organization. They are strong-acting and instant in their effect.

Amorphous

LAYERED

Layered, or plate-like crystals, such as Lepidolite, are helpful for working on several levels at once as they spread energy out in layers. Their energy can assist in getting to the bottom of things.

*Layered
Lepidolite*

TABULAR

A tabular crystal has two wide sides, resulting in a flat crystal which may be double terminated. Many tabular crystals have notches in them that can be rubbed to activate the information contained within the crystal. Energy flows freely through a tabular crystal, which offers little resistance. It removes confusion, misinterpretation, and misunderstanding and is an excellent aid to communication at all levels, both inner and outer. It is said that a tabular crystal is the finest tool for communication with other realms.

In healing, a tabular crystal links two points, bringing about perfect balance, and they can be used to enhance telepathy. This crystal activates other crystals.

Tabular

ELESTIAL

An elestial has many natural terminations and folds over a multilayered crystal. It has a gently flowing energy that removes blockages and fear, balancing the polarities and opening the way to necessary change. Sustaining and comforting, it is helpful in overcoming emotional burdens and in connecting to the eternal self. This crystal can take you into other lives to understand your karma or deep into yourself to give an insight into the spiritual processes at work.

Elestial

332

OCCLUSION*

An occlusion is usually formed from
a deposit of another mineral within
a Quartz crystal (see Chlorite, page
108). It is a cloudy spot or patch
depending on the mineral. Minerals may
also be deposited on an external face and
show through when viewed from the other side.
An occlusion radiates the energy of the mineral,
focused and amplified by the Quartz surrounding it.

*Tibetan Quartz
with occlusions*

ABUNDANCE

An abundance crystal consists of one long Quartz crystal
with many small crystals clustered around its base. Its
function is to attract wealth and abundance into your
life. It is best positioned in the wealth corner of a house
or business—the point at the farthest rear left of the
front door.

Abundance

333

Large
generator
point

GENERATOR

A single generator crystal has six facets meeting equally in a sharp point. Large or small, this powerful crystal is the optimum shape for generating energy. A generator crystal optimizes healing energy. It aids focus and clarity of intention.

A generator cluster is very large with many long points, each of which can be programmed for a specific purpose. A generator cluster brings a group together in peaceful harmony—each person can have a point programmed specifically for them. It is extremely useful for generating healing energy and is often placed in the center of a healing group.

Generator
cluster

MANIFESTATION

A manifestation crystal is a rare and precious thing. One or more small crystals are totally enclosed by a larger crystal. When you are absolutely clear as to what you want to manifest, this crystal will aid you, especially if it is carefully programmed. If you have any ambivalence or confusion over what you want, or are asking for purely selfish reasons, the crystal cannot work. The manifestation crystal can also be used to stimulate creativity and original thought, promote visualization, and invoke planetary healing. It is an excellent crystal for group work and functions to its highest purpose when programmed for the good of all.

Manifestation

*Large Cathedral
Quartz*

CATHEDRAL QUARTZ

Cathedral Quartz is a cosmic computer that contains the wisdom of the ages. It is a Light Library*, holding a record of all that has occurred on earth. Many of the Cathedral Quartzes are extremely large—the one pictured here is longer than a forearm. Even a small piece will give you the information you need, however. Parts of this book were written with the assistance of a palm-sized Cathedral Quartz natural generator studded with bridge crystals.

Cathedral Quartz may appear to be composed of several convoluted or separate pieces, but these are in fact all part of the main crystal which has multiple terminations with at least one point at the apex.

The Light Library can be accessed by meditating with a Cathedral Quartz. It aids attunement to the universal mind, and acts as a receptor and transmitter for group thought, which is raised to a higher vibration through contact with the pure energies of the crystal. It also provides access to the Akashic Record*.

It is believed that Cathedral Quartz makes itself known every two thousand years to aid the evolution of consciousness by raising thought to a higher vibration. Cathedral Quartz can be programmed to bring about a better world.

Placed over the site of pain, Cathedral Quartz has been found to bring significant relief.

RECORD KEEPER

A record-keeper crystal has clearly etched pyramid shapes on its side or sides. Sometimes these shapes are separated, so that the face is covered with triangles, others show only one, and some are grooved around each other in a chevron pattern. These crystals are often, but not necessarily, clear Quartz. They symbolize the perfect harmony of mind, body, emotions, and spirit and the all-seeing eye.

Record keepers hold the imprint of all that has gone before and are portals for spiritual wisdom. Discrimination and integrity are needed when working with a record keeper. Placed with a triangle on the third eye*, this crystal can be meditated with to access the personal or collective past or reattune to your own wisdom, and to facilitate insights for evolution. The crystal can be held and gently rubbed with a finger over the pyramid, which will "open the book."

Record keepers are an excellent way to explore your inner self. They can act as a catalyst for growth and aid in removing obstacles to progress. Reenergizing your whole being, they can prevent burn-out. (*See also* Record-Keeper Cerussite, page 98.)

Quartz record keeper

ETCHED

An etched crystal looks as though hieroglyphs or cuneiform writing have been inscribed on its faces. Used when meditating, this crystal takes you back to the ancient civilizations to access wisdom and knowledge of past lives. It can be extremely useful in attuning to spiritual training and initiations carried out at that time, reawakening inherent skills and healing abilities.

It is said that an etched crystal is a personal crystal and should be used by one person only but, appropriately cleansed and reprogrammed before and after use, it can skillfully guide another soul consciously to access their own past knowledge. It is especially helpful in past-life therapy when going to a time before dis-ease* or destructive emotional patterns set in, so that the regressee can feel what it was like to be without these heavy burdens, facilitating recovery of the state of inner perfection.

Quartz etched

SCEPTER QUARTZ

A scepter Quartz is a large central rod around one end of which another crystal formed. Scepter Quartz is also available in a smaller form in which the Quartz rod has a distinctive ridge and wider top, and as a reversed scepter in which a small crystal or opaque point emerges from a larger base stone.

Large scepter Quartz is a very special stone. Used as a meditation tool, it links into the wisdom of the ages and facilitates channeling high vibrations. Generating and amplifying energy, scepter Quartz is an excellent healing tool, as it directs healing to the core of a problem or to the center of the subtle bodies*. Dis-ease* is dissolved and the energies restructured at the physical, mental, emotional, or spiritual levels of being as appropriate. It is particularly useful where energy has to be transmitted in a specific direction.

Legend has it that these stones were used as a symbol of spiritual authority in Atlantis and Lemuria* and that they have reemerged to bring crystal power to the present day. A natural lingam, they can be used for fertility problems and to balance male and female energies.

Reversed Quartz scepters transmit healing energy, cleanse it, and then return it to the healer. They free the mind from false illusions and bring it to a point of stillness.

Other crystals may be found as scepters. Long and delicate natural Selenite wands are sometimes attached to another crystal to form a powerful healing tool that resonates at a high frequency and imparts deep wisdom and ancient knowledge. A Selenite scepter can be used to cut out dis-eased or damaged parts of the etheric blueprint* that carry the imprint of past-life wounds from the physical or emotional level and that have impinged on the present-life body.

Large scepter

Reversed scepter

TIME LINK (ACTIVATOR)

Time link or activator crystals can be found in two forms, right and left. From the unique helical atomic structure of Quartz, a small parallelogram forms a window that inclines to either right or left. This formation teaches that time is an illusion that we use to organize our experiences while on earth but that, in reality, there is no time as we know it. A left-inclined time link takes you into "the past" to explore other lives and the spiritual dimensions, and a right-inclined time link takes you to an apparent future or futures, showing that the future is what we make it. Some crystals display both.

A matched pair of activator crystals is an excellent tool for synthesizing the left and right hemispheres of the brain and can be used to heal disorders on different sides of the body, especially those caused by brain damage or dysfunction—a left-inclined activator treating problems on the right, and a right-inclined reversing dis-ease* on the left. Activators can also be used to align the chakras*, right-inclined treating the chakras from the back and left-inclined from the front of the body.

Time link (left)

Time link (right)

DIAMOND WINDOW

Flat faces at the top of a crystal are called windows. Windows may form in a diamond shape, some large, some small, which facilitate clarity of mind and the organization of information received from different levels of being. Gazing into a diamond window takes you deep inside yourself or enables you to read information for someone else.

A true diamond window is large and connected to the apex and the base, but even small diamond windows can assist the balance between the spiritual and the material worlds, facilitating living in everyday reality while at the same time being connected to a greater reality. Diamond windows provide a doorway into other levels of being and a deep connection with the self. They reflect the inner state of being and causes of dis-ease and can help to find a missing person's whereabouts or surroundings if a strong enough picture of the person is projected into the center of the diamond. (*See also* pages 352–353.)

Diamond window

Self-healed

SELF-HEALED

A self-healed crystal has many small terminations where it has been broken above its base and has then healed the break by laying down fresh crystals. A wound-healer, this crystal has an impressive knowledge of self-healing, which it is happy to share. It teaches how to heal and become whole again no matter how damaged and wounded one may have been.

ANCESTRAL TIME LINE

An ancestral time-line crystal has a very clear flat ledge going up from the base of the crystal toward the apex. It frequently has a fault line showing exactly where the family pain is located and how far back into the ancestral line it goes. Attuning to this crystal brings the source of the family dis-ease* to the surface so that it can be healed and the healing can then be sent back through the generations to a point before the dis-ease manifested. This transforms the whole family line, sending its benefits forward into future generations.

Time line

GATEWAY (APERTURE)

A gateway, or aperture, crystal has a cup-shaped depression within it that is large enough to hold liquid. Gazing into the liquid center provides a gateway to other worlds and enables one to travel through past, present, and future. It is an excellent stone for preparing a gem elixir that aids spiritual vision and psychic faculties.

KEY (APERTURE)

A key crystal has an indentation or aperture in one of its sides, which narrows as it penetrates the crystal. This indentation is usually, but not necessarily, three- or six-sided. It provides a doorway to unlock parts of the self that are normally kept hidden or to access hidden information of any kind. Meditating with one of these crystals reveals what is being hidden from you, especially by your subconscious mind, sweeping away illusion. It is an excellent tool for letting go of anything that holds the soul back and for tie-cutting.

Key

LIFE PATH

A life path crystal is a long, thin, clear Quartz crystal with one or more absolutely smooth sides. This crystal accesses your life purpose and helps you to go with the flow and follow your bliss, leading you to your spiritual destiny. This stone teaches you to follow what your soul, not your ego, wants.

SPIRAL QUARTZ

A spiral Quartz has a distinct twist down its axis and is beneficial for maintaining balance at any level. It draws universal energy into the body and anchors it during meditation. This crystal can stimulate the rise of kundalini* through the chakras*, clearing any energy blockages that impede the rise of kundalini energy.

Life Path

Spiral

SHEET QUARTZ

Sheet Quartz is laid down as a clear, flat layer, often between two crystals. It provides a window into other dimensions, facilitating communication, and it accesses the Akashic Record*. It can be used to contact relevant past lives and to go deep within the self. This crystal encourages the fullest use of psychic potential, stimulating the third eye* and enhancing visualization and spiritual vision. Used in meditation, it takes you to a place where answers can be found.

Sheet Quartz

COMPANION

A companion crystal has two crystals entwined and partly growing in each other, or a small crystal that grows out of the main crystal. Occasionally, one crystal will totally surround another. Companion crystals are nurturing and provide enormous support, particularly during difficult times. They can help you to understand a relationship better and to recognize how one partner can best support the other.

Companion

Tantric Twin

Soulmate

SOULMATE (TANTRIC TWIN)

A soulmate crystal does exactly what its name suggests—draws a soulmate to your side—although this soulmate may not be a sexual partner. Soulmate crystals, or tantric twins, are a pair of crystals approximately the same size growing from a common base, joined together along one side but with distinct and separate terminations. Tantric means "union of energies." Soulmate crystals are beneficial for all kinds of relationships. The closer they are in size, the more harmonious will be the partnership.

These stones have a powerful message concerning the bonding of two people into a close and intimate relationship. They teach how to be unique and separate, while united in equal partnership. To be in a

348

successful union, you need to be comfortable with yourself. If not, you will project your unresolved issues onto your partner. Tantric twins help you truly to know and accept yourself. As a result, interdependence and deep intimacy with another person are possible.

A twin crystal of unequal-sized sections is useful when working on a relationship such as mother–daughter, father–son, employer–employee. It helps more unconditional love to manifest in the situation and brings the two people into greater harmony.

If you are fortunate enough to find a soulmate or tantric twin Quartz crystal that has vivid rainbows across the intersection, then your relationship will be particularly harmonious. You will find a true soulmate. Place your soulmate crystal in the relationship corner of your house or bedroom—the farthest right from the door.

A true tantric twin crystal has two absolutely identical crystals aligned side by side. It is an excellent stone for two people working together as equals, whether spiritually or materially. They can also be used to harmonize and integrate the different levels of the self. A double-terminated tantric twin is the perfect stone for ascension— raising your vibration, it brings the higher self into line with the soul's purpose.

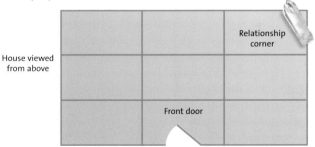

House viewed from above

Relationship corner

Front door

The relationship corner is the farthest back right point from your front door or the door into an individual room

Bridge

Tabular

Cross

Barnacle

This formation is a double terminated tabular crystal with bridge, barnacle, and cross crystals overlaid

BARNACLE

A barnacle crystal has many small crystals covering or partially covering a larger crystal. The large crystal is said to be the "old soul" whose wisdom attracts the younger crystals. It is a useful crystal for meditating on family or community problems and for people who are employed in service industries. It provides a cohesive group energy that enhances common purpose and promotes working together. It is said to be an extremely comforting crystal after the loss of a loved one.

BRIDGE

A bridge crystal grows out of another, larger crystal. As its name suggests, it bridges gaps and brings things together. It can be used to join the inner and outer world, the higher self with the ego, or yourself with another. It is helpful for public speaking, especially when trying to communicate new ideas.

CROSS

A cross formation has one crystal at right angles to another, usually larger crystal. Stabilizing you within yourself, it opens to the multiplicity of worlds and facilitates spiritual study. This formation removes energy implants* and clears and activates any chakra.

BUDDHA

A Buddha crystal is distinguished by a formation closely resembling a Buddha sitting in the crystal's upper quadrant. It occurs in clear crystals such as Quartz and Danburite and is an excellent crystal for enlightenment and deep meditation, especially by a group taking it to the highest levels of awareness. A Buddha crystal assists in treading your path and acts as a guide in the physical, mental, and spiritual worlds. This crystal facilitates the transfer of ancient wisdom from the East into the pineal gland and from there into consciousness.

Buddha

CHANNELING

A channeling* crystal has a seven-sided facet at the front of the termination and a triangular face on the opposite side. As its name suggests, it channels healing energy or information from higher sources and then assists in expressing what is learned. Channeling crystals can facilitate trance channeling but should only be used by those who are experienced in such matters.

TRANSMITTER

A transmitter crystal has two seven-sided facets with two perfect triangles between them. They can be used to send long-distance healing or for energy or thought transmissions. Linking to the purest possible vibrations, they open the intuition and attract wisdom and communication from higher realms.

Transmitter

TRANS-CHANNELING

A trans-channeling crystal combines the channeling and the transmitter crystal. It has a rare formation of three seven-sided facets, between each of which is a perfect triangular face. This is said to be a highly creative crystal, which is dedicated to the service of humankind and which can access the highest personal and collective wisdom, bringing intuitive awareness into any situation.

Trans-channeling

SEER STONE

A seer stone is a natural, water-polished stone that is cut to reveal an inner world.

This is an excellent aid to scrying* as it shows past, present, and future and can take you deep into your own inner self. It is also said that you can program a seer stone to take you back to a specific time frame to access its knowledge.

Seer Stone

ISIS (GODDESS)

The Isis crystal has a dominant face which is five-sided, with a tall sharp point rather like an arrowhead. This crystal is extremely useful for healing anything that is broken—body, mind, emotions, or spirit. It can be used to integrate spiritual energies into the emotional body, bringing in more balanced and joyful emotions, and to ameliorate overidentification with the suffering of others. This crystal can take you deep into your own heart for healing, insights, and acceptance. Helpful for men who want to get more in touch with their feeling nature, it can also assist sensitive children to stabilize their nature. An Isis crystal is beneficial for anyone who is facing transition, especially to the next world.

Isis

Artificially shaped wand

WANDS

Wands are the traditional healing tools of shamans, healers, and metaphysicians. The magic wands of myth and legend, they are believed to have been used by the highly evolved crystal healers of Atlantis, and many practitioners today believe that wands from those far-off times are surfacing once again, complete with their powerful programming.

Wands have the ability to focus energy tightly through their tip. Most wands are artificially shaped but naturally formed. Long pointed crystals such as the powerful laser Quartz are excellent healing tools.

The healing ability of wands is vastly expanded when programmed with intent (see page 29). When using a wand, it is important consciously to allow universal healing energy to flow in through your crown chakra*, down your arm to the hand holding the wand, and then into the wand where it is amplified and passed into the patient. Using your own energy for this purpose is shortsighted and inefficient, as you will become weak and depleted and need healing yourself.

QUARTZ WAND

A long, clear Quartz wand, whether natural or shaped, emits both positive and negative energy. It strongly amplifies energy and focuses this where it is needed, or draws it off and dissipates it as appropriate. Quartz can be used to reach the underlying cause of dis-ease* and to transform it. It points to, and then treats, areas of blockage or weakness in the physical body or the aura*.

LASER QUARTZ

Laser Quartz is a naturally formed, long, slender Quartz crystal that tapers toward the termination, which has very small faces. Its sides are often slightly curved. This is an extremely powerful instrument that should be used with caution. It should never be randomly pointed at anyone else and must be used only with clarity of intention. If this advice is followed, it is an amazing healing tool.

A laser Quartz focuses, concentrates, and accelerates the energy passing through it into a tight beam that acts like a laser. Suitable for psychic surgery, it stimulates acupuncture points and can reach tiny structures deep within the body, such as the pineal or pituitary gland, or perform precision work on the physical or subtle bodies. This wand can detach entities or attachments and ties to other people, and cuts away negativity of all kinds. It provides powerful protection for the aura and physical body. At a mental or emotional level, it removes inappropriate attitudes, outmoded thought patterns, and energy blockages.

Laser Quartz

TOURMALINATED QUARTZ

A Quartz wand with strands of Tourmaline running through it is extremely effective for anyone who is "buttoned down tight," whether from stress or trauma. It gently creates an opening for healing energy to flow into the body, realigning and reenergizing the meridians* and the organs. It cleanses and replenishes the chakras* and the aura*, providing excellent protection. Tourmalinated Quartz dissolves destructive patterns and behavior that has been carried forward from other lives, and alleviates negativity from the present life that is becoming fixed and will pass on to future lives. It fills the gap with self-confidence and a sense of self-worth that prevents the negativity from returning.

TOURMALINE WAND

Natural Tourmaline wands are useful healing tools. They clear the aura, remove blockages, disperse negative energy, and point to solutions for specific problems. They are excellent for balancing and connecting the chakras. At a physical level, they rebalance the energy meridians.

Natural Tourmaline wands

VOGEL WAND

Vogel (and vogel-type) wands have a
very precise vibratory signature. They
have specially created, indented facets
with specific angles down the sides of
a Quartz wand to create a superbly
efficient healing tool that has a very
high and pure vibration. The powers and
properties of Vogel wands vary with the
number of faces. The shorter, "fatter" end is
female and draws pranic energy which is amplified
as it spirals through the facets. The longer, thinner end is
male and transmits energy out in a strongly focused laser-like beam.
Vogels are excellent for connecting the chakras, removing attached
entities*, and removing negativity. They detect and rectify energy
blockages and strongly cohere the energy fields around and within
the body.

Vogel-type wands

Vogels need to be programmed and employed in a very precise
manner and they are best used after appropriate training.

FLUORITE WAND

Fluorite wands are artificially shaped, most often from a mixture of
Green and Purple Fluorite. They have a wonderfully soothing energy
and can be stroked over the skin to relieve pain and inflammation.
Even a small wand will absorb an enormous amount of stress and,
if not cleansed, may crack under the strain. It is often suggested that
the wand be immersed in water to cleanse it, the water then being
returned to the earth for transmutation of the pain.

OBSIDIAN WAND

An Obsidian wand is ideal in cases where there are negative energies within the emotional body that require removal and the patient is ready for these to surface. Once they have been released, the Obsidian wand then protects the aura* and connects to the earth, pointing the way forward. Obsidian wands can also be used for diagnosis and location of blockages.

AMETHYST WAND

An Amethyst wand is the perfect tool for opening the brow chakra* and activating the pineal gland to stimulate intuitive vision. It will also remove blockages from the sacral chakra and from the aura. It can be used to heal a weak aura and to provide protection.

Specially formed crystal wands

ROSE QUARTZ WAND

A Rose Quartz wand is imbued with wonderful peace. It is excellent for calming emotional distress and for healing a broken heart, but it works equally well for any state of agitation or anxiety. A racing pulse is quickly normalized and raised blood pressure returned to normal under this stone's gentle influence. If the chakras are spinning erratically, Rose Quartz will instantly stabilize the energy and bring things into harmony.

SMOKY QUARTZ WAND

Smoky Quartz is an excellent crystal for grounding negative energy and providing protection. A Smoky Quartz wand grounds the energy of the base chakra by linking it to the earth chakra beneath your feet. It purifies this chakra* in the etheric body and neutralizes the effect of any geopathic stress*. It can be used anywhere on the body where negative energy needs to be removed.

Natural Smoky Quartz wand

SELENITE WAND

Selenite wands have a very pure vibration. They can be used to detach entities from the aura or to prevent anything external from influencing the mind.

Natural Selenite wand

QUICK REFERENCE

In the pages that follow, you will find quick reference guides to the correspondences between crystals and the zodiac and crystals and the body, their links with the chakras* and the aura*, suggested layouts and grids, and how to make gem remedies. These are designed to help in your selection of crystals and to show you some general principles.

   The healing and protection layouts, for instance, can easily be adapted to your purpose. Find the layout closest to your intention, look in the body correspondences or the Index, and find the crystals you need. Checking their properties in the Directory will help you to refine your choice. Place as shown in the layout, or vary slightly according to your specific need. If you are looking for love, for example, you could adapt the heart chakra* healing layout with crystals such as Rose Quartz, Rhodochrosite, Rhodonite, and Kunzite. If you are of mature years, you could add Green Aventurine as this encourages love in later life. If it is passion you are after, Red Jasper and Green Tourmaline stimulate this. You will quickly learn to use your intuition to select exactly the right combination of crystals for your needs.

CRYSTALS AND THE ZODIAC

Birthstones ground and amplify celestial energies. Each of the twelve signs of the zodiac has traditional crystal affinities. Some arise from a month of birth, others from the planets connected to a sign. As new crystals are found they are assigned to a sign. Use the chart below.

Garnet

ARIES March 21 – April 19	Ruby, Diamond, Amethyst, Aquamarine, Aventurine, Bloodstone, Carnelian, Citrine, Diamond, Fire Agate, Garnet, Jadeite, Jasper, Kunzite, Magnetite, Pink Tourmaline, Orange Spinel, Ruby, Spinel, Topaz
TAURUS April 20 – May 20	Emerald, Topaz, Aquamarine, Azurite, Black Spinel, Boji Stone, Diamond, Emerald, Kyanite, Kunzite, Lapis Lazuli, Malachite, Rose Quartz, Rhodonite, Sapphire, Selenite, Tiger's Eye, Topaz, Tourmaline, Variscite
GEMINI May 21 – June 20	Tourmaline, Agate, Apatite, Apophyllite, Aquamarine, Blue Spinel, Calcite, Chrysocolla, Chrysoprase, Citrine, Dendritic Agate, Green Obsidian, Green Tourmaline, Sapphire, Serpentine, Tourmalinated and Rutilated Quartz, Tiger's Eye, Topaz, Variscite, Zoisite, Ulexite
CANCER June 21 – July 22	Moonstone, Pearl, Amber, Beryl, Brown Spinel, Carnelian, Calcite, Chalcedony, Chrysoprase, Emerald, Moonstone, Opal, Pink Tourmaline, Rhodonite, Ruby, Moss Agate, Fire Agate, Dendritic Agate
LEO July 23 – Aug 22	Cat's or Tiger's Eye, Ruby, Amber, Boji Stone, Carnelian, Chrysocolla, Citrine, Danburite, Emerald, Fire Agate, Garnet, Golden Beryl, Green and Pink Tourmaline, Kunzite, Larimar, Muscovite, Onyx, Orange Calcite, Petalite, Pyrolusite, Quartz, Red Obsidian, Rhodochrosite, Ruby, Topaz, Turquoise, Yellow Spinel
VIRGO Aug 23 – Sept 22	Peridot, Sardonyx, Amazonite, Amber, Blue Topaz, Dioptase, Carnelian, Chrysocolla, Citrine, Garnet, Magnetite, Moonstone, Moss Agate, Opal, Peridot, Purple Obsidian, Rubellite, Rutilated Quartz, Sapphire, Sardonyx, Sodalite, Sugilite, Smithsonite, Okenite

LIBRA Sept 23 – Oct 22	Sapphire, Opal, Ametrine, Apophyllite, Aquamarine, Aventurine, Bloodstone, Chiastolite, Chrysolite, Emerald, Green Spinel, Green Tourmaline, Jade, Kunzite, Lapis Lazuli, Lepidolite, Mahogany Obsidian, Moonstone, Opal, Peridot, Sapphire, Topaz, Prehnite, Sunstone
SCORPIO Oct 23 – Nov 21	Topaz, Malachite, Apache Tear, Aquamarine, Beryl, Boji Stone, Charoite, Dioptase, Emerald, Garnet, Green Tourmaline, Herkimer Diamond, Kunzite, Malachite, Moonstone, Obsidian, Red Spinel, Rhodochrosite, Ruby, Topaz, Turquoise, Hiddenite, Variscite
SAGITTARIUS Nov 22 – Dec 21	Topaz, Turquoise, Amethyst, Azurite, Blue Lace Agate, Chalcedony, Charoite, Dark Blue Spinel, Dioptase, Garnet, Gold Sheen Obsidian, Labradorite, Lapis Lazuli, Malachite, Snowflake Obsidian, Pink Tourmaline, Ruby, Smoky Quartz, Spinel, Sodalite, Sugilite, Turquoise, Wulfenite, Okenite
CAPRICORN Dec 22 – Jan 19	Jet, Onyx, Amber, Azurite, Carnelian, Fluorite, Garnet, Green and Black Tourmaline, Jet, Labradorite, Magnetite, Malachite, Onyx, Peridot, Quartz, Ruby, Smoky Quartz, Turquoise, Aragonite, Galena
AQUARIUS Jan 20 – Feb 18	Aquamarine, Amethyst, Amber, Angelite, Blue Celestite, Blue Obsidian, Boji Stone, Chrysoprase, Fluorite, Labradorite, Magnetite, Moonstone, Atacamite
PISCES Feb 19 – March 20	Moonstone, Amethyst, Aquamarine, Beryl, Bloodstone, Blue Lace Agate, Calcite, Chrysoprase, Fluorite, Labradorite, Moonstone, Turquoise, Smithsonite, Sunstone

Smoky Quartz

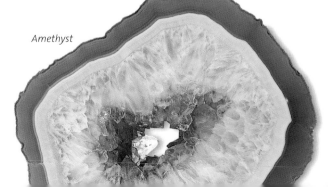

Amethyst

Citrine

CRYSTALS AND THE CHAKRAS

When healing and balancing the chakras*, an appropriate stone is placed on the chakra—on the front or back of the body, whichever is more comfortable. Leave for 15 minutes. Stones can be placed on all the chakras, or above the head and below the feet to perform certain tasks.

Pink Kunzite

GROUNDING ENERGY FROM CROWN TO BASE: Smoky Quartz
OPENING AND CLEANSING ALL: Amber, Dendritic Agate, Malachite
CLEANSING AND PROTECTING ALL: Tourmaline, Garnet
ALIGNING: Boji Stone, Yellow Kunzite, Kyanite
ELEVATING: Turquoise
CLEANSING LOWER CHAKRAS: Bloodstone

HIGHER CROWN	Kunzite, Apophyllite, Celestite, Muscovite, Selenite, Petalite, Azeztulite, Phenacite
CROWN	Moldavite, Citrine, Quartz, Red Serpentine, Purple Jasper, Clear Tourmaline, Golden Beryl, Lepidolite, Purple Sapphire
BROW/THIRD EYE	Apophyllite, Sodalite, Moldavite, Azurite, Herkimer Diamond, Lapis Lazuli, Garnet, Purple Fluorite, Kunzite, Lepidolite, Malachite with Azurite, Royal Sapphire, Electric Blue Obsidian, Azeztulite, Atacamite
THROAT	Azurite, Turquoise, Amethyst, Aquamarine, Blue Topaz, Blue Tourmaline, Amber, Kunzite, Amethyst, Lepidolite, Blue Obsidian, Petalite
HIGHER HEART	Dioptase, Kunzite
HEART	Rose Quartz, Green Quartz, Aventurine, Kunzite, Variscite, Muscovite, Red Calcite, Rhodonite, Watermelon Tourmaline, Pink Tourmaline, Green Tourmaline, Peridot, Apophyllite, Lepidolite, Morganite, Green Quartz, Pink Danburite, Ruby, Chrysocolla, Green Sapphire
SOLAR PLEXUS	Malachite, Jasper, Tiger's Eye, Citrine, Yellow Tourmaline, Golden Beryl, Rhodochrosite, Smithsonite

SACRAL	Blue Jasper, Red Jasper, Orange Carnelian, Topaz, Orange Calcite, Citrine
BASE	Azurite, Bloodstone, Chrysocolla, Obsidian, Golden Yellow Topaz, Black Tourmaline, Carnelian, Citrine, Red Jasper, Smoky Quartz
EARTH	Boji Stone, Fire Agate, Brown Jasper, Smoky Quartz, Cuprite, Hematite, Mahogany Obsidian, Tourmaline, Rhodonite,

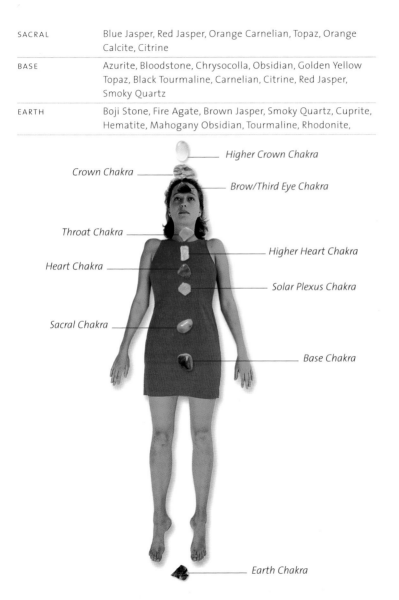

Higher Crown Chakra

Crown Chakra

Brow/Third Eye Chakra

Throat Chakra

Higher Heart Chakra

Heart Chakra

Solar Plexus Chakra

Sacral Chakra

Base Chakra

Earth Chakra

CRYSTALS AND THE AURA

Wear or place the following crystals around your body about
a handspan away to perform the functions listed.

Apache Tear

Bloodstone

AMBER	An ancient protector. It aligns the aura* with the physical body, mind, and spirit. It draws off negative energy and so cleans the aura.
AMETHYST	Gently cleanses the aura, heals holes, and protects it, drawing in divine energy.
APACHE TEAR (CLEAR BLACK OBSIDIAN)	Gently protects the aura from absorbing negative energies.
BLACK JADE	Guards the aura against negativity.
BLOODSTONE	Etheric cleanser that greatly benefits the aura.
CITRINE	Cleanses and aligns the aura, filling in gaps.
FLUORITE AND TOURMALINE	Provide a psychic shield.
GREEN TOURMALINE	Heals holes in the aura.
JET	Protects the aura against other people's negative thoughts.
LABRADORITE	Prevents energy leakage. It provides protection by aligning to spiritual energy.
MAGNETITE	Strengthens the aura.
QUARTZ	Cleanses, protects, and increases the auric field, sealing any holes.
KUNZITE AND SELENITE	Detach mental influences from the aura.
PETALITE	Highest vibration. Releases negative karma and entities from the aura.
SMOKY QUARTZ	Grounds energy and dissolves negative patterns encased in the aura.

THE BIOMAGNETIC SHEATH

The aura and its etheric bodies with the chakra linkage points (see page 364).

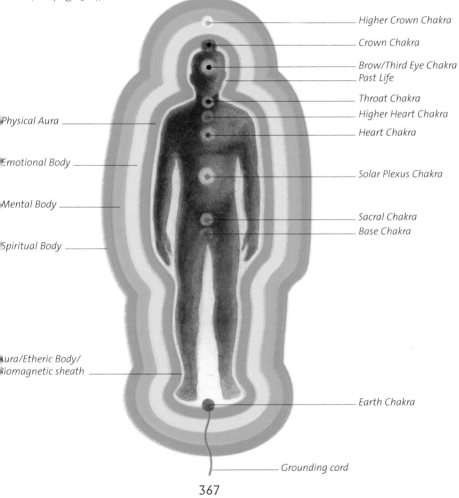

Higher Crown Chakra

Crown Chakra

Brow/Third Eye Chakra
Past Life

Throat Chakra
Higher Heart Chakra
Heart Chakra

Physical Aura

Emotional Body

Solar Plexus Chakra

Mental Body

Sacral Chakra
Base Chakra

Spiritual Body

Aura/Etheric Body/
Biomagnetic sheath

Earth Chakra

Grounding cord

CRYSTAL CORRESPONDENCES

Place an appropriate crystal over the organ to bring it back into balance or to stimulate or sedate it as required.

Red-Black Obsidian

Peridot

BRAIN	Amber, Green Tourmaline, Dark Blue Tourmaline, Beryl, Blue Lace Agate
EAR	Amber, Red-black and Snowflake Obsidian, Celestite, Rhodonite, Orange Calcite
EYES	Aquamarine, Beryl, Chalcedony, Chrysoprase, Sapphire, Charoite, Dark Blue Tourmaline, Celestite, Blue Fluorite, Fire Agate, Cat's Eye, Orange Calcite
TEETH	Aquamarine, Rutilated Quartz, Fluorite
NECK	Aquamarine, Quartz
SHOULDERS	Selenite
MUSCLE TISSUE	Cuprite, Magnetite, Danburite
LUNGS	Beryl, Pink Tourmaline, Peridot, Rhodonite, Amber, Dioptase, Kunzite, Lapis Lazuli, Turquoise, Rhodochrosite, Sardonyx, Blue Tourmaline, Chrysocolla, Emerald, Morganite
SPLEEN	Amber, Aquamarine, Azurite, Bloodstone, Chalcedony, Red Obsidian
STOMACH	Green Fluorite, Fire Agate, Beryl
INTESTINES	Beryl, Peridot, Celestite, Green Fluorite
APPENDIX	Chrysolite
ARMS	Malachite, Jadeite
PROSTATE GLAND	Chrysoprase
TESTES	Jadeite, Topaz, Carnelian, Variscite
HANDS	Moldavite, Aquamarine, Moonstone
SKELETAL SYSTEM	Amazonite, Azurite, Chrysocolla, Calcite, Cuprite, Fluorite, Dendritic Agate, Purple Fluorite, Sardonyx, Iron Pyrite
NERVOUS SYSTEM/ NEUROLOGICAL TISSUE	Amber, Green Jade, Lapis Lazuli, Green Tourmaline, Dendritic Agate

BONE MARROW	Purple Fluorite
PINEAL GLAND	Gem Rhodonite
PITUITARY GLAND	Pietersite
JAW	Aquamarine
THROAT	Aquamarine, Beryl, Lapis Lazuli, Blue Tourmaline, Amber, Green Jasper
THYROID	Amber, Aquamarine, Azurite, Blue Tourmaline, Citrine
THYMUS	Aventurine, Blue Tourmaline
HEART	Cuprite, Rose Quartz, Charoite, Rhodonite, Garnet, Dioptase
LIVER	Aquamarine, Beryl, Bloodstone, Carnelian, Red Jasper, Charoite, Danburite
GALLBLADDER	Carnelian, Jasper, Topaz, Calcite, Citrine, Yellow Quartz, Tiger's Eye, Chalcedony, Danburite
KIDNEYS	Aquamarine, Beryl, Bloodstone, Hematite, Jadeite, Nephrite, Rose Quartz, Citrine, Orange Calcite, Smoky Quartz, Amber, Muscovite
PANCREAS	Red Tourmaline, Blue Lace Agate, Chrysocolla
SPINE	Garnet, Tourmaline, Labradorite, Beryl
FALLOPIAN TUBES	Chrysoprase
FEMALE REPRODUCTIVE SYSTEM	Carnelian, Moonstone, Chrysoprase, Amber, Topaz, Unakite
BLADDER	Topaz, Jasper, Amber, Orange Calcite
CIRCULATORY SYSTEM AND BLOOD	Amethyst, Bloodstone, Chalcedony, Cuprite, Hematite, Red Jasper
VEINS	Variscite, Pyrolusite, Snowflake Obsidian
KNEES	Azurite, Jadeite
JOINTS	Calcite, Azurite, Rhodonite, Magnetite
SKIN	Azurite, Brown Jasper, Green Jasper
FEET	Onyx, Smoky Quartz, Apophyllite

Beryl

*Red
Carnelian*

Fire Agate

ENDOCRINE SYSTEM	Amber, Amethyst, Yellow Jasper, Pink Tourmaline, Fire Agate
IMMUNE SYSTEM	Amethyst, Black Tourmaline, Lapis Lazuli, Malachite, Turquoise
DIGESTIVE TRACT	Chrysocolla, Red Jade, Green Jasper
METABOLISM	Amethyst, Sodalite, Pyrolusite
BACK	Malachite, Sapphire, Lapis Lazuli
LOWER BACK	Carnelian
CAPILLARIES	Dendritic Agate

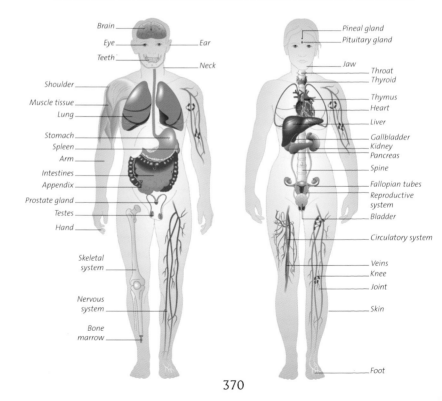

Brain
Eye
Teeth
Ear
Neck
Shoulder
Muscle tissue
Lung
Stomach
Spleen
Arm
Intestines
Appendix
Prostate gland
Testes
Hand
Skeletal system
Nervous system
Bone marrow

Pineal gland
Pituitary gland
Jaw
Throat
Thyroid
Thymus
Heart
Liver
Gallbladder
Kidney
Pancreas
Spine
Fallopian tubes
Reproductive system
Bladder
Circulatory system
Veins
Knee
Joint
Skin
Foot

GEM REMEDIES

As crystals have powerful vibrations, it is easy to transfer these vibrations to water. Gem remedies, also known as elixirs or essences, can be taken internally—unless the stone is toxic. They can also be applied to the skin or put into bathwater. Remedies such as Black Tourmaline can be put into a mister in water and sprayed into the room.

TO MAKE A GEM ELIXIR

Place a cleansed, nonfriable crystal in a glass bowl with spring water. (Place friable or toxic stones in a small glass jar and then in the glass bowl. This is the indirect method.) Stand the bowl in sunlight for twelve hours. Remove the crystal and bottle the mother tincture in a glass bottle with an airtight stopper. To keep for more than a week, add fifty percent brandy or vodka as a preservative. Store in a cool, dark place. Add to bathwater or make a dosage bottle (see page 372).

Direct method of gem remedy preparation

Bottling the elixir

TO MAKE A DOSAGE BOTTLE

Add seven drops of the mother tincture to a glass dropper bottle. Fill with one-third brandy to two-thirds water if taking by mouth or putting on the skin. If using as an eye drop, do not add alcohol. Take seven drops three times a day. (Note: Certain remedies should be used externally only.)

BLUE LACE AGATE	Treats eye infections.
BLACK TOURMALINE	Provides psychic protection and screens from electro-magnetic smog*. Relieves jet lag. releases toxic energy from emotions, mind, and body.
MALACHITE	Harmonizes physical, mental, emotional, and spiritual; grounds the body. Use tumbled stone only.
FLUORITE	Breaks up blockages in the etheric body. Anti-viral.
JADEITE	Heals eye conditions, brings peace.
AMAZONITE	Balances the metabolism.
GREEN JASPER	Restores biorhythms and natural sexuality.
HEMATITE	Strengthens boundaries.
KUNZITE	Opens the heart.
AMBER	Acts as an antibiotic, heals throat problems.
GOLDEN BERYL	A gargle for sore throats.
BLOODSTONE	Releases constipation and emotional stagnation.
CHAROITE	An excellent cleanser for the body.
HERKIMER DIAMOND	Aids psychic vision and dream recall.
MOSS AGATE	Treats fungal infections.

Moss Agate

Black Tourmaline

CRYSTAL LAYOUTS AND GRIDS

Laying crystals on or around your body quickly brings relief from dis-ease*.
You can also grid crystals around your bed or to protect your house. You
can use crystals to stimulate the immune system or to alleviate stress.
You can protect yourself from geopathic stress* or electromagnetic smog*
or sharpen your memory. Remember to program your crystals before use.

ALLEVIATING STRESS

Relaxation is the best antidote to stress. Take eight Amethyst points and
lay them around your body about a handspan away, point inward. Place
one between and slightly below your feet, one above your head, two
level with your neck, two at your hips, and two at your ankles. Close
your eyes and relax for at least ten minutes—twenty would be better.
You can leave them in place overnight, or position around your bed.

STIMULATING THE IMMUNE SYSTEM

Short treatment Place Pink Smithsonite over your heart, Green
Tourmaline over the thymus above the heart, and a Quartz point-up
above your head. Place eight Malachites around your body. Leave for
fifteen to twenty minutes.

Long treatment During sleep tape Green Tourmaline over your thymus.
Place Pink Smithsonite at each corner of your bed and a piece under
your pillow.

*Pink
Smithsonite*

CHAKRA LAYOUT

Place a brown stone between and slightly beneath your feet,
a red stone on base chakra, an orange stone below navel, a
yellow stone on solar plexus, pink stone on heart, Kunzite on
higher heart, blue stone on throat, indigo stone on third eye,
purple stone at crown, and white high-vibration stone above head.

*Green
Tourmaline*

GRIDDING THE HOUSE

Place Black Tourmaline (for protection, geopathic stress*, or electromagnetic smog*), Selenite (for protection and angelic guidance), or Sardonyx (guards against crime) at each corner of the house, or room. Where possible, place a large piece outside the front door.

MEMORY LAYOUT

You will need two Citrine or Yellow Fluorite to strengthen memory, Green Calcite for mental clarity, Azurite for insight. Place yellow crystals either side of your head at ear level. Place Green Calcite on top of your head and Azurite over the third eye*. Leave in place for twenty minutes.

HEALING THE HEART

Place seven Rose Quartz, one Dioptase, and one Watermelon Tourmaline as shown and leave in place for twenty minutes. Four Amethyst points can be added, point facing outward, to draw off any emotional imbalances that may be blocking the heart.

Heart layout

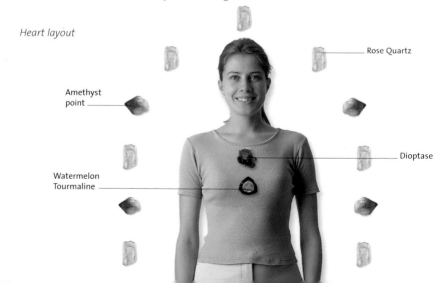

Rose Quartz

Amethyst point

Dioptase

Watermelon Tourmaline

DIVINATORY MEANINGS

Crystals have traditional meanings associated with them. For a quick answer to a question, place a selection of the crystals listed below in a bag. Concentrate on your question. Pick out a crystal at random; look at the meanings associated with that crystal to find your answer. If two or three crystals fall into your hand, read all the meanings.

AMETHYST	A life change and shift in consciousness. Faithfulness in love, freedom from jealousy.
AGATE	Worldly success or a pleasant surprise. Good health, wealth, and long life. Particularly lucky for people connected with the land.
BLUE LACE AGATE	Healing is needed.
BLACK AGATE	Needs and will find courage and prosperity.
RED AGATE	Health and longevity are yours.
BLOODSTONE	Unpleasant surprise, unlikely to be an illness.
RED JASPER	Pay attention to earthly affairs.
AVENTURINE	Future growth and expansion are possible.
GARNET	A letter is on its way.
CITRINE	Celestial wisdom is advising you.
DIAMOND OR CLEAR QUARTZ	Permanence. Business advancement. If the crystal loses its sparkle, betrayal.
EMERALD	Fertility or a secret admirer. If color pales, love is fading.
HEMATITE	New opportunities await.
JADE	Needs and will find immortality and perfection.
LAPIS LAZULI	Divine favor is yours.
QUARTZ	Be sure to clarify issues you asked about and those that arise.
ROSE QUARTZ	Love and self-healing are needed and will come.

Moss Agate

Opal

SNOW QUARTZ	Profound changes are coming.
RUBY	Power and passion, good fortune and friendship, but beware of strangers.
SAPPHIRE	Truth and chastity and the past will catch up with you.
SNOWFLAKE OBSIDIAN	End of challenging time.
TIGER'S EYE	All is not as it appears to be.
UNAKITE	Compromise and integration.
OPAL	Death or endings. If the crystal loses its brilliance, an unfaithful lover.
SARDONYX	A wedding may be in the offing.
TOPAZ	Exercise caution.
TURQUOISE	A journey is imminent.

Snowflake Obsidian

376

INVOKING LOVE

Crystals can be used in ritual; here is an example using Rose Quartz to invoke love. You need four pieces of Rose Quartz and a large Amethyst. You also need candles and candleholders—which could be fashioned from Rose Quartz.

1 Place your crystals and four candles on a table covered with a silk cloth. Place one candle to the north, welcoming the spirits of that direction as you light it. Then place the others to the south, east, and west, again welcoming the spirits of each direction as you light each candle. Ask that these spirits act as guardians and keep you safe.

2 Take your Rose Quartz crystals into your hands and sit facing your table (if the crystals are large, do one at a time.) Close your eyes and quietly attune to the crystals. Let their energy flow through your hands, up your arms, and into your heart. As the energy reaches your heart, feel it open and expand. Touch the crystals to your heart. Rose Quartz is a powerful heart cleanser and healer, so allow your heart to be purified by the energies of the crystals.

3 Then say, out loud: "I am a magnet for love. I welcome love into my heart." Place the crystals around the Amethyst on the table and say out loud: "And love into my life." Sit quietly for a few moments with your eyes focused on the crystals. When you are ready to complete the ritual, get up and blow out each candle in turn, saying: "I send your light and love into the world." Either leave the crystals on the table or place them around your bed.

GLOSSARY

AKASHIC RECORD In ESOTERIC THOUGHT, a storehouse that exists beyond time and space that contains information on all that has occurred, and all that will occur, in the universe.

ANCESTRAL LINE The means by which family patterns and beliefs are inherited from previous generations.

ANGELIC REALM The energetic level where angels are said to live.

ASCENDED MASTERS Highly evolved spiritual beings who may or may not previously have been incarnated, who guide the spiritual evolution of the earth. People on earth who seek to raise their spiritual and physical vibrations are embarking on the ASCENSION PROCESS.

ASTRAL TRAVEL The soul is able to leave the physical body behind and travel to distant locations. Also known as OUT OF BODY EXPERIENCE or SOUL JOURNEYING.

ATTACHED ENTITIES Spirit forms can become attached to the aura of a living person.

AUDIBLE ORACLE An oracle that conveys its prophecies through sounds such as cracking.

AURA The subtle biomagnetic sheath that surrounds the physical body, providing a protective zone that extends for about eighteen inches to three feet from the body and contains information about a person's physical, mental, emotional, and spiritual state of being. This traditional name for the human energy field comes from the Greek *avra*, meaning "breeze." The intuitive eye can see dis-ease in the aura. *See also* ETHERIC BODY.

AUTOMATIC WRITING A type of writing that occurs when a loosely-held pen moves across the page of its own accord, or when the person holding the pen is impelled to write by thoughts passing through the mind into the pen.

BIOMAGNETIC FIELD/SHEATH The energy field that surrounds all living things.

BETWEEN-LIVES STATE In esoteric thought, the state into which the soul moves out of a physical incarnation (i.e. has died on earth). The soul exists in this state in a subtle energy body, which carries the imprint of what happened to it in former lives. Here the soul formulates its plan for the next life. The between-lives state can also be accessed by the soul during a physical incarnation. While in this state it is possible to heal the past and to access the purpose and plan for the present life.

BLISSED OUT Describes a sensation of heightened awareness in which the subject is excessively joyful, ungrounded, and light-headed, unable to function properly in the physical, everyday world.

BLOWN CHAKRA A chakra that has been damaged by drugs, unwise psychic practices, or meditating for too long a period of time. The chakra remains open and cannot perform its functions of energy filtration and mediation.

CELESTIAL DOORWAY The means of access to the higher, spiritual realms. *See also* CELESTIAL REALM.

CELESTIAL REALM In New Age thinking, the abode of the higher beings.

CHAKRA A spinning vortex of subtle energy. The term comes from the Sanskrit word *chakram*, which means "wheel," because these centers appear to clairvoyants and yogis as whirling disks of light. The system of subtle energy channels and centers is the basis for the MERIDIANS and energy points used in acupuncture, yoga practice, and energy healing. There are eight main chakras, located in a line aligned with the spine. These centers connect the energy of the physical body with that of the SUBTLE BODY. The eight chakras are located in the crown of the head, the center of the forehead (third eye), the throat, the solar plexus, the base of the spine, the genitals, and beneath the feet (earth) (*see pages* 364–365). When the chakras are functioning properly, the body's physical and subtle energies are in balance and harmony. Malfunctions can lead to physical, mental, emotional, or spiritual disturbances. Many energy workers believe that the chakras can be healed by the interaction between the vibrations of crystals and the energies of the body's BIOMAGNETIC or subtle energy FIELD. *See also* BLOWN CHAKRA.

CHANNELING The process whereby information is passed from a discarnate being (souls not in physical incarnation) via the voice and mind of an incarnate being.

CHRIST CONSCIOUSNESS In Christian thought, a belief in our own divinity (similar to that manifested by Christ) that links us with all life forms of the universe. In esoteric thought, the highest awareness and manifestation of divine energy. *See also* COSMIC CONSCIOUSNESS.

CHRONIC FATIGUE SYNDROME (CFS) A debilitating, virus-associated disorder, characterized by extreme fatigue, muscular pain, lack of concentration, memory loss, and depression, for which there is no known conventional medical cure at present.

CLAIRAUDIENCE Clear psychic hearing—the ability to hear things that are inaudible to the physical sense of hearing.

CLAIRSENTIENCE Clear psychic feeling—the ability to feel things that are physically intangible.

CLAIRVOYANCE Clear psychic vision— the ability to see things that are not visible in the physical world.

COSMIC CONSCIOUSNESS A very high state of awareness in which the subject is part of nonphysical, divine energies.

DEVIC KINGDOM The home of the devas, or nature spirits, believed in esoteric thinking to inhabit or rule over natural objects such as trees, rivers, or mountains. Though devas are generally invisible, people with clairvoyance can sometimes see or communicate with them or gain intuitive access to the devic kingdom, the energetic level at which these spirits exist.

DIS-EASE The state that results from physical imbalances, blocked feelings, suppressed emotions, and negative thinking.

DYSPRAXIA A condition characterized by clumsiness, lack of coordination, and the inability to distinguish left from right. Often occurs in combination with dyslexia.

EARTH CHAKRA The chakra located between and slightly below the feet which holds the soul into incarnation and links the physical body to the earth. *See also* GROUNDING and GROUNDING CORD.

EARTH HEALING The attempt to rectify the distortion of the earth's energies caused by pollution and the destruction of its resources.

ELECTROMAGNETIC SMOG A subtle but detectable electromagnetic field that can have an adverse effect on sensitive people. The smog is given off by electrical power lines and items such as computers, cell phones, and televisions.

ENERGY IMPLANT Thoughts or negative emotions that are implanted in the SUBTLE BODIES from an external, alien source.

ESOTERIC THOUGHT Nonscientific, nonmaterial thought based on a belief in the existence of metaphysics rather than any one school of thought.

ETHERIC BLUEPRINT The subtle program from which a physical body is constructed. It carries imprints of past-life dis-ease or injury from which present-life illness or disability can result.

ETHERIC BODY The subtle biomagnetic sheath surrounding the body, also known as the AURA. *See also* AURA; BIOMAGNETIC FIELD.

FAULT LINE An inner flaw or break in a crystal that refracts light and appears to divide the crystal into sections.

GEOPATHIC STRESS Stress that is created by subtle emanations and energy disturbances from undergound water, power lines, and negative earth energy lines (LEY LINES). Geopathic stress runs through the earth and can affect or pollute people and buildings. It contributes to dis-ease of all kinds. *See also* LEY LINES.

GRIDDING The placing of crystals around a building, person, or room for protection or enhancement of energies.

GROUNDING Creating a sound connection between oneself and the planet Earth that allows excess and out-of-balance energies to flow from the body.

GROUNDING CORD A vibratory energetic cord that hooks into the earth and holds the etheric bodies and the soul in incarnation.

HEALING CRISIS A positive sign that symptoms will soon disappear, marked by a brief intensifying of those same symptoms

HOMEOPATHY A system of healing, first practiced by the Greek physician Hippocrates (c. 460–377 B.C.E.), that stimulates the body's healing power by introducing minute, diluted amounts of a substance that can cause the symptoms of a particular illness or disease. German doctor Samuel Hahnemann (1755–1843) was the modern founder of homeopathy.

HYPNOTIC COMMANDS Unconscious programs instilled by an external source can "run" a person, causing them to act in automatic mode.

INNER CHILD The part of the personality that remains childlike and innocent, or that can be the repository of abuse and trauma and may therefore need healing.

INNER LEVELS The levels of being that encompass intuition, psychic awareness, emotions, feelings, and subtle energies. *See also* OUTER LEVELS and SUBTLE BODIES.

KARMIC Arising from or appertaining to a past incarnation. Debts, beliefs, and emotions such as guilt can be carried over into the present life.

KARMIC SEEDS The residue of past-life trauma, attitude, or illness that lodges in the etheric body and has the potential to develop into dis-ease or illness in the present life.

KIRLIAN CAMERA A Russian invention that takes photographs of the BIOMAGNETIC SHEATH or AURA surrounding the body. This method of photography was discovered in 1939 by Semyon Kirlian.

KUNDALINI An inner spiritual and sexual energy that resides at the base of the spine but can be stimulated to rise to the crown chakra.

LEMURIA In esoteric thought, an ancient civilization believed to predate Atlantis.

LEY LINES Subtle energy lines, straight or spiral, that connect ancient sites or prominent points in the landscape.

LIGHT BODY A subtle energy body vibrating at a very high frequency. It is the vehicle for the soul and higher consciousness.

LIGHT LIBRARY An energetic repository of healing and knowledge.

MATRIX The bedrock on which crystals are laid down in their natural state.

MENTAL INFLUENCES The sometimes powerful effect other people's thoughts and opinions can have on some minds.

MERIDIAN In Chinese Medicine, a subtle energy channel that runs close to the surface of the skin and contains the acupressure points.

MIASM The subtle imprint of an infectious dis-ease from the past, such as TB or syphilis, that has been passed down through a family or place. The term was coined by Samuel

Hahnemann, the founder of homeopathy. *See also* HOMEOPATHY.

NEGATIVE EMOTIONAL PROGRAMMING "Oughts" and "shoulds," along with guilt, that are instilled in childhood or in past lives and remain in the subconscious mind to influence present behavior. They sabotage efforts to evolve unless released or reprogrammed.

OCCLUSION A mineral deposit within a crystal, which usually shows up as cloudy patches, spots, or a ghostlike image, depending on the color of the material. *See* Tibetan Quartz, page 228.

OUTER LEVELS The levels of being that are physically and environmentally orientated. *See also* INNER LEVELS.

OVERSOUL The part of a SOUL GROUP that resonates at a higher frequency and directs the spiritual progress of the group. *See also* SOUL GROUP.

PRANIC ENERGY The energy that permeates everything. It is particularly useful in healing work as it revitalizes and reenergizes. From the Sanskrit word *prana*, meaning "breath."

PLEOCHROIC In a crystal, appearing to have two or more different colors, or shades of color, depending on the angle from which it is viewed.

PRE-BIRTH STATE The dimension inhabited by human beings before birth. *See also* BETWEEN-LIVES STATE.

PSYCHIC ATTACK The direction of malevolent thoughts or feelings toward another person, whether consciously or unconsciously, that can create illness or disruption in that person's life.

PSYCHIC VAMPIRISM A person's ability to draw or "feed off" the energy of others.

PSYCHIC GIFTS Abilities such as clairvoyance, telepathy, and healing.

QI (OR KI) The life force that energizes the physical and subtle bodies. Chinese, pronounced "chee."

RADIONICS A method of diagnosis and treatment at a distance, using specially designed instruments, based on the premise that all dis-ease is a distortion of the electromagnetic field surrounding the body. The method originated in the research of the nineteenth-century U.S. physician Dr. Albert Abrams.

REFRAMING Returning to see a past event in a different light so that the situation it is creating in the present life can be healed.

REIKI A natural, hands-on healing technique that feels like a flow of a high frequency of energy trasmitted to the patient through the hands of the practitioner. The word REIKI comes from *rei*, meaning "a supernatural force or spiritual intelligence," and *ki* (*qi*), meaning "life energy." The technique was first used in Japan in 1922 by Mikao Usui.

SCRYING Discerning images in a crystal that reveal the future or the secrets of the past or present.

SICK-BUILDING SYNDROME The set of symptoms, including headaches, dizziness, nausea, chest problems, and general fatigue, associated with buildings with actual air pollution or inadequate ventilation, or negative environmental energies.

SMUDGING A method of purification, used by Native Americans, for the preparation of oneself and one's sacred place for spiritual practice. The process involves wafting about the smoke of slowburning herbs.

SOUL GROUP A cluster of souls who are in incarnation.

SOUL LINKS The connections between the members of a SOUL GROUP.

SOUL RETRIEVAL Trauma, shock, or abuse can cause a part of the soul energy to leave and remain "stuck." A soul retrieval practitioner or shaman retrieves the soul, bringing it back to the physical body or, temporarily, to a crystal.

SPIRIT GUIDES Discarnate souls who work from the between-lives state to provide assistance to those on earth. *See also* BETWEEN-LIVES STATE.

STAR CHILDREN Evolved beings from other planetary systems who have incarnated on the earth to help its spiritual evolution.

STAR GATE The access point through which extraterrestrial contact can be made.

SUBTLE BODIES The layers of the BIOMAGNETIC SHEATH that relate to the physical, emotional, mental, and spiritual levels of being. *See also* BIOMAGNETIC SHEATH.

SUBTLE ENERGY FIELD The invisible but detectable energy field that surrounds all living beings.

THIRD EYE The chakra located between and slightly above the eyebrows. Also known as the brow chakra, it is the site of inner vision and intuition. *See also* CHAKRA.

THOUGHT FORMS Forms created by strong positive or negative thoughts that can exist on the etheric or spiritual level that can affect a person's mental functioning.

TRIPLE-BURNER MERIDIAN One of the body meridians used in Traditional Chinese Medicine. *See also* MERIDIAN.

TUMBLED The term used to refer to stones that have been polished in a large drum with grit, resulting in a smooth and often shiny stone.

VISION QUEST A Native American shamanic practice, involving isolation in a wild, natural environment, in order to commune with nature and confront fears. It should not be undertaken without proper guidance.

INDEX

USEFUL INFORMATION

BIBLIOGRAPHY

Gienger, Michael *Crystal Power, Crystal Healing* Cassell & Co., London, 1998

Hall, Judy *The Illustrated Guide to Crystals* Godsfield Press, Alresford, 2000

Hall, Judy *Crystal User's Handbook* Godsfield Press, Alresford, 2002

Hall, Judy *The Art of Psychic Protection* Samuel Weiser, Maine, 1997

Melody *Love Is In The Earth* Earth Love Publishing House, Colorado, 1995

Raphaell, Katrina *Crystal Healing Vols I, II, III* Aurora Press, Sante Fe, 1987

Raven, Hazel *Crystal Healing The Complete Practitioner's Guide* Raven & Co., Manchester, 2000

TRAINING ORGANIZATIONS

UNITED STATES
The Association of Melody Crystal Healing Instructors (TAOMCHI)
http://www.taomchi.com

UNITED KINGDOM
Institute of Crystal and Gem Therapists
MCS
PO Box 6
Exeter EX6 8YE
Tel: 01392 832005
Email: cgt@greenmantrees.demon.co.uk
http://www.greenmantrees.demon.co.uk/found.html

International Association of Crystal
Healing Therapists (founder Hazel Raven)
IACHT
PO Box 344
Manchester M60 2EZ
Tel: 01200 426061
Fax: 01200 444776
Email: info@aicht.co.uk
http://www.iacht.co.uk

AUTHOR ACKNOWLEDGMENTS
My knowledge of crystals has been acquired over thirty years, much of it from intuitive use. However, the books in the bibliography provided additional material for this directory. I would also like to thank Pat Goodenough, Trudi Green, and Dawn Robins for practical, hands-on teaching and crystal contact. As always, the assistance of Steve, Jackie, and the rest of the staff at Earthworks, Poole, has been invaluable in compiling this book and sourcing appropriate crystals. Clive at Earth Design, Broadwindsor, introduced me to some remarkable crystals, as did Mike at The Dorset Pedlar, Bridport. And finally, I could not work with crystals and much else besides without Crystal Clear, for which I thank David Eastoe.

PICTURE ACKNOWLEDGMENTS
Grahame Baker Smith p367
Kate Nardoni of MTG p370